ESSAYS ON PLATO AND ARISTOTLE

Essays on
Plato and Aristotle

J. L. ACKRILL

CLARENDON PRESS · OXFORD

1997

Oxford University Press, Great Clarendon Street, Oxford OX2 6DP
Oxford New York
Athens Auckland Bangkok Bogota Bombay
Buenos Aires Calcutta Cape Town Dar es Salaam
Delhi Florence Hong Kong Istanbul Karachi
Kuala Lumpur Madras Madrid Melbourne
Mexico City Nairobi Paris Singapore
Taipei Tokyo Toronto
and associated companies in
Berlin Ibadan

Oxford is a trade mark of Oxford University Press

Published in the United States
by Oxford University Press Inc., New York

British Library Cataloguing in Publication Data
Data available

Library of Congress Cataloging in Publication Data
Ackrill, J. L.
Essays on Plato and Aristotle / J. L. Ackrill.
Includes bibliographical references and index.
1. Plato. 2. Aristotle. I. Title.
B395.A29 1997 184—dc20 96–41722
ISBN 0–19–823641–7

1 3 5 7 9 10 8 6 4 2

Typeset by Best-set Typesetter Ltd., Hong Kong
Printed in Great Britain
on acid-free paper by
Biddles Ltd, Guildford and King's Lynn

To Margaret

ACKNOWLEDGEMENTS

We are grateful for permission to reproduce the following material in this volume:

'*Anamnesis* in the *Phaedo*: Remarks on 73c–75c', from E. N. Lee, A. P. D. Mourelatos, and R. M. Rorty (eds.), *Exegesis and Argument*. © 1973. Reprinted by permission of Van Gorcum & Co.

'Language and Reality in Plato's *Cratylus*', from A. Alberti (ed.), *Realta e Ragione*. © 1994. Reprinted by permission of Leo S. Olschki.

'Plato on False Belief: *Theaetetus* 187–200'. © 1966 *The Monist*, La Salle, Ill., USA 61301. Reprinted by permission.

'*ΣΥΜΠΛΟΚΗ ΕΙΔΩΝ*'. © 1955 *Bulletin of the Institute of Classical Studies of the University of London*. Reprinted by permission.

'Plato and the Copula: *Sophist* 251–259'. © 1957 *Journal of Hellenistic Studies*. Reprinted by permission of the Society for the Promotion of Hellenic Studies.

'In Defence of Platonic Division', from O. P. Wood and G. Pitcher (eds.), *Ryle*. © 1970. Reprinted by permission of Doubleday.

'Aristotle's Theory of Definition: Some Questions on *Posterior Analytics* II. 8–10', from E. Berti (ed.), *Aristotle on Science: The Posterior Analytics*. © 1981. Reprinted by permission of Editrice Antenore.

'Change and Aristotle's Theological Argument', *Oxford Studies in Ancient Philosophy*. Reprinted by permission of Oxford University Press.

'Aristotle's Distinction between *Energeia* and *Kinēsis*', from R. Bambrough (ed.), *New Essays on Plato and Aristotle*. © 1965 Routledge. Reprinted by permission of International Thomson Publishing Services.

'Aristotle's Definitions of *Psuchē*', *Proceedings of the Aristotelian Society*, LXXIII. Reprinted by courtesy of the Editor of the Aristotelian Society: © 1972/3.

'Aristotle on *Eudaimonia*'. © The British Academy 1975. Reproduced by permission from *Proceedings of the British Academy*, LX (1974).

'Aristotle on "Good" and the Categories', from S. M. Stern,

A. Hourani, and V. Brown (eds.), *Islamic Philosophy and the Classical Tradition.* © 1972. Reprinted by permission of Bruno Cassirer.

'Aristotle on Action', *Mind*, LXXXVII (1978). © John Ackrill.

'An Aristotelian Argument about Virtue', *Paideia.* © 1978. Reprinted by permission of the Editor of *Paideia*.

CONTENTS

Introduction

The papers collected in this volume were written over a period of 30 years or so. They are printed not in the chronological order of their composition but in the order suggested by their contents: papers on earlier dialogues of Plato come before those on later dialogues, while the Aristotle papers are ordered according to the traditional ordering of his works. Had the title not already been used (in a well-known and excellent set of essays in honour of Gregory Vlastos), I should have liked to entitle this volume 'Exegesis and Argument'; nearly all the essays start from a particular text and attempt to analyse and criticize it with a view to clarifying some point or points of philosophical significance. In some of them I was lucky enough to hit on questions that provoked wide interest and generated discussion, discussion which included (of course) criticism of my treatment of them. But my purpose here is not to reopen those interesting controversies, but to say something about how the study of ancient philosophy has changed since the Fifties. This is not offered as a serious—or even a non-serious—contribution to scholarship or historiography, but as a highly personal and selective account that may (it was suggested to me) be of interest to some contemporary readers. I shall start in the Fifties, and then look back on some of the more striking changes since then.

It may seem absurdly parochial to start in Oxford, but that is indeed where the story must begin. Several facts about Oxford in the Fifties conspired happily to make it a unique source of influence on the subsequent development of ancient philosophy as an academic field of study—more precisely on how the study of Greek philosophy developed in the English-speaking world.[1]

Oxford was distinguished both by the number of philosophers it had and by the character of the teaching they did. There were very

[1] In what follows 'ancient philosophy' will often mean 'the study of ancient philosophy', and 'ancient philosophers' will usually mean 'students of ancient philosophy', as in 'Ancient philosophers are now numerous'.

many more professional philosophers than in any other university. The University Calendar for 1952 lists 45 full-time tenured philosophy teachers. Eight (including the three professors) held University appointments, but the great majority held joint appointments, being both University lecturers and College Fellows and tutors. (Some had already graduated before the beginning of the war in 1939; many had graduated after its end in 1945.) As University lecturers they were obliged to give a small number of lectures each year (on subjects of their choice); but their main teaching activity was the tutorial teaching of the undergraduates in their own Colleges, and they would reckon to teach for most of the philosophy papers in the courses which included philosophy. In this capacity they were not specialist scholars but general practitioners in philosophical argument. In their research, of course, then usually called 'their own work', they were working and writing on a variety of different subjects. (A few names will be sufficient to indicate the variety: Anscombe, Austin, Grice, Hare, Hart, Kneale, Pears, Strawson.) But since as philosophy tutors they were all teaching for (and in turn examining in) the same examinations, and were discussing, in tutorials or with one another, the same range of authors and topics, there was a strong feeling of shared activity—and of shared excitement at new ideas in the air.

Of the undergraduate courses that included philosophy, the oldest and largest was Greats (*Literae Humaniores*). This was a four-year course that started with intensive work on classical language and literature, and moved on in its second part to ancient history (studied in the original texts) and to philosophy (including Greek philosophy). Of the three philosophy essay papers in the final examination, two were on modern philosophy, the third was on Plato's *Republic* and Aristotle's *Nicomachean Ethics*.[2] The undergraduate would have spent a whole term on each of these works, writing weekly essays for reading and discussion in tutorials. Since he had had a long classical training, he could readily grapple with the Greek; but because this was a philosophy paper, taught by the same tutor who taught for the other philosophy papers, it was approached not as literature or as history but as an integral part of philosophy. Since both the *Republic* and the *Ethics* raise questions of fundamental importance not only for ethics and politics but also

---

[2] Alternative works of Plato and Aristotle could be, but rarely were, chosen by the student.

for logic, metaphysics, and philosophy of action, there were plenty of connections to be made between the topics in this paper and those in the other (modern) philosophy papers.

The tutorial system, in which the tutor discussed an essay for an hour or more each week, was not directed towards the inculcation of a wide knowledge of different philosophers or philosophies, but to the training of the pupil in understanding and analysing and criticizing difficult philosophical books or papers. Respect for authorities was not expected; clarity of exposition and rigour in argument were. The examination papers in philosophy called for little factual knowledge (although a good knowledge of the *Republic* and *Ethics* was necessary for a good result in that paper), but rather for the ability to seize the point of a tricky question and to formulate a convincing, or at least plausible, way of dealing with it. Discussions were expected to take place—and essays to be written—in plain language, free from the sort of technical terms or esoteric jargon that serves to obfuscate (or perhaps impress).

The style of philosophy practised at Oxford in these years was often characterized as 'ordinary language philosophy' or 'linguistic philosophy'. Its practitioners paid close attention to ordinary linguistic usage, investigating its nuances with relish; and they demanded that philosophers should not depart from it without explicit explanation. It would be a mistake to suppose that all Oxford philosophers subscribed to this policy, or that those who did so spent all of their time on linguistic investigations. But devotion to ordinary language was widely regarded as distinctive of much Oxford philosophy. (After Quine had spent a very successful year in Oxford as a visiting professor, the appreciative faculty gave him a farewell dinner. At the end of his witty speech he asked us to stand and drink the health—of Ordinary Language.) This manner of philosophizing was vilified by some as trivializing and debasing a great subject. How could, for example, the problems of knowledge or of freedom be solved by close attention to the various ways in which the common man uses the words 'know' and 'free'? (Ernest Gellner wrote a passionate book diagnosing the psychological and sociological causes of the hateful phenomenon—an unphilosophical work that so incensed Ryle that he refused to have it reviewed in *Mind*.) No doubt time was sometimes spent on (enjoyable) linguistic expeditions that brought back no significant rewards; but the general approach did illuminate substantial problems. In any case, the main permanent influence of the movement was, I think, good. The idea was fostered that philosophers should try to formulate their questions, arguments, and answers precisely and in clear, plain English (or should explain technical terms in clear, plain English). This demand was sometimes used as a blunderbuss to knock out unfashionable doctrines (just as the logical positivists had a too-crisp argument to annihilate metaphysics). But the pressure for clarity and plain language in exposition and for rigour in argument could be, and regularly was, exercised beneficially in philosophy, and therefore in the philosophical interpretation of Plato and Aristotle.

I have said enough to indicate why Oxford philosophy in the Fifties was well placed to exercise a considerable influence outside Oxford. Circumstances were exceptionally favourable: universities and their philosophy departments were everywhere expanding, and the size and reputation of the Oxford philosophy faculty attracted increasing numbers of graduates (as well as visiting academics), especially from the United States. They returned home to teaching posts, and many of them distinguished themselves over the following decades. The particular magnet for such graduates was the newly established B.Phil. course. The main architect of this course was the Waynflete Professor of Metaphysics—though no one could be less metaphysical than Gilbert Ryle (or 'Uncle Gilbert'). He thought that it did nobody any good, and in particular did no philosophy student any good, to shut himself away for three years reading, thinking, and writing about a narrowly defined topic. For the development of philosophical culture and ability in graduates aiming at teaching posts, what was needed was a good acquaintance with several main areas and at least one major philosophical authority; the best method of achieving this was by the vigorous discussion of papers read to classes of fellow students, as well as by the preparation of papers for supervisors. Ryle had identified a real need, and there came into being a strong and lively population of articulate philosophy graduates destined to be active, influential teachers in their own universities.

A special blessing was that Ryle was himself enthusiastic about Plato and Aristotle, and when he advised new arrivals as to which 'chosen authority' they should choose, he regularly pressed the claims of these two. Since they were to be studied as philosophers, knowledge of Greek was not required (though there were always enough classicists at hand to warn against special pitfalls in the available translations). B.Phil. classes on Plato and Aristotle attracted many participants, and usually gave rise to stimulating and constructive discussions, often under Gwil Owen's vigorous leadership.

Such classes were very different from a graduate seminar on Plato which I had attended in Switzerland 1950. There the professor went through the dialogues, giving sympathetic exegesis and answering occasional requests for explanation; but when I suggested that a certain argument advanced by Plato was invalid, a shocked silence ensued—as though I had committed an embarrassing solecism. The professorial exposition then flowed on. It was evidently assumed either that no question of validity was allowable or that correct exegesis would necessarily show the argument to be valid. This very strong version of the principle of charity in interpretation used to be quite common in accounts of Plato and Aristotle.

Another experience comes to mind. In the Seventies I took a visiting German professor to a graduate class on the *Theaetetus* at which I was reading the opening paper. In the lively discussion that followed, those present challenged the views I had expressed, and made good criticisms of my paper in warm argument. I therefore found this a very successful meeting; but my visitor evinced amazement at the freedom with which I had been criticized. He said that he had never considered allowing, let alone encouraging, such comments from graduates in his seminars. (He thought he might make a tentative experiment.)

A graduate who had read Plato or Aristotle for the B.Phil. would go away not having been taught what their 'doctrines' were, but having been encouraged to study them as philosophers, to base analysis of their views on close attention to the texts, and to criticize and build on their discussions in clear, precise language without undue deference. These points, taken together, do something to characterize the main body of work on ancient philosophy in recent decades and to distinguish it both from some ancient philosophy done elsewhere in the period and from much ancient philosophy done in other periods.

There have been major developments since the war both in the scope, or range, of ancient philosophy studied in English-speaking universities and in the character of that study.

Large areas of ancient philosophy that were more or less neglected at Oxford (and in most other universities) in the Fifties have been taken seriously since then. It was natural, and not necessarily a Bad Thing, that for those philosophers Plato and Aristotle should be the centre of attention. It was equally natural, and certainly a Good Thing, that in the following years there should have been increased interest in other philosophers and philosophical movements, most of which were rooted directly or indirectly in the thoughts of Plato and Aristotle. I mention a few striking examples: first, Plotinus and Neoplatonism. The Regius Professor of Greek in the Fifties (E. R. Dodds) was (amongst other things) a distinguished Plotinus scholar, but most philosophers spoke of Plotinus in the same breath as Hegel, regarding them as virtually unreadable and barely intelligible. A great new critical edition by Henry and Schwyzer produced an excellent text, published in Oxford Classical Texts from 1964; and this enabled us for the first time to get a readable text at a reasonable price. Some of us were startled to find that the *Enneads* contained a large amount of strong and provocative argument which even the ordinary philosopher could grasp and appreciate. However, the Greek is fiendishly difficult, and the next great need was for an accurate translation; this came from Armstrong of Liverpool, published in Loeb volumes from 1966. The final infrastructure was provided by a word index, published by Sleeman and Pollett in 1980. Commentaries on individual works of Plotinus have begun to appear, and interest is spreading to other Neoplatonists, encouraged by the great enterprise (initiated by R. Sorabji of London) of translating all the Greek commentaries on Aristotle. Thus, on the basis of much splendid scholarly work, philosophical interpretation and criticism of Plotinus have begun to flourish—though much remains to be done.

Plotinus remains a special taste. Perhaps the most remarkable expansion of the scope of ancient philosophy in recent years has occurred in other post-Aristotelian areas. The importance of Stoicism, Epicureanism, and Scepticism in the history of philosophy has never been doubted; but the relevant texts are scattered, often fragmentary, often in Latin, and rarely a pleasure to read. The challenge to make philosophical sense of these important schools, and to get through to the philosophical greatness of their main proponents, was first taken up by a few enthusiasts (among whom it would not be invidious to mention Tony Long). Interest among philosophers gradually increased, and a group of 22 met at a conference on Hellenistic philosophy held at Oxford in 1978. This conference, and the subsequent publication of the papers read at it, stimulated further activity and major advances—in monographs, collections of papers, new texts, and translations. Together with work on the Neoplatonists, these studies are building the bridge to medieval philosophy, itself recently enjoying an overdue flourishing.

It is not only for post-Aristotelian studies that the availability of good texts (and translations) has been an essential condition for rigorous philosophical work. There were parts even of Aristotle that were hardly known to exist by most mid-century philosophers. Aristotle's biological works form a large part of his preserved work, and were clearly for him an important, integral part of philosophy. (I recall that in 1951 Harold Cherniss told me that Aristotle's biology was the key to his metaphysics; unfortunately I did not have the wit to interpret this Delphic utterance.) Between 1937 and 1965 good texts and translations were published in the Loeb Library (by A. L. Peck), and one important work was edited in the Oxford Classical Texts (by Drossaart Lulofs). Papers by D. Balme furthered philosophical discussion, and in 1976 A. Gotthelf wrote a paper that sparked interest in a larger group of philosophers, and stimulated a whole wave of activity, particularly in the United States; there have been conferences, collections of papers, and the preparation of new commentaries.

If the study of ancient philosophy has broadened by taking in new areas, it has also been enriched by its interaction with general philosophy. In the post-war decades an increasing number of serious workers on ancient philosophy has come to be found in philosophy departments rather than in classics departments, and this has naturally affected the work done. These people had colleagues teaching modern philosophy, and they themselves were often doing such teaching as well as having a special interest in Greek philosophy. They brought to their work on ancient philosophy the training and outlook of philosophers. It goes without saying that it is essential for our subject that scholarship and philosophy should both flourish and that they should co-operate. It is the balance between them that seems to me to have changed significantly within the last

50 years, tilting away from scholarly exegesis towards philosophical interpretation and criticism.

The techniques and ideas of contemporary philosophy have borne good fruit in our field. One particular example: the techniques of mathematical logic have been brought to bear with great effect upon the interpretation of Aristotle's logic and of Stoic logic. The contrast in style and content between Maier's *Die Syllogistik Des Aristoteles*, three volumes published in 1896–1900, and Patzig's *Die Aristotelische Syllogistik*, one volume published in 1958, could not be more striking.

More generally, in nearly all the central areas—of philosophical logic, metaphysics, philosophy of mind, and ethics—the lively investigations of contemporary mainstream philosophers have helped ancient philosophers illuminate and advance their own part of the subject. This was not a case of imposing alien ideas upon recalcitrant material, but of taking advantage of refined and subtle discussions of questions and concepts that were already to be found (in a more or less recognizable form) in the ancients. Take, for example, problems of identity and the notion of 'the same thing under a different description'. This notion is already in Aristotle, and indeed put to good use by him; but the diverse applications made by modern philosophers have increased the recognition and understanding of its importance in his work. Contemporary writings on such other topics as sense and reference, thought and desire, the 'is' of constitution, and the mind–body problem have had their effect. Recent work on ancient philosophy would have been very different, and much poorer, without the influence of such various philosophers as Anscombe, Grice, Hare, Putnam, Rorty, and Wiggins (to name a representative few). I do not think that it was equally true in the past that mainstream philosophy worked its way so naturally and powerfully into ancient philosophy—or that it is equally true everywhere today.

It is of course no accident—in that they had read Greats—that many of those associated with ideas central to modern philosophy themselves came to modern philosophy with a knowledge of Greek and of Greek philosophy. It is also happily the case that philosophers without Greek can more easily than ever before come to grips profitably with works of Greek philosophy and with modern books and papers on the subject. This was not so in the immediately post-war years. Most available translations were not accurate enough for close philosophical study, and secondary material usually made use of Greek in the text. There has been a striking change in these respects. In the late Fifties J. L. Austin recognized the need for new translations of Aristotle, made for philosophers and accompanied by philosophical commentary, and a new genre of work was initiated with the publication of the first volume in the Clarendon Aristotle series in 1962. There has since been a steadily growing number of such volumes on both Plato and Aristotle; and the same format has been adopted for other authors (e.g. Sextus Empiricus and Plotinus) and for collections of fragments (e.g. of pre-Socratics and of Stoics). I call this a new genre, because although the close commentary had long been a feature of classical studies, it had been attached to a Greek text, had itself made free use of Greek, and had had a strongly philological character. (Important forerunners of the more recent activity were volumes on some Platonic dialogues by Cornford and Hackforth.) Since English has become more and more a world language, the availability of good new translations of Greek texts has helped to spread interest in Greek philosophy well beyond Europe and North America.

The changes I have noted—in the scope of ancient philosophy and in its philosophical sophistication—have undoubtedly been good ones. Some other developments, due to external factors, have been a mixed blessing for ancient philosophy, and indeed for academic studies in general; and I will mention a few of them.

In the post-war years travel, especially international travel, was difficult and expensive. Few British academics had sabbatical leave, and still fewer could take their leave in the United States. (The journey there took four and a half days and was very enjoyable). Since that time air travel has become easy (a few hours and not very enjoyable), and academic trips across the Atlantic and within Europe are commonplace—not only for sabbatical terms but also for conferences (colloquia, workshops, symposia . . .). There can be dangers in too much rushing around—it will be remembered that Socrates preferred to stay at home—but the main effects of easy travel have surely been good. The sense of closeness and the benefit of easy exchange of ideas which characterized Oxford in the Fifties have now spread to the international academic community. People working on the same topic in different places can expect to meet one another and discuss work in progress, instead of receiving only the printed outcome. (Plato said the last word on the superiority of live discourse over written documents, which cannot answer your questions.) The possibility of meetings has been particularly important for new or highly specialized areas of study. Working alone on a little-studied subject can be dull or depressing; a conference with fellow students stimulates ideas, and renews enthusiasm. One of the most influential series of international conferences was initiated by Ingemar Düring in 1957, the triennial Symposia Aristotelica. In a succession of meetings, which continue, individual themes or works of Aristotle (including some that were previously neglected) have been given intensive study and discussion, the results being published as collections of papers.

Besides travel, other new means of communication have brought together in easy and swift conversation scholars who in the past would hardly have hoped to hear each other's voices. I can recall the difficulty and excitement and expense of making a phone call to San Francisco soon after the war. How different from today's tutor, who finds phoning easier than writing and for whom the miracle of e-mail is taken for granted—and the Internet beckons.

Some other technological advances have been less clearly welcome. Photocopying has made it too easy to produce a multiplicity of documents and to indulge in the circulation of insufficiently revised drafts. More seriously, the power of the computer and of sophisticated software may focus research attention on those questions for which the use of that power is helpful. (We are all too well aware of the danger that academic appraisal will take into account only those things that can be more or less quantified—how, after all, can one take into account what cannot be counted?) Janet and Super-Janet are excellent handmaidens, but useful for only limited purposes and in connection with only some problems. It is said—with what truth I do not know—that when Kenny was preparing his revolutionary study of Aristotle's *Eudemian Ethics*, he produced all the statistical material by counting occurrences of the relevant words and phrases while watching 'That Was The Week That Was' on television. For this he would no doubt have welcomed a handmaiden. But the value of his book is in the reasoning and argument, and for that activity not the hand but the head is required.

One must not, of course, adopt the Thamus reaction to the

invention of the computer. Plato tells us that when Theuth offered his invention of letters to Thamus, the king of the Egyptians, claiming that it would improve their memories, the king argued to the contrary: 'Those who use your invention will cease to use their own memory, relying on the written word; and they will acquire the appearance of wisdom but not real wisdom.'

Our subject, like others, has lately suffered from external pressures that are a serious threat to the quality of work. Competition for too few jobs and the demands of crude appraisal must lead to over-production of quickly produced papers, and make it more and more difficult for younger philosophers to develop at a natural pace and produce substantial works—substantial not necessarily in size but in the importance and originality of their contents. In the Fifties some people wrote many papers, other none. But nobody was having his publications counted by an authority, and nobody was deterred from working on a long-term project because of the need to give an annual account of his progress. Present pressures resemble the harmful pressures in the City of London for short-term gains rather than investment for long-term benefits. No doubt pressures keep academics (and managing directors) from being lazy, but they also make impossible those achievements for which more time and leisure are required.

Our subject has grown and flourished since the Fifties. I suppose that the most fundamental contrast between then and now is that then most teachers and pupils in Greek philosophy knew Greek; now the reverse is, in most universities, the case. There is clearly a loss here: direct confrontation with texts and close acquaintance with them must be the best foundation for the study of any philosopher. In the present case it is also an advantage in giving access to a long tradition of careful exegesis and discussion in writings where knowledge of Greek was taken for granted. (By the same token, nearly all specialists in ancient philosophy could read German; not so many now.) On the other hand, as the proportion of Greek-reading students of ancient philosophy has diminished, the proportion of students of ancient philosophy who are philosophers rather than classicists has increased. This has significantly affected the way in which the subject is studied, giving more emphasis to the purely philosophical and less to the purely philological than was previously the case. The happiest conjunction of course is where a philosopher co-operates with a classicist, either by being the same person or by being in co-operating departments of the same university.

I

Anamnesis in the *Phaedo*: Remarks on 73c–75c

INTRODUCTION

The Platonic doctrine of reminiscence, that what we call learning is really recalling what we already know, is argued for at length in two places. The argument in the *Meno* concerns our knowledge of necessary truths. Leibniz spoke well of this argument, saying that Plato's doctrine 'is very sound provided that it is taken aright and purged of the error of pre-existence'.[1] More recently Professor Vlastos has shown in detail how the *Meno* brings out the special character of a priori knowledge.[2] The *Phaedo* argument differs in that it is about our acquisition of concepts rather than of necessary truths. There is also this difference, that the pre-existence of the soul certainly cannot in the *Phaedo* be treated as a myth or metaphor; the context makes it impossible to see the doctrine of reminiscence as simply making a point about concept formation and not really referring to the passage of time and the recovery of what was already known.

Nobody supposes that the *Phaedo* argument does indeed prove the pre-existence of the soul. But it is of considerable interest as an argument; its structure is complex, and it involves a variety of philosophical points and difficulties. It has not, I think, been examined in print as fully and rigorously as it should be. I very much wish that I had been able in Gregory Vlastos's honour to offer a full-scale analysis and discussion of it. Instead I must confine myself to raising some questions that have puzzled me about the first part of it, and making a few suggestions. I do not present a single thesis

---

[1] G. W. Leibniz, *Discourse on Metaphysics*, XXVI, trans. P. G. Lucas and L. Grint (Manchester: Manchester University Press, 1953), p. 45.
[2] Gregory Vlastos, '*Anamnesis* in the *Meno*', *Dialogue*, 4 (1965), 143–67.
First published in 1973.

about the *anamnesis* argument in the *Phaedo*—unless you count as
a thesis the contention that there are some philosophically interesting questions about it that have not yet been sufficiently ventilated.
In the stretch of argument with which I shall be concerned,
Socrates first gives an account of *being reminded of something* and
illustrates it with various examples. He next brings in the theory of
Forms—that besides sensible particulars there are unchanging
knowable entities such as the Equal itself, a doctrine agreed to by
the interlocutors without discussion. Socrates claims that since we
acquire knowledge of Equality, etc. from our perception of something different (sensible particulars), what occurs must be
anamnesis. Moreover, we recognize that sensible particulars fall
short of Equality, etc. So we must have known Equality, etc. beforehand. In fact, our so-called learning or acquisition of concepts
in this life is really recovering or recalling concepts we already
possessed before this life.

Questions can be raised both about the general structure and
strategy of this argument and about many particular moves within
it. It will be best first to give a fairly literal translation.

TRANSLATION OF 73c1–75c6

73c1   SOCRATES. We agree, no doubt, that if anyone is to be *reminded*
       of anything he must have known it at some time previously.
       (SIMMIAS. Certainly.)

73c4   Do we also agree on this, that whenever knowledge comes along in
       a certain way it is recollection—I mean, in the following way. If a
       person, on seeing one thing—or hearing it or getting any other
       perception of it—not only recognizes it but also thinks of something
       different, which is the object not of the same knowledge but of
       another, do we not rightly say that he is *reminded* of the thing he
       gets the thought of?   (How do you mean?)

73d3   Take an example. Knowledge of a man is other than knowledge of
       a lyre?   (Of course.)

73d5   Well, you know what happens to lovers when they see a lyre or a
       cloak or some other thing which their favourites customarily use.
       They recognize the lyre, and they get in their thought the form of
       the boy whose lyre it is. This is recollection. Or again, one seeing
       Simmias is often reminded of Cebes; and there must be countless
       other such cases.   (Countless indeed.)

73e1 That sort of thing, then, is a kind of recollection? Particularly, however, when this happens to someone concerning items which have already been forgotten through time and not attending to them?   (Certainly.)

73e5 Now is it possible on seeing a picture of a horse[3] or a picture of a lyre to be reminded of a man, or on seeing a picture of Simmias to be reminded of Cebes?   (Certainly.)

73e9 And also to be reminded of Simmias himself on seeing a picture of Simmias?   (Yes indeed.)

74a2 With regard to all these, then, isn't it a fact that there is recollection from like things but also from unlike things?   (It is.)

74a5 But whenever it is from like things that anyone is reminded of something, does it not also necessarily happen to him, that he thinks whether or not *this* falls short, in respect of likeness, of that thing of which he has been reminded?   (Yes, necessarily.)

74a9 Consider now whether this is correct. We say that there is such a thing as equal—I don't mean a stick equal to a stick or a stone to a stone or any other thing of that sort, but something different apart from all those, *the equal itself.* Are we to say that there is such a thing, or not?   (We are indeed to say so, most emphatically.)

74b2 And do we know it, what it is?   (Certainly.)

74b4 Whence did we get the knowledge of it? Was it not from the things we were just mentioning—seeing either sticks or stones or other equal things, *from* these we thought of *that*, which is different from these.

    Or does it not seem to you different? Look at the question thus: equal stones and sticks sometimes seem—the very same ones— equal to one person but to another not. Agreed?   (Certainly.)

74c1 But now, have equals themselves ever seemed to you unequal, or equality inequality?   (Never.)

74c4 Therefore these equals are not the same as the equal itself.   (Definitely not.)

74c7 Yet it is *from* these very equals, that are different from *that* equal, that you have nevertheless thought of and got the knowledge of it?   (Very true.)

74c11 It being either like these or unlike them?   (Certainly.)

74c13 It makes no difference. So long as, on seeing one thing, from this perception you think of another thing—whether like or unlike— what has occurred is necessarily recollection.   (Yes.)

74d4 Now then, does something of this sort happen to us with regard to the sticks and the equal things we were just speaking of? Do they

---

[3] Literally 'a pictured horse', and similarly in the following examples. This may be important for certain purposes, but not (I think) for mine.

seem to us to be equal precisely as that which is equal itself is, or do they fall short somehow of it—fall short of being just like the equal—or don't they?   (They fall short a great deal.)

74d9 Do we agree on this: whenever a person on seeing something thinks that 'this that I now see wishes to be just like some other thing there is but falls short and cannot be just like it, but is inferior'—is it not necessary that the person thinking this should have known beforehand that thing which he says this one resembles but falls short of?   (It is necessary.)

74e6 Well now, does something of this sort happen to us in fact, or not, with regard to the equals and the equal itself?   (It certainly does.)

74e9 It is necessary, therefore, that we should have known the equal *before* that time when we first saw the equals and thought that 'all these want to be like the equal, but they fall short'.   (That is so.)

75a5 But on this too we agree, that we have thought of it—and it is impossible to do so otherwise—precisely from seeing or touching or from some other sense; I count all these as the same.   (So they are for the purposes of the present argument.)

75a11 Yet it is in fact *from* the senses that we have to think that all the things in the senses both strive after it—that which is equal—and fall short of it. Is that what we say?   (Yes.)

75b4 So before we began to see and hear and use the other senses, we must surely have possessed knowledge of the equal itself, what it is, if we were going to refer to it the equal things from the senses, thinking that they all do their best to be just like it but are inferior to it.   (This necessarily follows from what was said before.)

75b10 Now we were seeing and hearing and were in possession of the other senses from the moment we were born, weren't we?   (Certainly.)

75c1 And *before* those we must, we maintain, have possessed the knowledge of the equal?   (Yes.)

75c4 So before being born we must necessarily, it seems, have possessed it.   (It seems so.)

NOTES ON THE TRANSLATION

First, a remark about the translation of the noun *anamnesis* and the corresponding verb. Translators are embarrassed by not having in English a single word, in both noun and verb form, which covers both *recalling* and *being reminded of*. That these are different is of course obvious. Recalling something does not entail being reminded of it or having been reminded of it; one may just recall something without any particular object or experience having reminded one of it. (To say this is not to deny that there must have been some *cause* of one's recalling so-and-so.) Plato may well be aware that reminded recall is only one kind of recall. At any rate, 73c4 ff., which is clearly about being reminded, purports to give a sufficient condition of *anamnesis*, not a necessary one; and at 73e1 it is said, with reference to the reminding situation, that 'that sort of thing . . . is *a kind of anamnesis*'.

It is clear enough that the arguments we are to consider are in fact about being reminded. Translators tend to oscillate, using 'recollection' for the noun *anamnesis*, and 'being reminded of' for the corresponding verb. I have followed this practice in the foregoing translation. It is harmless provided that the Greekless reader understands that both English expressions render one and the same Greek root, which itself covers both the general concept of recall and the more particular one of recall through being reminded.

Secondly, the Greek contains many expressions of the forms 'Seeing *x*, he thought of *y*' and 'From seeing *x* (or: from *x*), he thought of *y*'. Most translations gravely overtranslate these expressions, using such turns of phrase as 'Seeing *x* made him think of *y*' or 'put him in mind of *y*'. These overtranslations are dangerous where the very topics under discussion are the concept *being reminded of* and the question of how we come to think of things. It is important in this context to *distinguish* the mere statement 'Seeing *x*, I thought of *y*' from such statements as:

(a) 'Seeing *x* made me think of *y*';
(b) 'Seeing *x* put me in mind of (or: reminded me of) *y*';
(c) '*x* reminded me of *y*'.

Statement (a) says more than that the seeing was followed by the thought, though it does not carry the implication that I had already previously perceived or thought of *y*. Statement (b) says still more than (a), since it does carry this implication. Statement (c) is different in several ways. In particular, in a case like 'Your village-hall reminded me of a garage' a similarity between the *x* and *y* items is implied; which is why one can speak here of being reminded slightly, very much, etc. It is clear, I think, that forms like (a), (b), and (c) should not be used to render the colourless Greak expressions mentioned above.

PHAEDO 73C1–D1

Two theses about *anamnesis* are stated at 73c1 and 73c4 respectively. The first need not detain us: if at time *t* someone is reminded of *y*, he must have known *y* at a time prior to *t*.[4] The second thesis, another appeal to ordinary correct usage, says in effect: if a man, perceiving *x*, not only recognizes *x* but also thinks of some other thing, *y*, which is the object of a different knowledge, he is correctly said to be reminded of *y*. This second thesis, then, purports to state a sufficient condition for *being reminded of*. I wish to make three comments on it.

(a) What is the meaning and importance of the phrase 'not only recognizes *x*'? This is not a question that agitates the commentators. Yet one would hope that the words were doing some definite work in what appears to be a rather carefully composed sentence. Allusion to recognition recurs in the first example, at 73d7: someone recognizes the lyre and thinks of its owner.

Plato may here be touching on a point that is indeed important if an adequate account of conditions for *being reminded of something* is to be given. I can attempt no more than a very rough indication of the issues involved. A man might have a visual experience correctly describable as 'seeing a lyre', and it might be followed by the thought of Simmias; it might even cause him to think of Simmias, without its being natural to say that *seeing a lyre* put him in mind of, or reminded him of, Simmias. For the person may not have had the faintest idea that the thing he saw—the dark thing sticking out from under the curtain—*was* a lyre. To invoke the notion of reminding is to imply the availability of an explanation in terms of associative laws connecting thought-contents. So it must be features of *x* that I noticed, not features that I didn't notice, that *reminded* me of something, though features that I didn't notice—and indeed, features that I could not have noticed—may have *caused* anything whatsoever (including thoughts in me).

The similarity of colour of two objects *a* and *b* would not be offered as the explanation why a man on perceiving *a* thought of *b*, if his perceiving *a* consisted of his touching it in the dark. That you have often in the past seen him with her will not explain why now

---

[4] It will be convenient always to use '*x*' for the reminding item and '*y*' for the item one is reminded of.

on seeing him you think of her, if when you see him now (in the dusk) you take him to be a pillar-box. To return to Simmias's lyre: it might indeed be that seeing the dark lumpy object sticking out from under the curtain reminded someone of Simmias without his suspecting that the object was a lyre. For perhaps Simmias, like Orson Welles, commonly looks dark and lumpy; or perhaps he has been seen on some important occasion carrying a dark lumpy parcel. But a condition of either of these explanations' holding is that the person should have noticed what he saw to be *dark and lumpy*. It would clearly be wrong to suggest that the blank in 'seeing . . . reminded me of Simmias' can be properly filled only by an expression which actually reveals the explanation. Indeed, we can say that seeing something reminded us of something else when we do not know but are wondering what it was about the something that reminded us. But in saying that and in wondering this, we are implying and assuming that the explanation will be in terms of features or aspects which we noticed, identified, or recognized.[5]

I suggest, then, that something like a recognition requirement is indeed necessary if Plato is to give an adequate account of 'Seeing *x* reminded him of *y*', and is to bring out the ways in which it goes beyond 'He saw *x* and then thought of *y*'. It will not be surprising if Plato touches on the matter, a complicated one, only lightly, particularly since he is giving a sufficient condition for being reminded: the complexities arise when one enquires into minimum conditions necessary for being reminded. There may, however, be a difficulty that threatens Plato's whole programme. For if reminding is to explain concept formation, can a pre-condition for reminding be recognition or something akin to it?

In Plato's first example, 73d5, the lover, seeing his friend's lyre and recognizing it, thinks of him. Does Plato suppose him to have recognized it as his friend's lyre, or only perhaps as a lyre? No doubt the thing might occur either way. But the distinction has some interest for the following reason. Recognizing *x* as a lyre is logically independent of thinking of Alcibiades, even though it may naturally lead one to think of him if one has often seen lyres in his possession or him in possession of a lyre. On the other hand, recognizing *x* as Alcibiades' lyre is not logically independent of

---

[5] This flurry of verbs will serve as a reminder—were one necessary—that many distinctions which a proper investigation of the topic would call for are being neglected or blurred in my brief remarks.

thinking of Alcibiades. A temporal and causal relation can hold between thinking 'This is a lyre' and thinking of Alcibiades, but not between thinking 'This is Alcibiades' lyre' and thinking of Alcibiades; for in thinking 'This is Alcibiades' lyre', one is already necessarily thinking of Alcibiades.

(b) The second question I wish to raise about the sentence at 73c6–d1 concerns the phrase 'which is the object not of the same knowledge but of another' (οὗ μὴ ἡ αὐτὴ ἐπιστήμη ἀλλ' ἄλλη). Why does Plato add this emphatic phrase to the words 'something different' that precede it? What condition or requirement does it add? Burnet writes: 'This is an important reservation. Certain things, notably opposites, must be known together or not at all (τῶν ἐναντίων μία ἐπιστήμη). It proves nothing that odd reminds us of even, or that darkness reminds us of light; for in this case the knowledge of the one is *ipso facto* knowledge of the other.'[6] Hackforth summarizes Burnet's note and goes on: 'In view, however, of the instance in D3 ('knowledge of a man is other than knowledge of a lyre') I think he (Socrates) more probably means that the perception of, for example, a man may remind us of things that we know about him but do not perceive: the perceived characters and those of which they remind us would all alike be included in our total knowledge of the man, and therefore are objects of the same knowledge. This kind of reminder Socrates rules out as irrelevant.'[7] Thus both Burnet and Hackforth suppose that the situation described would be a case of being reminded even without the qualification 'the object of another knowledge', and that Socrates adds this simply to rule out a type or types of reminding that he does not want in play.[8]

[6] J. Burnet, *Plato's* Phaedo (Oxford: Clarendon Press, 1911), note on 73c8.
[7] R. Hackforth, *Plato's* Phaedo (Cambridge: Cambridge University Press, 1955), 67 n. 4.
[8] I cannot fully understand R. Loriaux's note on our phrase, in *Le* Phédon *de Platon*, vol. 1 (Namur: Presses universitaires de Namur, 1969). He writes: 'La condition est importante. Il faut qu'à l'occasion de la première connaissance (ἐκεῖνο γνῷ), surgisse une connaissance intellectuelle d'autre chose (ἕτερον ἐννόηση). Une seule connaissance ne suffirait pas (et ce serait le cas si, de la connaissance de "vrai", par exemple, on passait à la connaissance de "non vrai", qui est la simple négation de "vrai".) D'autre part, il n'est pas requis, pour l'instant, que ces deux connaissances soient différentes de nature; il suffit qu'il y ait deux actes de connaissance. Cf. 74A, φαμέν που.' How could one be said to *pass from* the knowledge of 'true' to the knowledge of 'not true' unless two 'acts of knowledge' (in *some* sense of this hazardous expression) were involved? What are the criteria for 'une connaissance' and for 'une acte de connaissance'?

It would, I think, be more natural to see in the phrase we are considering a condition that really is required if it is to be correct to speak of *being reminded* at all. I suggest that Plato wants to exclude, as *not* a case of being reminded of something, a situation where thinking of *y* is already necessarily involved in perceiving and recognizing *x*. This would not be an unreasonable exclusion. One would not want to say that something brings so-and-so to mind if so-and-so is necessarily in mind when the something is. There are, of course, a host of difficult problems in this neighbourhood, problems about what counts as a different thing and problems about what counts as thinking of the same or a different thing. I am not suggesting that Plato has these matters clear, or even that he has the relevant questions clearly formulated. I am suggesting only that the qualification we are considering may show an awareness— which it is quite easy to have in an unsophisticated way—that there can be cases where one would say that there are two different things but would not be willing to speak of *passing from* the thought of the one to the thought of the other, or of being *reminded of* the other by the thought of the one, because the thought of the one already includes the thought of the other.

On this interpretation, while the relation *being something different* is symmetrical, the relation *being the object of another knowledge* is not. Thus the concepts *bachelor* and *man* are different from one another. But it is only if I go from the thought of man to the thought of bachelor that I go to something that is the object of another (a further) knowledge. The thought of bachelor includes that of man; so here there can be no such going from the first to the second. Again, thinking that this is Simmias's portrait, I am already thinking of Simmias; but not vice versa.

To put together these two comments. Both in his mention of *recognizing* and in his qualification about *another knowledge* Plato shows an awareness that being reminded of something is more complicated than it might appear. What is involved is not just a causal sequence, nor yet a case of entailment. The reminding item has to be recognized *as* so-and-so or such-and-such, and the other item has to be such that the thought of it is not already given in the thought that the reminding item is so-and-so or such-and-such.

Do the examples in 73d3–74a1 satisfy the conditions laid down? As mentioned above, the first particular example—seeing a lyre and thinking of its owner—can be taken in two ways, according to whether one is supposed to recognize it as a lyre or as his lyre. If the latter, it is in breach of the condition about *another knowledge*. The next example presents no difficulty: seeing Simmias I think of Cebes. The third case raises the same doubt as the first: seeing a picture of a lyre, I think of its owner. The fourth is unproblematic: seeing a picture of Simmias, I think of Cebes. The fifth and last example, however—seeing a picture of Simmias, I think of Simmias—is in blatant breach of one of the conditions. If we suppose that the thing is recognized as a picture of Simmias—as is certainly taken for granted—we cannot satisfy the 'other knowledge' condition. Saying to myself 'This is a picture of Simmias' may lead me to think about Simmias for the next three hours; but it cannot bring Simmias to my mind, since in saying this to myself I already have him in mind.

If there is indeed something suspect about Plato's fifth example, this may be of importance for the appraisal of the whole *anamnesis* argument. For when he comes to apply the account of *anamnesis* to the case of perceiving equal things and recovering knowledge of Forms, he treats this last as of the same type as the case of Simmias's picture and Simmias.

(c) My third and last comment on the thesis about *anamnesis* at 73c4–d1 is simply this: that the thesis is false. For the account it gives of *anamnesis*—or of the kind of *anamnesis* that is *being reminded*—does not include the condition that the *y* item must have been already known to a person if it is to be correct to say that he is reminded of it. The first thesis, at 73c1, did indeed lay down that '*A* is reminded of *y*' entails '*A* knew *y* before'. But the second thesis offers itself not as stating some *additional* requirements for *being reminded of*, but as stating a sufficient condition. Clearly the thesis is not in the least plausible unless the assumption that *y* was already known is added. But this is not mentioned as a necessary additional condition. And when at 74c13 Socrates comes to appeal to the present discussion he says: 'So long as, on seeing one thing, from this perception you think of another thing—whether like or unlike—what has occurred is necessarily *anamnesis*.' Thus, because of this second thesis he does not think it necessary to show that the person knew *y* before in order to show that it is a case of *anamnesis*. Yet, of course, having so 'proved' that it is *anamnesis* he would be in a position, by appealing to the agreed *first* thesis, to infer that the person had in fact known *y* before. This would clearly be a major deception. It would in particular beg the question against alternative explanations for a person's thinking of *y* on seeing *x*: e.g. that he now invented, made up, the idea of *y*. To beg this question in the context of an enquiry into the origin of our general ideas would indeed be reprehensible.

Plato could of course repair the disastrous omission in the second thesis by just adding the requirement that *y* be already known. It is, however, difficult to see how he could do this without frustrating the strategy of the whole argument towards pre-existence of the soul. If the point of appealing to the notion of *anamnesis* is to infer from certain facts about our recognition and classification of things that we *must* have known *y* (Forms) beforehand, the project would collapse if we had to *show* that we knew *y* beforehand in order to show that we had a case of *anamnesis*. What Plato needs is that the second thesis (73c4–d1) should give a sufficient condition for *anamnesis* (without mentioning the necessity of past knowledge of *y*), yet that the first thesis (that *anamnesis* entails prior knowledge) should also be true.

In the examples about Simmias and lyres it is all too easy just to assume the condition of prior knowledge to be satisfied. There are explicit references to forgetting. At 73e1: 'That sort of thing, then, is a kind of recollection, particularly when this happens to someone concerning items which have already been forgotten through time and not attending to them.' Again, at an important later stage (76a1): 'This did certainly appear possible, that a man on perceiving something . . . should from this think of something different, which he had forgotten, and to which this was closely related.' Whatever the acceptability of these statements, and of the assumptions in the examples, the fact remains that the official characterization of *anamnesis* in the second thesis, appealed to at 74c13, does not include the crucial point that *y* must have been known beforehand.

I have dwelt upon this radical defect in the *Phaedo* argument because, though it is obvious, it has received surprisingly little recognition from commentators. It is of course true that after the appeal at 74c13 Socrates does not in fact proceed to draw the inference ('since we are reminded of the Forms, we must have known them before') that the reader expects; he does not, in short, exploit the position he has built up. Instead, he introduces and exploits a new principle at 74d9–e4. Perhaps—or, even, presumably—Plato side-steps here precisely because he sees that the second thesis cannot after all serve his purpose. However that may be, the first thing for the analyst is to make clear that the second thesis is false, and that the appeal to it at 74c13 must be fruitless.

PHAEDO 73d2–74a8

It will be convenient to list here the examples Socrates gives:

	the *x* item, the *item perceived*	the *y* item, the *item thought of*
(1)	a lyre	a man
(2)	Simmias	Cebes
(3)	a pictured lyre	a man
(4)	pictured Simmias	Cebes
(5)	pictured Simmias	Simmias

In the light of these examples Socrates points out at 74a2 that *anamnesis* can occur from likes or on the other hand from unlikes; and he adds a comment about *anamnesis* from likes (74a5). Since perceiving equal things and getting the thought of equality will be treated as a case of *anamnesis* from likes, it is important to look rather closely at this earlier passage in which the notion is introduced.

(a) '*Anamnesis* from likes' might refer to *anamnesis* where the *x* item is like the *y* item; or it might refer to *anamnesis* where the thought of *y* arises *because of x*'s likeness to *y*. In the latter case—but not in the former—the phrase mentions the associative mechanism involved in certain instances of *anamnesis*. There can, I think, be little doubt that Plato does have this point in mind, even though the mere words 'from likes' do not clearly express it. But if so, it must be confessed that he is somewhat confused. For if 'from likes' is intended to mark off cases where perception of *x* leads to the thought of *y* by the similarity principle, the alternative ought to comprise cases where some other associative principle is operative (e.g. contiguity). In fact, however, when Plato says that there is recollection from likes 'but also from unlikes', it is obvious that this last phrase refers not to an alternative associative principle or mechanism (it is not *because* the lyre is *unlike* Simmias that seeing it makes me think of him), but simply to those *x*'s that are as a matter of fact unlike their respective *y*'s. The phrase 'from likes or from unlikes' appears to make an obvious and exhaustive dichotomy; but this appearance is deceptive.

The same point can be made in another way by consideration of Ross's note on a passage in Aristotle's *De Memoria*. Aristotle says that when trying to recall something, we go from something similar to it or contrary to it or close to it (451b19). In his note Ross says:

This is the earliest general formulation of the laws of association. But A. is to some extent only summing up what Plato had said by way of examples in *Phaedo* 73d2–74a4 ... [here Ross lists Plato's five examples]. Plato remarks that in some of these cases we proceed ἀπὸ ἀνομοίων [from unlikes], in some ἀφ' ὁμοίων [from likes]. Cases (1) and (2) are instances of association ἀπὸ ἀνομοίων [from unlikes], by contiguity. Case (5) is an instance of association ἀφ' ὁμοίων [from likes], by similarity. In cases (3) and (4) both similarity and contiguity are involved. The novel element in A.'s statement is his recognition of association by *contrast*.'[9]

Thus Ross takes Plato in the *Phaedo* to be talking about types of association, and he takes 'from likes' as a reference to association by similarity. But he does not take 'from unlikes' as a reference to association by dissimilarity—as if it were a weak form of association by contrast—but speaks as though it referred to association by contiguity. However, though that may indeed be the principle involved in the relevant examples, the description of them as cases of *anamnesis* 'from unlikes' cannot possibly be construed as a reference to that principle (in the way in which 'from likes' *can* be construed as a reference to the similarity principle).

The very same lack of parallelism is, I suspect, to be found at a later place in the *Phaedo*. At 76a3 Socrates remarks that they had seen that it was possible for a person on perceiving something to get from this the thought of something else which he had forgotten, something 'which this was close to, being unlike, or close to, being like' (ᾧ τοῦτο ἐπλησίαζεν, ἀνόμοιον ὂν ἢ ὅμοιον). Here it is natural to take 'being like' as giving the *nature* of the closeness—the association—in question; but it is not natural to take 'being unlike' in that way. If 'close to it, being like' is to mean 'connected with it in virtue of being like it', a proper parallel would be a phrase that mentioned

---

[9] W. D. Ross, *Aristotle's* Parva Naturalia (Oxford: Clarendon Press, 1955), 245.

some other type or types of association. But Plato's 'close to it, being unlike' certainly does not mean 'connected with it in virtue of dissimilarity'.[10]

(b) In which of the examples does Socrates intend us to see *anamnesis* from likes? Surely the last. In it the *x* item fulfils its role precisely through its likeness to the *y* item. This is not so in any of the other cases. Of course, in each of them there is some similarity between *x* and *y*; and in some the reminding mechanism includes similarity as well as contiguity or past association. But only of the last example could it be said that the *x* makes you think of the *y* because it is like it. That Socrates does indeed treat this as the example for *anamnesis* from likes is confirmed by his next remark (74a5), that in *anamnesis* from likes one necessarily considers whether the reminding item falls short of the other item as regards likeness. We need not now discuss this alleged necessity. But it is clear at once that the suggestion can only hope to apply to the fifth and last kind of case. When reminded of Cebes by seeing a picture of Simmias, you certainly will not ask whether the latter falls short of the former as regards likeness; nor will such a question arise in the other examples. Only in the last example, where *x* represents or depicts *y*, is the question whether the perceived item *falls short* of the item thought of, in regard to likeness, a sensible (and often very natural) question.

While the remark at 74a5 shows that Plato means the fifth example to be *anamnesis* from likes, the fact is that his point about falling short presupposes an asymmetrical relation which cannot properly be extracted from the description '*anamnesis* from likes', even when we construe this as a reference to the similarity mechanism ('from likes, *because* they are likes'). The example is a case of *a likeness*, and the relation of a likeness to its original is indeed asymmetrical. But 'from likes' cannot possibly *mean* 'from likenesses'. A proper straightforward case of *anamnesis* from likes would be this: seeing your cat makes me think of my cat, because they are very alike. Plato's array of examples contains no such case. The *only* example he gives which even looks like a straightforward

[10] Hackforth does, however, take both 'unlike' and 'like' as referring to associative mechanisms: 'something with which the first object was connected, whether by resemblance or contrast'. Bluck, on the other hand, avoids this implication in both cases: 'something similar or dissimilar, but anyhow in some way related' (*Plato's* Phaedo (London: Routledge and Kegan Paul, 1955) 70).

case of the similarity principle is the last. But this is in fact a very special case—where *x* is not simply *like y* but is *a likeness of y*. It is only with respect to such special cases that the subsequent remark about falling short could even possibly be thought to hold.

There are, then, two weaknesses in Plato's talk of *anamnesis* from likes. First, he fails to distinguish between saying that in some cases of *anamnesis x* is like *y* and saying that in some cases of *anamnesis* it is because *x* is like *y* that perceiving *x* provokes the thought of *y*. Secondly, because he fails to include a straightforward example of reminding by similarity (your cat, my cat), he is led to say about *anamnesis* from likes what can really be said sensibly only about the special case where the *x* item is a like*ness* of the *y* item.

(c) But is the remark at 74a5 correct even for the special case of likenesses? Why should it be thought *necessary* that one should raise the question whether *x* falls short of being a perfect likeness of *y*? If the point is that recognizing *x* as *a picture of y*—and not taking it to *be y*—involves seeing that it falls short in some way of complete and perfect likeness to *y* (*Cratylus* 432), how can there be the question *whether or not* it falls short? These and connected problems have been subtly discussed by J. C. B. Gosling.[11] I will simply set out very roughly the basic contrast which, it seems, Plato has not in this passage kept clearly enough in mind.

(i) Two things that are in a straightforward way similar (my cat and your cat) *can* be perfectly alike.

If the question whether they are is raised, the answer may be 'Yes' or 'No'. But the question need not be raised, and usually isn't. When it is said of two things that they are alike, there is, of course, no suggestion that either of them wants to be or ought to be exactly like the other.

(ii) A likeness *cannot* be in every way like its original.

So if the question were raised, the answer would have to be 'No'. The question how good a likeness it is can always be asked, and it often is; for a likeness, in general, wants to be or ought to be as true to its original as possible.

---

[11] J. C. B. Gosling, 'Similarity in *Phaedo* 73B seq.', *Phronesis*, 10 (1965), 151–61.

PHAEDO 74a9–b3

'We say that there is such a thing as *the equal itself*' (74a9–b1). Here and in what follows it is important to know whether 'we' and 'you' refer to people in general or to believers in the theory of Forms. In this passage there is little doubt that Socrates is appealing to a doctrine—the theory of Forms—acceptable to him and his associates but not, of course, to the man in the street. 'We say' means in fact (though Socrates could hardly have put it so) 'We Platonists say'. It is true that phrases like 'the equal itself' and sentences of the form 'There is such a thing as . . .' could be used in ordinary Greek without any metaphysical implications. But, given that the theory of Forms is introduced into the present argument as a crucial premiss—and later remarks confirm this[12]—it is hard to deny that 74a9 is the place at which it is introduced.

But if the 'we' at 74a9 means 'we Platonists', what about the 'we' at 74b2? 'We know it, what it is'—we Platonists or we ordinary people? The following passage, about how we have acquired this knowledge, and particularly the section 74e–75b with its talk of our use of sense perception since infancy, are surely meant to apply to people in general. Plato seems to be drawing attention to ordinary familiar facts about how we all grow up classifying and recognizing perceptible objects. If so, the 'we' at 74b2 ought also to have this wide reference. Yet this would involve a very awkward switch from the esoteric 'we' of 74a9.

Connected with this little difficulty about 'we' is the apparent contradiction between the statement here (74b2) that we know it, what it is, and the statement later (76b5–c3) that nobody (except perhaps Socrates) has knowledge of the equal, the good, etc. We need, perhaps, to distinguish three propositions:

(a) The ordinary person gets to know the correct use of the ordinary word '*X*' and thereby acquires, as we should normally say, knowledge of *X*-ness: he knows that there is such a thing as *X*-

---

[12] Particularly 76d–77a and 92d. I cannot agree with G. Prauss, who writes as follows in his rewarding book *Platon und der logische Eleatismus* (Berlin: Walter de Gruyter & Co., 1966), 108: 'Die Theorie der Anamnesis ist letztbegründende Voraussetzung sowohl für die Lehre von der Präexistenz der Seele wie für die von der Existenz der Ideen, an die wiederum die Unsterblichkeitsargumente anknüpfen.'

ness, and he knows what it is (in the unloaded sense of these expressions).

(b) Platonists hold that *X*-ness is an eternal, unchanging Form, an independently existing entity.

(c) Few if any Platonists can give account of the Form *X*-ness: few if any know what *X*-ness is (in the rich sense).

Where Socrates is talking about what people in general have been doing since infancy, and saying that we know what equality is, he is advancing the first of these propositions. In introducing the theory of Forms, he is relying on the second. When he says that we do *not* know what equality is, he is asserting the third.

A GENERAL QUESTION

I should like finally to take a bird's-eye view of the whole argument of which the passage I have so far discussed is only the first part. I shall raise a general question about the strategy of the argument, in particular about the way in which the theory of Forms is supposed to combine with other premises to generate the required conclusion. I shall pass over many details and difficulties, and just try to bring out one main point.

The basic ingredients of the argument seem to be:

(a) the account of the ordinary concept of *anamnesis*;
(b) the theory of Forms;
(c) a metaphysically unloaded description of what we all do from infancy:
  (i) perceiving sensible particulars, we think of universals; and
  (ii) we realize that the particulars fall short somehow of the universals.

We have already noted that (a) and (c)(i) together will not get us to the conclusion that we must have known universals before infancy.[13] That the situation described in (c)(i) satisfies the requirements of the thesis about *anamnesis* at 73c4 is compatible with its being the case that we think up universals for ourselves—and do not *recall* them. Moreover, if (a) and (c)(i) together did the trick,

---

[13] Quite apart from the notorious fallacy in the argument of 75b4–c6.

there would be no role for the theory of Forms in the argument. But there clearly is. So can we bring in this further ingredient (b), and thereby get to the wanted conclusion?

In the present context the theory of Forms presents itself as an existential statement or a set of existential statements; and for our purposes a sufficient formulation may be this: that there really exist perfect equality, perfect beauty, etc. I am not, of course, suggesting that this is absolutely clear; but it is close enough to the text, and, with luck, it may serve.

'Perceiving x, he thinks of y' does not entail 'He recalls y'. He may be making up what he thinks of; there need not have been any actual y that he once knew and now remembers. But suppose we now add to the premiss 'Perceiving x, he thinks of y' the further premiss 'There really is such a thing as y', can we infer that *what he is thinking of is a real thing*, and therefore *not* just something he is making up? And can we infer further that, if it is not just something he is making up—and also not something he is currently perceiving—he must have got to know it somehow in the past? Part of what is involved can be brought out by a case like this: that people fear the Loch Ness monster does not entail that there really is such a monster; add the premiss that there really is; surely we can conclude that what they fear is a real monster? Here, as before, the question is what happens when an existential premiss is added to a premiss involving an intentional verb: what one can then truly say, and what inferences can safely be drawn from that. In the *Phaedo* the final inference depends on the assumption that if one is thinking of something which one is not currently perceiving, *either* one is making it up *or* one is recalling something one previously made up or encountered, the first possibility being ruled out by the first conclusion—that what one is thinking of is something real.

Let us now return to consider (c)(ii), the premiss that we realize particulars to fall short of universals. Though brought in in connection with one type of *anamnesis*, that 'from likes', the argument from it rests essentially not on anything said about *anamnesis*, but just on the principle agreed to at 74d9: 'whenever a person on seeing something thinks that "this that I now see wishes to be just like some other thing there is but falls short and cannot be just like it, but is inferior"—is it not necessary that the person thinking this should have known beforehand that thing which he says this one resembles but falls short of?' In fact, the appeal at 74c13 back to the *anamnesis* analysis is not carried through; and the principle just quoted *replaces* what would have been a different, independent argument (an argument apparently relying on the [mis]use of criteria for *anamnesis*, but covertly depending upon the use of the theory of Forms in the way just considered).

What are we to say about the principle agreed to at 74d9? Surely someone seeing something can think that it falls short of some ideal or possibility that he conceives at that moment, that he then makes up? So if he says 'This falls short of perfect *F*-ness', we cannot infer that there really is such a thing as perfect *F*-ness and that it is that which he sees this to fall short of. Let us, however, as before, add a further premiss: 'Perfect *F*-ness really exists.' Can we now infer that what he is thinking and speaking about really exists, that what he believes this to fall short of is a Form, *not* something he is just making up, but something he must be recalling? The question here is clearly parallel to that raised above in connection with (c)(i): the intentional context there was '. . . thinks of . . .'; here it is '. . . thinks that . . . falls short of . . .'. The existential premiss in each case is provided by the theory of Forms.

Plato does not of course discuss the weighty problems that grow like weeds in this area; nor shall I. I have only wished to indicate a pattern of reasoning—not unplausible and not without philosophical interest—that seems to me to lie not far below the surface of the *Phaedo* argument, and to suggest what role the emphatic assertion of the existence of Forms plays in that argument. A sign of Plato's grasp of what his argument requires is, I think, to be found in the precise wording of 74d9: 'this that I now see wishes to be just like some other thing *there is*' (ἄλλο τι τῶν ὄντων). In making the person himself say this, Plato makes him commit himself to there *actually being* the thing of which he takes this to fall short; and that *is* incompatible with its being something (an ideal, a blueprint) he is just now making up. 'He is very unlike the ideal candidate for this job' is compatible with there being no ideal candidate; but it is different if I add 'and the ideal candidate actually exists'.

It may be said that all the fuss about combining intentional premisses with existential ones is unnecessary, because it comes of treating as independent bases of Plato's argument, firstly the theory of Forms, and secondly the neutral description of what people do (thinking of one thing when they perceive another). Doesn't Plato rather take it that people *recognize things as falling short of Forms*?

But how could Plato *get* this proposition? It is not what ordinary people would themselves say. It must result, therefore, from a conflation of what they would say and readily agree, with something 'we' know and can add—namely, the theory of Forms. But the propriety of making this conflation is precisely the issue raised above.

2

Language and Reality in Plato's
Cratylus

INTRODUCTION

The *Cratylus* is a curious dialogue, and it is perhaps not surprising that it has not been a favourite among scholars or among philosophers, at least until recently. About half of the dialogue, a great chunk in the middle, speculates about the etymology of Greek words in a manner that is sometimes amusing, but often just boring. The arguments in the other half used to be interpreted in a rather narrow way, as concerned with the origin of language, or with the suitability of particular names to particular things. More recently, serious and complicated philosophical issues have been found to be raised by these argumentative parts of the *Cratylus*, though there remains dispute as to how many of the issues were in Plato's own mind, and also as to how the various parts of the dialogue hang together. The typical modern approach will regard the etymological section of the dialogue as only mildly interesting, but will discover in the rest of it material relevant to a number of important topics in the philosophy of language, philosophical logic, and metaphysics—topics carried forward in the *Theaetetus* and *Sophist*. As usual with Plato, fundamental ideas are presented in a very simple way; but it is often instructive to get back from sophisticated modern discussions to the basic essentials.

The *Cratylus* opens with a confrontation between Hermogenes and Cratylus, who hold opposed views on a *linguistic* question, whether names are purely conventional or have some natural correctness; and the dialogue mainly consists in an examination of the two rival answers to these questions. But it ends with a confrontation between two *ontological* theories, the Heraclitean doctrine of flux and the Platonic doctrine of Forms. It is not obvious that there

First published in 1994.

is any correlation between the two linguistic theses and the two ontological theses. It is true that the historical Cratylus, presented in the dialogue as an exponent of the nature theory of language, was in fact (and is presented as) an exponent of an extreme flux view of reality; but there seems no necessary or rational connection between that theory and this view. For the one is a theory about how names name *whatever* there is; the other is a theory about what there is. Nor does Hermogenes' rival conventionalist view seem to involve the rival ontological view, the theory of Forms.

If the contrast between flux and Forms is somewhat surprising as the outcome of a discussion of the two linguistic views, it is also somewhat surprising in itself, in that the obvious alternative to the view that everything is in continuous flux is that *not* everything is in continuous flux, that there is some stability in reality. But the thesis that there are unchanging Forms goes much further than that.

In this essay[1] I discuss some of the arguments and ideas about language which the *Cratylus* contains, partly for their own interest and partly in the hope of throwing light on the question how the arguments about language are related to ontological theses.

It may be useful to give first a brief outline of the structure of the dialogue. In 383–391a Socrates argues against Hermogenes, who holds that anyone can call anything what he likes, and that there is no '*natural* correctness' of names; and the outcome of the whole section seems to be that there must be *some* such 'natural correctness', though it is not yet clear what this is.

391b–421d is a long etymological section designed to show, by analysing compound words and tracing them back to their elementary parts, what the original or basic words were, and thus to show why compound words have the meanings they have. This section leaves untouched the question why and how the elementary or 'primary' words had (or have) the meanings *they* had (or have). And this question leads into the next section.

421d–427 concerns the primary, elementary names or words, and considers the suggestion that *they* successfully and correctly do their job in so far as they imitate (or represent by *likeness*) the things they stand for—a sort of picture theory of meaning.

---

[1] This essay is based on two lectures delivered in Florence in April 1990. The lectures did not argue for a single thesis, but were designed as an introduction to the *Cratylus* and a stimulus to thought about some of the issues it raises. I hope that this published version may serve the same purposes.

428e–435c attacks Cratylus's contention that there is a natural correctness of names, that only naturally correct names are names at all, and that falsity is impossible.

435d–440 argues that knowledge of things is prior to knowledge through language, and that language and knowledge would be impossible on the flux theory, but are possible if there are unchanging Forms.

I

I shall first analyse the argument against Hermogenes and make some comments on it. In the second part of the essay I shall pick out for discussion certain main ideas from the rest of the dialogue, before finally drawing some general conclusions.

The main argument may be divided into seven sections, preceded by three short preliminary passages:

Preliminaries	(a)	383a3–385a	The two views
	(b)	385b–c	Truth and falsity
	(c)	385d	Hermogenes' view
Sections	(1)	385e4–386e5	Things
	(2)	386e6–387b7	Doings
	(3)	387b8–c5	Saying
	(4)	387c6–d9	Naming
	(5)	387d10–388c8	Teaching
	(6)	388c9–389a4	Name making
	(7)	389a5–391a	Ideal names and the dialectician

Preliminaries (a) and (c) are mainly concerned with setting out the rival views. At the beginning of the dialogue (383a4–b2) Cratylus is said to hold 'that for each thing there is a correct name that belongs to it by nature: a name is not whatever any set of people have agreed to call a thing and do call it . . . , but there is some natural correctness of names which is the same for all, both Greeks and barbarians'. Hermogenes, on the other hand, says (384d1–8): 'correct naming is simply a matter of convention and agreement. . . . Whatever name anyone gives a thing is its correct name; and if he then changes to another name and stops using the first one, then the new name is no less correct than the old one was, as when we rename our servants. No name ever belonged to anything by nature, only by custom and habit, that is, through people becoming habituated to its use.' Further formulations of Hermogenes' view are to be found at 385a and 385d–e3.

Hermogenes' thesis is not as precise as one would wish. Firstly, the word *onoma* (translated 'name') can cover both proper names and general or abstract names ('dog' or 'generosity'); it can even be extended to include adjectives, or indeed any words. So the exact scope of Hermogenes' thesis is unclear. In what follows I shall usually speak of *names*, though many of the examples discussed in the *Cratylus* would not usually be called names by us, but *words*; and I shall myself sometimes speak of *words* in discussing Plato's arguments and ideas. Secondly, there are differences, to which Hermogenes is not attentive, among such ideas as agreement, convention, stipulation, and custom. These differences are perhaps unimportant for his essential thesis, which is not about the exact way in which names are initially introduced *into* a language, but about what enables them to be correct names *in* a language. This depends, Hermogenes will maintain, on the language-users' all *using* the names to stand for certain things, and *not* on the existence of any *natural* relation between the names and those things.

It *is*, however, a defect in Hermogenes' statements that they do not emphasize sufficiently the crucial distinction between (i) the word introduction (whether by fiat or by agreement or in any other way) that establishes rules for the use of a word, and (ii) the subsequent use of the word, which is correct if it is in accordance with those rules. The clearest expression of this distinction in the Greek is at 385d8–9, the contrast between the past event of introducing a word (ἐθέμην) and the continuous present custom of using it (καλεῖν). Hermogenes' thesis is not that every subsequent use of a word that has been introduced is a correct use (i.e. a use in accordance with the established rules for its use), but that there are no natural constraints on what rules may be established when a word is introduced.

The little section I have labelled (b), 385b–c, is an argument to the conclusion that there are true and false names. It contains a number of difficulties, but I will make just two points, one about the content of the passage, the other about its relevance in the dialogue.

Socrates infers from the fact that there are true and false *logoi* (sentences or statements) to the conclusion that there are true and false *onomata* (names or words), on the ground that a *logos* is a whole and *onomata* are its parts. This is altogether too crude as a general argument, since wholes often have characteristics that do *not* attach to their parts. But it does suggest an important point. Consider a standard basic statement such as 'Callias is a man'. This statement is *true* if and only if 'Callias' is *true* of something and 'a man' is also *true* of that thing. The truth of such statements cannot be analysed or understood without the notion of *true of* which applies to names. And conversely, this notion of a name's being *true* (or *false*) *of* requires an understanding of the whole speech-act (e.g. the statement) of which naming forms a part. We shall meet again later (in sections 3 and 4 of the main argument) the move from saying to naming.

But what is section (b) doing in the *Cratylus*? Is it put forward as in itself an argument against Hermogenes? Its conclusion is that there are both true and false names. Is Socrates implying that on Hermogenes' view there could not be false names? If so, the implication is unfair. Just as Hermogenes is not committed to the view that every use of an established name is a correct use, so he is not committed to the view that in every correct use of a name it is true of that to which it is applied.

Perhaps, however, it is wrong to regard this section as a separate argument. The point that Socrates here gets agreed is that there *is* truth and falsity of statements and so of names. This is the linguistic counterpart of the ontological point (in section 1) that will serve as the foundation of the main argument against Hermogenes, the point that *things* have independent characters of their own. The argument that then follows is designed to show that Hermogenes' thesis of absolute freedom in naming is inconsistent with there being truth and falsity and (equally) with there being things with objective natures of their own.

I turn now to the main argument against Hermogenes, and begin by giving a summary of the first four sections (i.e. up to 387d9).

Section 1 (385e4–386e5)

Socrates gets Hermogenes to reject both Protagoras's relativism—that things are just as they seem to anyone—and Euthydemus's paradox—that things both are and aren't anything whatsoever. He does this by appealing to the distinction we all draw between the wise and the foolish, the good and the bad. (Compare *Theaetetus* 152a, 161cff.) So things do have some fixed being, independent natures of their own (386e1–4).

Section 2 (386e6–387b7)

Socrates now applies this conclusion to *praxeis*, or 'doings'; for doings are themselves one kind of thing there is. They must therefore be done *according to their own nature*. For we shall *succeed* in doing this or that only if we do it according to the nature of this or that doing, and with the naturally appropriate instrument (*organon*). Otherwise we shall fail and 'get nowhere' (οὐδὲν πράξομεν).

Socrates illustrates this with the examples of cutting and burning; and with these examples it is easy to see what he means. If we want to do some cutting, it is no good trying to use a feather, we must use a knife; and if we want to cut wood, it is no use trying to do it with a butter-knife. What *cutting is*, and what the character of the candidate for *being cut* is, limit or even determine how we must proceed, and with what *organon*, if we are indeed to (e.g.) cut wood.

Section 3 (387b8–c5)

Saying things (λέγειν) is one kind of doing. So if *it* is to be achieved, it must be done in the *way* in which it is *natural* to say this or that thing (and for them to be said)—and with the naturally appropriate *tools* (*organa*).

Section 4 (387c6–d9)

Since in *saying* things we *name* this or that, naming is a part of saying. So naming itself is a kind of 'doing with regard to things' (387c6–11). Therefore we shall succeed in naming things only if we do it in the way in which it is natural to name things (and for them to be named), and with the naturally appropriate tools (387d1–8).

I will now comment on the argument so far. The idea of *words as tools* with which we do something seems promising, but is not

Plato's comparison of naming with other activities seriously misleading?

The most obvious objection is that naming x is a very different *type* of 'doing' from cutting or burning x, and that this difference prevents the argument by analogy (which purports to show that nature dictates how and with what we must name a given thing) from doing what Socrates wants it to do. My naming x is not a causal transaction between me and x; I am indeed doing something in naming x, but not doing something *to* x (not effecting a change in x). And so my success—the effectiveness of the name I use—does not depend on the character of x in the way in which my ability to cut or burn something with this or that tool does depend on the character of the thing (and on my using a tool appropriate to that character).

There are of course numerous cases—indeed, kinds of case—where though ϕing may be counted as a doing, ϕing x is not doing anything *to* x: for example, recalling an event, buying a book, dancing a waltz, playing chess, bidding three clubs, imagining a city free of traffic. (There are also, of course, plenty of cases of ϕing that would be counted as doing, but where there is *no x* at all: walking, talking, voting, gardening.) (Note the variation in terminology between 'saying things' at 387c1 and 'a doing *with regard to things*' at 387c10. The former suggests an analogy with transitive verbs like 'burn' and 'cut'; the latter does not.)

That dancing a waltz and bidding three clubs are not activities in which one does something *to*—acts causally *upon*—a waltz or three clubs does not of course exclude the possibility that they are activities in which one does something to—acts causally upon—*something*. After all, making a marble statue is bringing a statue into being, and not doing something to a statue; yet it necessarily involves doing something to the marble. In such a case the nature of whatever *is* acted upon can determine the method and tools necessary for success in the activity.

The essential point, however, is this, that though the analogy between naming and burning (or cutting) is defective, *every* distinguishable kind of doing (as of thing) has *some* objective criteria of success, or of what counts as that kind of doing (or that kind of thing). It is not up to me to decide that I have danced a waltz or done some gardening; there are objective criteria to settle the question. So for naming also we must ask what *are* the objective criteria for success in naming things, and ask whether these criteria are such as to rule out Hermogenes' thesis.

Socrates does not in fact make *im*proper use of the argument from analogy with burning and cutting. For he does *not* say that because success in cutting *x* depends on using a tool naturally suited to cut *x*, success in naming *x* must depend on using a name naturally suited to name *x*—and that Hermogenes is thus refuted. Instead, he approaches the question about the objective criteria for success in the case of naming by asking what kind of activity it is, what we are really up to when we do it (388b8). When we shuttle, we are dividing the weft and warp. When we name we are . . . doing what? An understanding of *this* should reveal whether there are—contrary to Hermogenes' view—*natural* restrictions on what can be used as names for this or that naming task.

Before turning to Socrates' account of what we *are* doing in naming, I want to make a comment on section 4 (387c6–d9), in which Socrates moves from saying to naming. Why does he first introduce saying as a kind of doing, and then *argue* that naming is a kind of doing—on the ground that it is a 'part' of saying?

It will be helpful at this point to ask what we are to think of as a case or episode of naming (i.e. of name using). Take a simple situation in which I point to my cat Benjamin and say to you (in an assertive tone of voice) 'cat'. What is necessary if this is to be a thoroughly *successful* performance? One requirement is that I should convey my thought to you; and for this to be so, I must use the word 'cat' correctly—according to some settled usage—and you must recognize my adoption of that usage.

Communicative success depends on shared conventions, by which one person can come to know what another one thinks. (This point is made later against Cratylus, 434e–435b: provided the conventions are shared, successful communication of thoughts is possible, no matter what the conventions are.)

However, another sort of success in naming concerns *truth*. For this success I must have used a name that does actually apply, in virtue of its meaning, to the item to which I have applied it. In this case I have not only expressed my thought correctly and conveyed it successfully, I have also expressed (by my gesture and naming) a *true* thought—the same in fact as would be expressed by the true statement 'That is a cat' (or 'Benjamin is a cat').

This is, of course, a highly oversimplified account of one particular naming context, but it will serve to bring into view the point I wish to make. The use of sentences to make statements involves the use of names to pick out or apply to things; and the point of using names to pick out or apply to things is to contribute to the making of statements. Telling someone something is a complex operation whose simplest form is '*S* is *P*', and to perform this operation, we use terms '*S*' and '*P*'. If what I tell is *true*, '*S*' and '*P*' must both be *true of* the same thing. (I can, of course, as in the cat example, convey a truth using only one name—but that is because my gesture and the context serve to pick out the subject item.) These matters, discussed further by Plato in the *Theaetetus* and *Sophist*, in connection with the analysis of truth and falsity, are only touched on in the *Cratylus*; but the elements of the later discussions are to be found here.

So much for the questions why Socrates argues from saying to naming and why naming is a part of saying. I shall return to the distinction between the requirements for communicative success and the requirements for success in stating the truth. Meanwhile, I go on to sections 5 and 6 of the argument (387d10–389a4), which may be summarized as follows.

Section 5 (387d10–388c8)

We shuttle with a shuttle, we name with a name. When we shuttle, we separate out the warp and the weft; what exactly are we trying to do when we use names as tools and do some naming? 'We teach one another something, dividing things as they are' (388b10–11). So a name is a tool for teaching and dividing things as they are.

Section 6 (388c9–389a4)

Where do these tools, the names we use, come from? From *nomos* (law or established custom). They are therefore the product of the lawmaker (the *nomothetes*), who must obviously—like any other tool-maker—have the necessary special skill.

Do we think self-evident, or even plausible, the thesis that the essential aim of name using is 'teaching one another and dividing things as they are'? (I take it that the second part of this formula is intended to elucidate the first part, and is not specifying a further thing we do in addition to teaching.) Surely we use names for a great variety of purposes. However, the notion of teaching does combine two features that seem to be fundamental and essential to language: communication and truth. Of course, not every speech-act is an assertion, still less a didactic assertion intended to convey truth to another. But it may well be held that assertion is the fundamental speech-act—and an assertion certainly makes a claim to truth; and it will probably be agreed that the possibility of use in communication is essential to language. If so, the apparent narrowness of Socrates' answer to the question 'What are we doing when we use names?' will not matter. He is directing us to the two central ideas in the philosophy of language: truth and the communication of thoughts. The rest of the *Cratylus* revolves round these two ideas.

In section 6 talk of a personal 'law-giver' or 'word-maker' carries on the analogy with ordinary crafts, but the real questions are not in any way historical, but are: what are the criteria for *being* a name (or a good name); and what (therefore) are the natural limitations or conditions upon word *introduction* (requirements for *becoming* a name)?

Conveying truth about various things by using names requires that the names distinguish things there *are*. So here there is a 'natural necessity' which is a constraint upon name introduction— if an essential purpose of using names is to convey truth. Names must stand for items there really are and for characteristics there really are, if we are to be able to use names to ascribe characteristics to things—and to do so truly. This is, then, a necessary condition of effective name using, and hence a requirement for successful name introduction: the 'law-giver's' task is to assign names to *things there are*. This task is discussed in the next section.

Section 7 (389a5–391a)

The name-maker must, if he is to make names that are capable of doing their job, (i) identify the various real natures there are (what for example shuttling *is*), and (ii) express or embody each of them in a name appropriate to its nature. Whether he has done this successfully will be judged by the expert name-user, the dialectician.

The two aspects of the task here assigned to the name-maker are in effect two conditions which Plato says must be fulfilled if language is to serve its purpose, which is to communicate truth. They concern *what* is named, and *how* it is named. (i) Names must designate characters or kinds there really are, and (ii) a name must be naturally appropriate to the character or kind it corresponds to. I shall discuss these points in reverse order.

The *second* claim would seem simply to contradict Hermogenes' thesis; and surely he ought simply to reject it. He can perfectly well allow that, if language is to serve its purpose, names must designate kinds and characters there really are; but he must insist that it is up to anyone (or any group) *what* name is attached to some kind or to some character. Take the dog: it is entirely conventional (no 'natural appropriateness') whether the word 'dog' or 'chien' or 'cane' is used to stand for that kind of animal—and any other word would have done just as well. Nature may determine what kinds or properties are to be found in reality; but that is not to say that there are any natural restrictions on the names that may be introduced, and used successfully, to *stand for* this or that kind of property. For designating *x* is not a casual operation upon *x*, and a name's ability to designate *x* is not determined in any way by the *character* of *x*.

Now, Socrates' discussion of the name-maker's work contains a difficult but interesting notion in the passage 389d–390a7: a notion of *what a name really is* that distinguishes it from ordinary so-called names in particular languages. The 'name itself' or the 'form of name' is distinguished from its particular embodiments. The name itself for the species *dog* is not the English word 'dog', nor is it the French word 'chien'; these are two different expressions of one and the same name itself. Is this perhaps a manœuvre, designed to meet Hermogenes' claim that the choice of names is purely conventional by redefining what a name (really) is? But first, what exactly does the notion of a name itself amount to?

Socrates is introducing a notion of name according to which a name is to be *identified* solely by reference to the job it does—what it stands for. If 'dog' and 'cane' *mean the same*, they are to be counted as one and the same *name*, in spite of the differences of letters (and sounds). This idea, given briefly in our passage, recurs later at 394a–c. The doctor, it is there said, counts two tablets as the *same medicine*, even if they differ in shape and colour, provided that they have the same power (*dunamis*)—that is, produce the same medical effect. So, Socrates suggests, we should regard names that have the same *force* (*dunamis*) as being really the same name. (The term *dunamis* here corresponds to *eidos* and *idea* at 389e3 and 390a6.)

We might call the name identified by the idea that it expresses the *ideal* name (as opposed to the ordinary name). An ordinary name is made of particular sounds or letters; but the ideal name is a *semantically defined* unit not made of sounds or letters. It is in effect the meaning of all the ordinary names in a group of synonyms; and one might well call it the *name-as-concept*, in that what synonyms all express is *the same concept*.

So could this idea form part of an argument against Hermogenes? Surely not. If one uses meaning as the sole criterion of identity of 'names' (i.e. considers *ideal* names, or concepts), Hermogenes' original thesis is side-stepped rather than denied or refuted. For *his* thesis was about the conventionality of the *ordinary* words that *have* meanings (or *express* concepts), not about the meanings or concepts themselves. His thesis was that various ordinary words can be equally good for expressing a given concept (embodying a given ideal name)—and this is not contradicted by the suggestion that a concept itself is identified by what it is the concept *of*. So whatever the value of Socrates' idea about the identity conditions of concepts (or 'ideal names' or 'synonym groups'), Hermogenes' actual thesis about *ordinary* names still awaits discussion. And in fact, most of what follows in the *Cratylus* is about the sounds and letters of ordinary Greek names, and whether there is any 'natural correctness' about *them*.

Nevertheless, it seems to me that in the passages we are considering, Socrates puts his finger on a point that is essential for the understanding of language and of how it works. A primitive account of language is tempted to treat names as directly standing for things; and some notorious paradoxes about the impossibility of falsity arise from this assumption. So it is a matter of fundamental importance that there is a third element in the situation, an intermediary between names and things: the meaning or concept or thought. Because you know the meaning of a word I use, the concept I express by it, you can grasp the thought I am trying to communicate to you. A common conceptual scheme is the condition of the communication of thoughts. But the question of truth depends on the relation of concepts or thoughts to the external world, the fit between concepts or thoughts and things. This is, of course, a very crude statement. But we are, in the *Cratylus*, at the birth of the philosophy of language; and it would not be helpful to use in exegesis the more sophisticated apparatus of modern analysis. Indeed, my crude statement already goes beyond what Plato makes explicit. In particular, it is a serious question to what extent he himself drew a clear distinction (here or elsewhere) between concepts and universals, and between the existence of concepts and the existence of universals. But in any case it is certainly right to emphasize the philosophical importance of the contrast Socrates draws between ordinary words in particular languages and the identical meanings that different ordinary words can have.

I return now to the first of the conditions we noted: that names must correspond to *real* characters or kinds, if we are to be able to 'teach each other and divide things as they are'. When this phrase was first used to describe what we are doing when we use names, it was natural to understand it in an entirely untechnical way, and to interpret the condition correspondingly. We use language to tell each other that the cat is on the mat. This could not convey information if there were no cats or mats. We say that lions are brave; this could not convey information if there were no lions and no such thing as bravery.

Perhaps, however, in the section we are now considering, a somewhat deeper meaning must be sought. For now the person said to be expert in using names—and hence the best judge of their correctness—is the *dialectician*, 'the man who can ask and answer questions' (390c10). A surprising assertion, and it is necessary to draw upon other dialogues to interpret it. I summarize familiar points. The dialectician does not ask and answer such questions as 'Where is the cat?' or 'Is the cat on the mat?' He asks after definitions or essences: 'What *is* justice?' 'What *is* a cat?' His use of language is not identical with the ordinary use of it, but is somehow of a higher level; it is *critical*, as it were, not of individual statements or misstatements (like 'The cat is on the mat'), but of the language and its words in general. One such type of criticism might direct itself to practical requirements; it might bring out, for example, that some words are ambiguous, and therefore bad tools of communication. But another type of criticism will direct itself to individual concepts or a group of concepts, or to the whole conceptual structure expressed in a language, which can be tested for clarity and coherence and objective validity. If questions such as 'What is justice?', 'What is a cat?' can be answered (on this level and in this way), it is established not just that the words 'justice' and 'cat' have clear meanings, but that justice is a real, objective characteristic, and that the cat is a real natural kind. A successful language (one the dialectician commends) will be one that correctly mirrors the structure of reality.

II

The main argument against Hermogenes inferred from the fact that language-using is an activity with a definite purpose that there is a 'natural correctness' of names, but it left unanswered the question what that correctness consists in. Socrates drew an important distinction between ordinary names, made up of Greek (or other) letters or sounds, and 'ideal names' or names-as-concepts, the meanings that ordinary names (in whatever language) serve to express. It will be helpful to correlate these two types of name with the two elements in the function (*ergon*) of language. That function is 'teaching and dividing things as they are', and the two elements are communication and truth. If a language-user is to perform successfully, there are two main conditions—natural necessities—that must be satisfied. (1) The language must contain a stock of words (ordinary names) that are understood and therefore service-able for communication of thoughts to others. (2) The words in the language must express concepts that relate to reality in such a way as to be serviceable for the communication of *truth*. This truth requirement lays a condition upon names-as-concepts. To convey truth about things and characteristics, a speaker needs concepts of qualities and other characteristics that are actually instantiated and concepts of kinds of things that actually exist.

Something more will be said about truth and reality. But in the meantime Socrates turns (in 391b–421d) to a long discussion of the ordinary (Greek) names that are the immediate tools of communication. The details of his often fanciful etymologizing do not concern us; but the main lessons derived from them, as regards conditions for having and using ordinary language, deserve some attention.

How is it possible for (ordinary) names to express and convey concepts? How might one learn such names—and learn to use them to express the concepts others use them to express? One obvious aid to rely on would be *natural likeness*. This pictorial or imitation principle is relied on as often as possible in international traffic signs; Socrates gives some basic examples at *Cratylus* 422e–433a. So one suggestion would be that ordinary names, to be effective in communication, must be learnable and teachable, and that to be learnable and teachable, they must be like what they stand for—they must *carry their meanings on their faces*.

Socrates plays with the idea that Greek names express the conceptual scheme of Heracliteans, and sets out to show how names do by their sounds imitate or represent what they stand for. The attempt breaks down in two ways. First, in more and more examples Socrates is forced to claim that, although the original words were like the things they stood for, our present words have been much changed from their original composition—letters have been added and subtracted. But if this is so, then even if names did once have a natural likeness to what they stood for, that cannot be a necessary condition of their usability now—since we successfully learn to use them for communication, even though they no longer have that natural likeness. Secondly, Socrates draws attention to a bit of vocabulary where the very idea of natural likeness is absurd—the indefinitely large number of names for numbers (435b6). The first lesson of the etymologizing is that the necessary and sufficient condition of success in communication is that the speaker and hearer have come to the custom and usage of attaching the same names to the same concepts (434e–435b). How this can be brought about is another question, which Socrates does not go into. He does, however, recognize that natural likeness is desirable as far as possible (435c2–3), since it obviously facilitates the acquisition of concepts, the learning of meanings; but it is neither necessary nor sufficient to ensure such learning.

Some words are easily intelligible to one who hears them for the first time because they are like what they stand for; but there is another way in which words may be instantly intelligible—they may be *compounds* of words already known to the hearer. Socrates offers etymologies of many compounds. He makes clear that the possibility of understanding this kind depends on there being already a common understanding of the primary words (*prōta onomata*) from which the compounds are built (425d–426a). (We may add that it is helpful in a language—it makes it easier to learn and easier to use for communication without misunderstanding—if the ways in which compounds are built are regular, so that analogies are reliable. English is notoriously unhelpful in this respect: a butter-knife is a knife for cutting butter, but a pocket-knife is not a knife for cutting pockets. But here again, although such regularity in compounds is desirable, it is neither a necessary nor a sufficient condition of the word's being understood and used successfully to communicate thought. For this a common custom or usage, however achieved, is the sole requisite.)

The core of a language, then, is a set of basic words which the language-users have learned to employ in the same customary way, to express the same concepts. This provokes two large questions, one epistemological and one ontological. (1) How is such learning possible? Can we (say, Greek-speakers) be sure that we do indeed all have the same thoughts—express the same concepts—when we use these words? And (2), supposing that we do all think of the same characters and kinds when we say '*leukon*' or '*hippos*', can we safely infer to the reality of the characters and kinds we think of? (Is it clear that you and I mean the same when we speak of 'a ghost'? And, supposing that we do, can we infer from the existence of the concept *ghost* to the existence of ghosts?)

The first of these questions, the epistemological one, is not examined in the *Cratylus*. Part of the answer, no doubt, is that we find ourselves applying the same words to the same things around us; and that we can teach and learn the meanings of many words by applying them to examples easily identified by pointing. But in other cases—and these the more important—there is dispute in applying the words and disagreement as to the identification of examples (*Phaedrus* 263a–c, *Politicus* 285d–286a). Another part of Plato's response is to be found in his doctrine of *anamnesis*. He uses it in the *Phaedo* (73c–77a) to explain in particular our capacity to conceive universals of which we have met no actual (perfect) instance, in the *Meno* (80d–86b) to explain our capacity to see logical connections, and in the *Phaedrus* (249b–c) to explain in general our capacity to seize the universal in the particular. *Anamnesis* is the forerunner of Locke's doctrine of innate ideas and of more recent theories of innate grammatical programmes. The ability to revive common knowledge of general ideas is presented as an innate and distinctive power of human beings. It must of course be recognized that such a doctrine cannot constitute a refutation of the sceptic who questions whether we do indeed have common ideas; it takes for granted that we do, and offers a sort of theoretical—or mythical—basis for that fact.

The second question—about the relation of concepts to reality—becomes prominent in the *Cratylus* when Cratylus, following up his thesis that names are naturally connected to the things they stand for, says that one who knows the names knows the things—and that this is indeed *the* way to know things (435d). Since our expert name-giver, competent to introduce names, attached them to things they were really like, we can infer from the names to the real things (436b12). Cratylus claims that his thesis is confirmed by the way in which Socrates has been able in his etymologizing to find a consistent theory of reality—namely, the flux theory—expressed in language (436c2–6).

The assertion that our expert name-giver correctly put into verbal form concepts that fit reality combines two claims: first, that an expert name-giver is one who is competent to introduce correct names; second, that *our* name-giver was an expert name-giver. (Put otherwise, the claims are that a good language fits reality, and that our language is a good one.) The first of these claims might be thought a necessary truth; but it is far from clear how the second is to be supported.

Against Cratylus's position Socrates makes several powerful points, which may be summarized thus. (1) It is true that in our etymologizing we found a flux theory expressed in our language. But we could just as easily have developed alternative etymologies that suggested a non-flux theory (437a–c). (2) Supposing that a language did consistently and certainly express one particular theory of reality, that would show that its word-marker had that view of reality (436d). How could we be sure that his view was correct (that he was an expert word-maker and that his language, therefore, is a good one)? (3) And how, if his view *was* correct, did *he* come to that view? (Reference to divine inspiration is a notorious dead-end.) If the name-giver was to name realities correctly, he must have been able to know realities, to grasp universals, independently of and prior to framing concepts and naming them. And so, if we ourselves are to claim that our language represents reality correctly—is a good one—we ourselves must claim an ability to grasp reality independently of language (438b5–9). Only if we know the original can we say that a picture or description is an accurate picture or description of it; similarly, in general, with realities and names (439a). Therefore, if we are to have knowledge of realities and thus the ability to see whether a given language expresses them correctly, we must have a way of studying realities not just *through* language (438d–e). What is this way? We must learn about realities 'through each other, if they are somehow related, and themselves through themselves' (438e7).

Discussion of Cratylus's views has led us right into ontology. The argument has been abstract, and has contained no conclusions about the nature of what there really is; and the prescription for studying realities ('through each other and through themselves') is far from clear. But the last pages of the dialogue notify us that the realities are Plato's Forms (439c–d, 440b6); and other dialogues can help us to interpret the prescription.

The task of the dialectician or philosopher is (according to *Phaedrus*, *Sophist*, *Politicus*, and *Philebus*) to divide reality at its natural joints, and to determine how various Forms are related to one another. He will necessarily—as does Plato in his examples of such dialectic—*use* language; but his enquiry is not taken to be about words or about mere concepts (the ideas and thoughts we use words to express), but about the real kinds and qualities that our concepts are (we hope) concepts *of*. But how can we be sure that our hope is realized—that if we clarify by careful discussion the structure of the conceptual scheme embodied in our language, we have thereby discovered the structure of reality? Plato himself recognizes that not every general word stands for a real kind (*Politicus* 262d–263b), but fails to tell us how to distinguish those that do from those that do not. 'How are we to distinguish the *eidos* or *genos* from the mere *meros*? This is not an easy task, and we will take it up again when we have time' (263a5–b2). Dialectical method may, by a rigorous process of question and answer, clarify and improve our conceptual scheme; but once concepts are distinguished from realities (universals, kinds, or characters), it is impossible to see how such a process can give an access to realities which is independent of the concepts, and which can therefore make it possible to see whether the concepts fit the realities.

In fact, Plato seems to rely on the idea that the skilled dialectician will eventually come to 'see' what the real kinds are. He often uses this metaphor of sight, and he speaks of *noesis* as if it were a sort of intellectual vision (or grasp) which the philosopher achieves after methodical dialectical enquiry. He assumes that just as our eyes have the power, in good conditions, of seeing ordinary phenomena as they are, so our minds (in good conditions) can see the Forms there really are: dialectic removes confusion and fog, and enables the intellect to see reality clearly. Having so seen, the philosopher would be able to judge whether a given language or a given conceptual scheme was or was not a faithful and adequate representation of reality. It is obvious that this 'theory' of *noesis* is in an important respect like the doctrine of *anamnesis* referred to earlier. For it is a way of making a certain claim—the claim that we can grasp realities directly and not just through our own language and concepts; it is not a way of justifying that claim.

CONCLUSION

In conclusion I will pick out four points, not unconnected with one another, which seem to me to throw some light upon the drift of the *Cratylus* and its achievement.

(1) The notion of teaching, given as the essential function of language, is well suited to move discussion from the linguistic controversy with which the dialogue begins to the ontological confrontation with which it ends, since it combines the ideas of communication and truth. Moreover, it opens the way to a dissolution—at least, a partial dissolution—of the original disagreement between Hermogenes and Cratylus: the conventionalist thesis dwells on what is necessary and sufficient for any interpersonal communication, but the requirement of truth involves non-conventional constraints.

(2) The important distinction between ordinary names and 'names themselves' assists in that dissolution. With respect to ordinary names, questions about origin, etymology, and composition can arise; and there is plenty of scope for the influence of convention and custom: the understanding of ordinary words depends on shared conventions and custom. But for the 'ideal names' no such questions arise—meanings have no etymology. Good concepts are ones that actually apply—that is, are serviceable for the grasp of objective reality; conventions and custom do not determine this.

(3) The distinction between words and meanings or concepts corresponds to a distinction between two types of discourse—or

two senses of *dialektike*. In ordinary discourse, people use language to talk about ordinary things. In the philosophical discourse that Plato calls 'dialectic', philosophers use language to talk about meanings or concepts (or indeed, taking the point further, about Forms).

(4) The realities at which philosophical dialectic is aimed are the Forms, celebrated at the end of the *Cratylus* as things that are and are knowable. The things which ordinary talk is about, particular objects in this world, are not given a place at the end of the *Cratylus*, save perhaps by implication. Contrasted with the Forms is the (imaginary) world of complete flux, of which it is argued that in it there would be nothing of any kind or character, nothing that could be spoken of or known. What, then, of the inhabitants of our actual world, the subject-matter of ordinary discourse? The answer is no doubt that they fall, as it were, between Forms and absolute flux: they have a degree of stability sufficient to make them objects of discourse and belief (true and false), but they lack the complete stability which enables the Forms to be objects of unshakeable knowledge. This element in the Platonic ontology is missing from the last pages of the *Cratylus*, but it would suggest itself readily enough as a corollary of the dialogue, even if one did not have other Platonic texts to rely upon.

3

Plato on False Belief: *Theaetetus*
187–200

1. The paradox that there can be no such thing as falsity is treated by Plato in a number of places. As exploited in the early dialogue *Euthydemus* (283e–284c), it appears to rest on a simple equivocation. A false statement would be one that stated what is not (τὸ μὴ ὄν), but to state what is not is to state nothing; so a false statement would in fact be a non-statement, no statement at all.

The paradox recurs in the *Cratylus* (429), and here a rather more subtle error seems to be involved. Cratylus's denial that there can be false statements derives from his doctrine that there cannot be incorrect or false names. If 'Hermogenes' is really somebody's name, then, Cratylus holds, in saying 'Hermogenes', I name that person. I may have had in mind the man who is actually not Hermogenes but Socrates; but I have neither named nor misnamed *that* man, I have named the man Hermogenes. Were there nobody whose name was 'Hermogenes', I should have named nobody; I should have failed to perform an act of naming. Now if a sentence is thought of as a complex name, the paradox about statements follows. In saying, for example, 'Hermogenes is asleep', *either* I have correctly named a state of affairs (the state of affairs that consists in Hermogenes' being asleep) *or* I have failed to name anything (there being no such state of affairs as the expression 'Hermogenes is asleep' would name if it named anything). There is thus no such thing as false statement, because stating is a kind of naming, and all naming is necessarily correct naming.

In his response to Cratylus (430–1) Socrates does something to clear up the muddle, in that the introduces the notion of *assigning* a name or description *to* a given individual. He begins to bring to light the special type of complexity that distinguishes a sentence from a name, even a complex name; and the way is prepared for

First published in 1966.

Plato's final account of false statement in the *Sophist* (261–4). In this late dialogue Plato makes clear the special grammatical and logical complexity of the sentence, a unit which interweaves a naming part (ὄνομα) with a saying part (ῥῆμα). A statement must be about something, and it must say something about it. But it can assert a real property of a real subject when that property does not in fact belong to that subject.

It is obvious that Plato's brief discussion in the *Sophist* does not say all that needs to be said about false statement. For example, his account does not cater for the possibility of false existential statements. Nor does he make clear in what sense each part of a sentence must stand for something 'real'. Nevertheless, he certainly makes an important advance in the *Sophist* by recognizing the special type of complexity which a sentence enjoys, and by tying the notions of truth and falsity to these specially complex units.

2. In this essay I wish to examine Plato's discussion of false belief in the *Theaetetus* (187–200). While this discussion undoubtedly has connections with the *Cratylus* (that probably precedes it) and with the *Sophist* (that certainly follows it), it raises some questions of its own, and tackles them in a distinctive manner.

Theaetetus having suggested that knowledge can be defined as true belief, Socrates asks whether false belief is in fact possible. The thesis that it is not possible was put forward earlier in the dialogue, in the context of Protagoras's relativist doctrine, and was briefly rebutted (170–1). But now, at 187d, Socrates says that they will attack the problem in another way; and he embarks upon a long discussion that has the following general structure.

Socrates first deploys two arguments against the possibility of false belief. Then, to meet the second of these, he suggests that false belief should perhaps be conceived of as *allodoxia*, mistaking one real thing for another. This proposal, however, proves vulnerable to the first of the two preceding arguments. Socrates seeks to save it by introducing the model of the mind as containing a waxen block. This seems helpful as far as perceptual mistakes go, but does not provide an explanation of the possibility of purely conceptual or intellectual mistakes, like the mistake of thinking that the sum of seven and five is eleven. A new model, that of the mind as an aviary, is put forward to handle this type of case, but it meets with objections from Socrates. He closes the discussion by saying that they ought not to have tried to examine false belief until they had established what knowledge was. The dialogue then continues with this, its main theme.

3. Before turning to an examination of the text I should like to make three preliminary remarks in self-defence. First, it is not possible in one short essay to discuss the passage at all fully. I shall offer an interpretation which seems to make some philosophical sense and which has a certain unity. But I recognize that it is open to many objections. I have touched on a few of these, but only briefly and in footnotes.[1] My purpose is to try out one particular line: the essay is intended as a stimulus to debate, not as a final summing-up or verdict.

Secondly, though I have tried to make *philosophical* sense of this text, I have not attempted a high degree of philosophical rigour or sophistication, either in my exegesis or in critical comments. The logical points that arise are obviously of great complexity and difficulty, and require very careful and subtle handling. I have stayed at a very elementary level.

Thirdly, I do not enter into the question whether Plato thought— or why anyone may have thought—that *all* statements are some-how statements of identity, all errors misidentifications. There are no arguments for this view in the *Theaetetus*, and the philosophical interest of the discussion does not depend on the adoption of this view. The fact is that Plato concerns himself here, at least primarily, with just one type of false belief, misidentifications.

4. The first argument (188a–c) starts from the assumption that anything whatsoever, and hence any possible object of a man's thought, must be either something known to him or something unknown to him. Suppose, then, that A and B are two different things. If I know them both, how can I possibly fail to know that they are different? If I know neither of them, how can I possibly entertain any thought about them? And if I know one but not the other, how can I possibly hold a belief that the one is the other? Since these cases exhaust the alternatives with respect to knowing or not knowing A and B, no room is left for the possibility of mistakenly thinking that A is B. We might put the argument in this way. If two expressions '*A*' and '*B*' stand for different things,

---

[1] I am indebted to a number of friends and colleagues for criticisms of an earlier version of this essay. Some of their comments are referred to in my footnotes.

nobody who knows what they both stand for could conceivably believe that they stand for the same thing. But one who does not know what they both stand for could not understand, let alone believe, the assertion '*A* is *B*'.

It is not difficult to find a class of cases for which an argument of this kind does hold. The sentence 'Cowardice is generosity' *could* not be uttered by anyone as the correct expression of a belief he has, not even of a false belief. We should say of one who uttered it in seriousness not that he wrongly believed that cowardice was generosity, but that he evidently did not know the meaning of the words he used. A person who does know the meaning of 'cowardice' and the meaning of 'generosity' cannot fail to know that they have different meanings, and that cowardice is not generosity. A person who does not know the meanings of both words cannot be correctly expressing any belief he holds when he says 'Cowardice is generosity' (or, for that matter, 'Cowardice is not generosity').

Now the examples Socrates gives in the passage we are considering do not involve names of properties like generosity, but proper names of individuals. Is it possible, he asks, 'that a man who knows neither Theaetetus nor Socrates should take it into his head that Socrates is Theaetetus?' (188b8–10).[2] Unfortunately, of course, with ordinary proper names the argument outlined above does not work. A man might be introduced to me at one time as 'Jo' and at another time as 'Smith', and it might be a matter for later discovery by me that Jo and Smith are one and the same person. Before this discovery, I might well think they were different people, and I could express this belief by saying 'Jo is not Smith'. The necessary conditions of my saying this as the correct expression of a belief do not imply that I must know that the person named 'Jo' is the person named 'Smith'. They involve only that I must be able to identify in at least one way the person named 'Jo', and again the person named 'Smith'. So since there are many different ways in which a person may be identified, the possibility is open that I may use both 'Jo' and 'Smith' quite correctly as names without knowing that Jo is Smith. This point about ordinary proper names (which I have of course stated only very roughly) is obvious enough to us. But I think that in this first argument Socrates is made to overlook (or

---

[2] I have generally followed F. M. Cornford's translation: *Plato's Theory of Knowledge* (London: Routledge and Kegan Paul, 1935), and subsequent page references are given in parentheses in the text.

conceal) it: he operates with ordinary proper names as though they were logically proper names applied to simple particulars. This error will be corrected in the later section on the wax tablet.

To summarize the main thought of the argument: for a man to hold a belief he could correctly express by saying '*A* ... *B*', it is necessary for him to know who or what '*A*' stands for and who or what '*B*' stands for. But if the two names '*A*' and '*B*' stand for different individuals, anyone who knows who or what '*A*' stands for and who or what '*B*' stands for cannot fail to know that they do stand for different individuals. Thus it is logically impossible for anyone to hold a false belief which he could correctly express by saying '*A* is *B*'.[3]

5. The second argument (188d–189b) is in a way a counterpart to the first. While that argument exploited the dichotomy knowing and not knowing, this one uses the dichotomy being and not being (κατὰ τὸ εἰδέναι καὶ μὴ εἰδέναι ... κατὰ τὸ εἶναι καὶ μή; 188c9). That argument sought to show that false belief cannot be made intelligible by the supposition that the person fails to know one or the other of the terms of his belief; this argument claims that false belief cannot be made intelligible by the supposition that one or the other of the terms of the belief is non-existent or nothing. The contention that each of the terms of a belief must be *something* is of course highly ambiguous. The passage is quite general—no examples are given—and it points forward to the *Sophist*. But in the present context the obvious application is to *names*, the proper names of the preceding argument or the names of universals or concepts which come up in the next section. Plato is saying that it could not be the explanation of the falsity of '*A* is *B*' that '*A*' (or that '*B*') names nothing; a name must surely have a nominee.

6. Socrates now makes a suggestion (189b12) designed to meet the point just made in the second argument. Perhaps false belief should be understood as *allodoxia*, taking one thing for another. Nothing non-existent is now to be brought into play. Both *A* and *B* really

---

[3] The text of this passage does not refer explicitly to sentences or statements, but only to beliefs. The connection is made in the *allodoxia* section (189e–190a). Is it unreasonable to assume it earlier?

Perhaps the first argument consists merely in asking how a man who knew both Socrates and Theaetetus well could mistake one for the other. But this is not the *sort* of question examined in the rest of the discussion; nor is there any explicit reference to knowing *well*.

exist, and when I say '*A* is (or is not) *B*', both of the names I use are
genuine names of things. But this suggestion is of course immediately vulnerable to the line of thought contained in the *first*
argument. If I am supposed not to be thinking of one or the other
of the two items *A* and *B*, I cannot correctly express my belief
by saying '*A* is (or is not) *B*'; but if I am thinking of both the
items I cannot possibly hold a belief that would be correctly expressed by my saying '*A* is *B*' if in fact *A* and *B* are different
items. This is so clearly the same line of thought as that in the first
argument that one must ask how the discussion of *allodoxia* is
supposed to advance our understanding. This question does not
seem to have exercised the commentators, but I think that it can be
answered.

This section (189b–190e) differs from the first argument (188a–c)
in two important and connected ways. First, the verb used in the
exposition of the argument here is διανοεῖσθαι ('to think of'), and
not, as in the earlier section, εἰδέναι ('to know', but particularly and
originally 'to be acquainted with an individual through having seen
him'). Secondly, the examples used in this *allodoxia* passage are not
individuals like Theaetetus, but properties and other universals
such as beauty, ugliness, the ox, the horse. Socrates explains (189e–
190a) that a judgement or belief is a statement uttered not aloud to
another but silently to oneself. He goes on:

> Now search your memory and see if you have ever said to yourself 'cer-
> tainly the beautiful is ugly' or 'the unjust is just'. To put it generally,
> consider if you have ever set about convincing yourself that any one thing
> is certainly another thing, or whether on the contrary you have never, even
> in a dream, gone so far as to say to yourself that odd numbers must be
> even, or anything of that sort. . . . Do you suppose that anyone, mad or
> sane, ever goes so far as to talk himself over, in his own mind, into stating
> seriously that an ox must be a horse or that two must be one? (190b–c)

Attention is still confined to sentences of the form '*A* is *B*', but
we are no longer restricted, as in the first argument, to cases where
'*A*' and '*B*' are names of individuals. Socrates is now considering
names of universals or concepts. He is making a sound point:
sentences like 'Justice is injustice' or 'An ox is a horse' *cannot* serve
as correct expressions of any possible belief.

It is sometimes said that in this section Plato makes Socrates
commit a very gross mistake, the mistake of thinking that because
nobody could ever say and mean 'An ox is a cow', it follows that

nobody could ever mistake an ox for a cow.[4] To think this would of course be a gross mistake. For one may well say and believe 'This animal is a cow' on an occasion when the animal at hand is in fact an ox. However, it is clear from the passage quoted above that Socrates is adverting precisely to *utterances* (aloud or silent) like 'An ox is a cow'. He is not considering what we may truly say of a man who says in the presence of an ox 'This animal is a cow', but what we may truly say of a man who says 'An ox is a cow'. He is pointing out that we do not describe this man as falsely believing that an ox is a cow. We just cannot construe what he says as the correct expression of a false (or indeed of any) belief.

In so far as Plato's advertised problem is the general problem of false belief, one may indeed complain that he is not confronting it when he dwells on the impossibility of certain special types of false belief. However, in isolating certain kinds of impossible sentence, he clears the ground. In what follows he will widen his conceptual and linguistic apparatus. To start with, he assumed an equipment simply of proper names together with the expression 'is' ('is identical with'); and he has now, in the *allodoxia* section, brought in also names of universals. He has argued that within these limits no sentence can be framed that could correctly express a false belief. The main thing wrong so far is his treatment of ordinary proper names as if they were logically proper names, and this error will be implicitly corrected in the next section on the wax tablet.

7. I will first summarize the wax tablet section (191–5). Let us suppose, says Socrates, that in the mind of each man there is a waxen block. This is the gift of Memory, mother of the Muses. Whatever we want to remember, of the things we see or hear or think of, we imprint on the block by holding it under the perceptions or thoughts, as if stamping impressions of seal-rings. Whatever is imprinted, we remember and know, so long as its image remains in the block. Anything that does not get imprinted or that gets rubbed out, we have forgotten and do not know.

I may, then, either know or not know Theaetetus—that is, I may or may not remember him, have a memory imprint of him. Again, I may or may not be now perceiving him. There are thus four situations I may be in with respect to Theaetetus: I know and

---

[4] Plato might of course be letting Socrates commit this mistake precisely in order to make us see that it is a mistake. Such is the beautiful flexibility of the dialogue form. But I do not think that this way out is necessary.

perceive, I know but do not perceive, I perceive but do not know, I neither know nor perceive. ('Know' here of course means 'remember'.) There are four similar possibilities with respect to Theodorus, and thus sixteen possible situations I may be in *vis-à-vis* the pair Theaetetus *and* Theodorus. Socrates enquires whether any of these situations offer the possibility of a misidentification on my part, and he concludes that a few of them do. The possibility arises where I have a memory imprint of one person and a sense perception of another, and I wrongly assign the sense impression to the memory imprint, supposing it to match, or fit into, that imprint. Where it is not the case that I have both a memory imprint of one person and a sense perception of another, no such possibility of misassignment exists.

This is a very summary summary of the wax tablet section. I cannot enter into all its details and difficulties. I want only to suggest what the main contribution of the section is, and how it is related to what precedes and follows it. Cornford, indeed, does not seem to find any philosophical interest in it. 'It does not appear', he writes,

> that Plato offers his waxen block as anything more than an illustration, a mechanical model which helps us to distinguish a memory image from a fresh impression of sense, and to imagine the process of fitting the one to the other correctly or incorrectly. The conclusion, that true and false judgements of this type do exist, rests simply on familiar experience. (p. 127)

These remarks surely do not do justice to the logical character of Plato's problem. Difficulties in understanding how there can possibly be misidentification do not arise from defects of the imagination, but from erroneous or confused assumptions about meaning, reference, identity, and the like. Such matters cannot be cleared up by an appeal to 'familiar experience', any more than Zeno's arguments against the possibility of motion can.

What, then, is the philosophical point of the wax tablet? One suggestion is that Plato is here recognizing the possibility of expressing a mistake about identity, not by saying, for example, 'Theaetetus is Theodorus' (ruled out by the first argument), but by using a sentence of a different logical form. There is certainly no assumption in the wax tablet section that a man making a mistake will say such a thing as 'Theaetetus is Theodorus'. The implication, rather, is that he will say something like 'The man I see is the man I remember seeing last week'. So we are now equipped not only with proper names, but also with descriptions. Thus the principle that led us to regard sentences of the form '*A* is *B*' as impossible sentences need no longer harass us. Without dropping that principle as far as proper names are concerned, we can find sentences that correctly express misidentification beliefs—sentences, namely, that make use of descriptions. The suggestion, then, is that the wax tablet introduces descriptions in addition to names, and implicitly recognizes that the necessary conditions for proper and successful use of descriptions are different from those for the proper and successful use of names.

The trouble with this tempting interpretation is that it makes it impossible to understand what happens in the dialogue *after* the wax tablet passage. For Socrates there goes on to say that we have handled only mistakes involving perception, that there are other mistakes (like that of believing that the sum of seven and five is eleven), and that therefore a further model and account of false belief is necessary. But the above suggestion attaches no special importance to the fact that the wax tablet section is about perception and memory, but reads into it a purely logical point that would seem as relevant to a mistake like 'The sum of seven and five is eleven' as to a mistake like 'This is the man I saw yesterday'. We must surely look for an interpretation of the wax tablet that will make clear why Socrates still finds a problem about mistakes like 'The sum of seven and five is eleven'.

A natural formulation of a false belief of the kind illustrated in the wax tablet would be 'The man I see is the man I remember seeing yesterday'; and Plato himself uses such formulations in his exposition. But if we consider the details of the model he offers, we can see that he is giving a certain *analysis* of such statements.[5] He provides us in every case with two objects of immediate experience: a memory imprint or image and a sense impression. What we do when we identify the man before us with the man we met yesterday is to connect *this* sense impression with *that* memory imprint. What then do we say to ourselves—what is it that we believe? We assert,

[5] This is a crucial—and disputable—contention. I take it that the 'tying together' of the model represents what we assert in a statement, not just a psychological operation we perform. I do not see how the description of such an operation could solve the philosophical problem about misidentification.

in effect: '*this* belongs to the same man as *that*.' We do not say or believe 'This *is* that'; but we suppose, perhaps wrongly, that there is a certain relation between these two individual items of experience. Plato is thus suggesting that what are normally called identity statements about people do not really assert the identity of two items, but rather a certain relationship between two items. He is meeting the difficulties raised earlier about the possibility of falsely thinking that *A* is *B*, not by replacing '*A*' or '*B*' by descriptions (and then distinguishing between the sense and the reference of descriptions), but by replacing the 'is' ('is identical with') by 'is related to' ('belongs to the same continuant as'). He is claiming that ordinary misidentification statements really assert a relationship (not of identity) between two items recognized to be different, a past and a present sense impression. So he is making a point about the nature of personal identity or the identity of a physical continuant. This solution to the problem about misidentification does not rest on any recognition of the difference between names and descriptions; so there is nothing surprising in the fact that Socrates still finds himself puzzled by cases like 'The sum of seven and five is eleven'. On the contrary, it is clear that the Hume-like analysis of misidentifications of people which the wax tablet gives does *not* afford a solution to the problem of purely intellectual error. For the number twelve is not a perceptible continuant presenting different appearances at different times; nor is it easy to see how the false belief that the sum of seven and five is eleven could be analysed so as to show that it is really the belief that two admittedly different items are related in a certain way.

Before we turn to the aviary, two further comments must be made on the wax tablet. Firstly, it must be confessed that Plato does not give to his account all the generality of which it is capable. He expresses the outcome by saying that false belief has been found not in perceptions alone or in thoughts (memory imprints) alone, but in the connecting of perception and thought (ἐν τῇ συνάψει αἰσθήσεως πρὸς διάνοιαν; 195d1). Now the crucial point here, if the above interpretation is right, is the notion of connecting two different experiences or data. Misidentifying this man as that man is wrongly relating this datum to that datum. But there is no reason why this analysis should not hold where the two different data are both memory imprints or both present sense impressions. I may wrongly think that yesterday's sense impression belonged to the same person as the day before yesterday's; and I may wrongly think that my present visual datum is 'of' the same person as is my present auditory datum. One cannot say that Plato's summary phrase 'the connecting of perception and thought' is just careless, because in his earlier careful survey of possible cases (192) he explicitly denied the possibility of mistaking one man for another where both are remembered and neither is perceived, or where both are perceived and neither is remembered. But why should he think that the two items to be wrongly connected, if what we should call a misidentification is to occur, must be not merely different but of two radically different types? The case of the two simultaneous perceptions is perhaps rather recherché; but the other case, that of misassociating two different memory imprints, is not at all recherché or even uncommon.

I can only suggest—while recognizing the feebleness of the suggestion—that Plato is the victim of his model. Connecting is represented in the model by the operation of fitting something into an existing mould, like putting a foot into a footprint. But this operation necessarily requires two different kinds of thing: you cannot fit a foot into a foot or a footprint into a footprint. Perhaps, then, it is because of a really irrelevant feature of the model he employs that Plato fails to realize (or anyway make clear) the full scope of which his analysis in terms of connecting is capable. Would it be easy to find a vivid model that did represent all the possibilities?

The second comment I want to make on the wax tablet is this. The passage has primarily to do with the misidentifying of persons or other continuants. Yet there are in it hints of a possible wider application of the model. Thus, at the very beginning (191d5), Socrates says: 'Whatever we want to remember, of the things we see or hear or *think of*, we imprint on the block.' Nothing is made of this last case within the wax tablet section. But at the transition to the aviary, it is clearly implied that items thought of and imprinted on the block are (or include) abstract or universal ideas. For in raising a question about 'five and seven themselves' ('I don't mean five men and seven men or anything of that sort'), Socrates says that we describe these as memory imprints on our block (196a1–3). Now such imprints as these, imprints representing concepts we have acquired, play no overt part in the account of misidentification of individuals. But they clearly could be helpful in accounting for other types of false belief. There were those who construed ordinary subject–predicate statements ('Socrates is wise', 'Socrates is a man') as statements of identity, and so got into paradoxical difficulties. We can explain to them that those statements do not assert an identity, but only a relationship, between the subject term and the concept 'wisdom' or 'man'. If I am wrong in thinking that this is a man, it is not that I have before my mind two items, the individual indicated by 'this' and the concept 'man', and suppose them to be one and the same item; it is that I wrongly connect the one item with the other.

Thus the account of misidentification in terms of the misconnecting of two items (recognized to be two) can be widened to cover misdescription and misclassification. These also can be regarded as the misconnecting of two items (recognized to be two); only here, one item is an individual, and the other is a universal or concept. That this extension is in Plato's mind, though not emphasized in the text, is perhaps suggested by the piece of dialogue which leads from the wax tablet to the aviary. Socrates asks whether a man could ever suppose that eleven, which he merely thinks of, is twelve, which again he merely thinks of. Theaetetus replies: 'Well, I shall answer that, if he saw or handled eleven things, he might suppose that they were twelve; but he will never make that judgement about the eleven and the twelve he has in his thoughts' (195e5–7). Socrates is here leading up to mistakes not capable of being explained by the wax tablet, while Theaetetus is speaking as one who is so far satisfied with wax tablet. If he happily accepts as possible, within the framework of the wax tablet account, the mistake of thinking that a group of people number twelve, when in fact they are only eleven, he is presumably construing 'These are twelve' as asserting wrongly a connection between these individuals and the remembered and known concept (imprint) *twelve*.

We can now summarize the drift of the whole argument so far. Let us use α and β to stand for names of individuals, ϕ and ψ to stand for names of universals or concepts. Plato has maintained the following theses:

(1) There can be no false belief correctly expressible by a sentence of the form 'α is identical with β'.
(2) There can be no false belief correctly expressible by a sentence of the form 'ϕ is identical with ψ'.

(3) There can be a false belief correctly expressible by a sentence of the form 'α belongs to the same so-and-so as β'. Ordinary misidentification statements can be analysed into this form.

(4) There can be a false belief correctly expressible by a sentence of the form 'α belongs to, falls under ϕ'. Ordinary misdescriptions and misclassifications can be analysed into this form.

In neither of the two types of false belief here admitted are the two different items mentioned asserted to be identical. The trouble with 'The sum of seven and five is eleven', the kind of case the aviary tries to deal with, is that here it does seem that two different items mentioned are being asserted to be identical. Nothing has yet been said to show the possibility of this kind of false belief, which has indeed been ruled out of court by earlier arguments.[6]

8. Having pointed out that the wax tablet fails to cater for purely intellectual error, Socrates draws a distinction between possessing knowledge and actually having it about one (197–8). If I have bought a cloak, I possess it; but I may not actually have it on. If I have caught some birds and put them into an aviary, I possess them, and have the power ($\delta\acute{v}\nu\alpha\mu\iota\varsigma$) to catch hold of any of them; but only when I exercise this power do I actually have a bird in the hand. Socrates asks us to think of the mind as an aviary. It is empty at our birth, but we gradually fill it with the pieces of knowledge we acquire by learning or discovery. Once we thus possess a piece of knowledge, we can subsequently look for it and catch it. An expert mathematician knows all numbers in the dispositional sense, but he will have to search on a given occasion to catch and grasp the number he wants.

---

[6] Can one say that the move from the wax tablet to the aviary is a move from empirical mistakes to error in the field of necessary truths? That Plato will now concern himself with error in this field is certainly of great importance in view of the doctrine he embraces elsewhere that belief (which permits of truth and falsity) is 'set over' the realm of change and appearance, while knowledge (necessarily true) is of changeless being. Unfortunately, Plato does not stop in the *Theaetetus* to discuss *empirical* statements like 'The number of men in the room is twelve' or 'The colour of her eyes is blue'. If he had considered such statements and shown that they are *reducible* to statements of the kind handled by the wax tablet—while statements like 'The sum of seven and five is eleven' are not—he would have made it clear that the problem left for the aviary is precisely the problem of error in the field of necessary truths. This is anyway what he now turns to—what I have called 'purely intellectual error'.

Socrates suggests that this model may explain the possibility of purely intellectual error. He says:

Having drawn a distinction between possessing knowledge and having it about one, we agree that it is impossible *not* to possess what one does possess, and so we avoid implying that a man may *not* know what he does know. But we say that it *is* possible for him to get hold of a false judgement about it. For he may not have about him the knowledge of *that* thing, but a different piece of knowledge instead, if it so happens that, in hunting for some particular piece of knowledge among those that are fluttering about, he misses it and catches hold of a different one. In that case, you see, he mistakes eleven for twelve, because he has caught hold of the knowledge of eleven that is inside him, instead of his knowledge of twelve, as he might catch a dove in place of a pigeon. (199a6)

But immediately after expounding this suggestion, Socrates makes objections to it. Is it not odd that the interchange of pieces of *knowledge* should ever result in a judgement that is false? It is strange that a man should have knowledge of something, and at the same time fail to recognize that very thing not for want of knowing it, but by reason of his own knowledge. Is it not absurd to suggest that when knowledge is present, the mind may fail to recognize anything and should know nothing?

Nobody will doubt the importance of the distinction between latent or potential knowledge and actualized knowledge. But it is far from clear how this distinction, and the aviary model that expresses it, could even be thought to provide a solution to the problem in hand. Let us, however, recall the wax tablet. The problem was that for a man to mistake Theaetetus for Theodorus, it seemed necessary that he should somehow know both of them, yet his knowing both of them seemed to preclude his failing to distinguish them. The solution depended on distinguishing two ways of knowing a person, remembering and perceiving. One can satisfy the conditions for *somehow* knowing both Theaetetus and Theodorus, and still make a mistake, wrongly connecting the perception of one with the memory of the other. The aviary seeks to find a solution to the problem of intellectual error by again distinguishing two ways of knowing (though we should speak rather of senses of 'know'). The man who mistakes one number for another can thus be said to know both of them *somehow*—one in the dispositional way, the other in the actualized way. Thus the requirement that for a man to mistake one thing for another, he must somehow know both is met, even though he is actually thinking of only one of them, and that the wrong one.

It is clear, however, that this solution will not work, and that it is not really a true parallel to the wax tablet solution.[7] *There* two ways of actually knowing a person were provided, and the man in error actually had in mind two different items, a memory imprint and a sense perception; his error was in associating these in a certain way. But here in the aviary we are not provided with two ways of actually knowing a number; nor can the mistake of thinking that the sum of seven and five is eleven be construed as the mistaken association of two actually known and really different items. Socrates' own objections are sound. In so far as a man is actually thinking of the number eleven, he is not in any sort of error; the fact that he could think of the number twelve is neither here nor there. If, to provide conditions for possible error, we say that the man is actually thinking of both of two different numbers, we are back at the original difficulty of seeing how one who knows both of two things can fail to see that they are different—and the distinction between potential and actualized knowledge is not in play, and again cannot help.

Cornford claims that 'the aviary apparatus is, after all, as adequate to explain false judgement where no perception is involved as the waxen block was to explain false judgement involving perception' (p. 137). The aviary, he says, can provide an explanation of the mistake 'The sum of seven and five is eleven' in terms of the misfitting of two pieces of knowledge, provided that the expression 'piece of knowledge' is taken in a sufficiently wide sense. He writes:

The expression covers objects (such as numbers) that I am acquainted with, as well as truths that I have been taught. All these are in my aviary. Does it also include a complex object such as 'the sum of 7 and 5'? This

---

[7] Why does a distinction that explains how you can fail to catch the right bird though you possess it prove of no help over conceptual mistakes? In the model it is presupposed that you know what you are looking for; you understand the request 'Bring a dove'. You combine this actualized understanding with a failure to actualize your dispositional 'having' of the dove. But in the situation being investigated— where understanding is the very topic—such a combination seems impossible: the actualized knowledge required for understanding the question ('What is the sum of seven and five?') seems to be *identical* with the actualized knowledge required for answering it. The model has concept catching (understanding the request) and bird catching or bird missing; the situation in view has concept catching and concept catching or concept missing. Here, if the concepts in question are identical, it seems impossible to catch the question and miss the answer.

ought to be included; it consists of terms I am acquainted with and it is
before my mind when I ask: what is the sum of 7 and 5? It is this object that
I identify with 11 when I make my false judgement. If it is a 'piece of
knowledge' and contained in the aviary, then the false judgement can be
explained as the wrong putting-together of two pieces of knowledge, as in
the waxen block false judgement was the putting-together of a fresh impression and the wrong memory-imprint. (ibid.)

Now it is of course obvious to us that the possibility of thinking
that the sum of seven and five is eleven, when it is not possible to
think that twelve is eleven, depends on the fact that 'the sum of
seven and five' and 'twelve' are different expressions—and indeed,
expressions of different types. But it seems very doubtful whether
this point can be successfully worked into the aviary model. For if
it is supposed that I have in my aviary *three* objects, corresponding
to the three expressions 'the sum of seven and five', 'eleven', and
'twelve', the suggestion that I may actually grasp or think of two of
them and wrongly believe them to be one, is open to Plato's original and pervasive difficulty. The notion of putting together evaded
this difficulty in the wax tablet, because false identification was
there construed as the wrong putting together of two different
objects recognized to be different. But the mistake in the aviary will
consist in straightforwardly identifying two different objects. The
man does not think that the sum of seven and five is connected in
some way with the number eleven; he thinks that it just *is* that
number. Moreover, not only does Cornford's proposal fail to explain the possibility of thinking that the sum of seven and five is
eleven; it makes it impossible to see how there could be the true
belief that the sum of seven and five is twelve. For if these are
different objects, it cannot be true to say that they are one and the
same object. I think, therefore, that Cornford's attempt to save the
aviary by making 'the sum of seven and five' and 'twelve' stand for
different objects is unsuccessful. What is required is the recognition
that they stand for one and the same object, but do so in different
ways; and of this there seems no hint in the aviary passage.

In response to Socrates' objections to the aviary model as an
explanation of intellectual error, Theaetetus suggests a modifi-
cation to it (199e2). Perhaps we should suppose that the aviary
contains not only pieces of knowledge but also pieces of non-
knowledge (ἀνεπιστημοσύναι). To be of interest, Theaetetus's suggestion cannot be the suggestion that the aviary should contain

such birds as the proposition that the sum of seven and five is eleven. For this would simply side-step the question how such a proposition could possibly be entertained or believed. But what then are these pieces of non-knowledge? Whatever concept I call to mind is precisely what it is, and there seems no sense in suggesting that it is in itself erroneous. But perhaps Theaetetus is playing with the idea that some of my concepts may be misconceptions, and that calling to mind any of these would in itself be a case of error. Socrates objects to Theaetetus that if we use his suggestion to try to explain intellectual mistakes, we find ourselves trapped once again in our original difficulty, the difficulty of seeing how a man could mistake one thing for another if he did *not* know both of them—or again if he *did* know both of them. I offer the following model as perhaps representing Theaetetus's suggestion and Socrates' refutation of it.

Suppose I have some cards, each containing a colour patch and the name of a colour: one card has on it a red patch and the name 'red', another has a blue patch and the name 'blue', and so on. (Having such cards represents having colour concepts.) The impossibility of intellectual error will be represented in terms of the model by the following principle: if I am asked to bring a card containing a colour patch and the name 'red', and I understand this request, it must be the case both that I have such a card and that I know which of my cards it is. I cannot both understand the request and unwittingly bring the wrong card.

To introduce the possibility of mistakes, Theaetetus supposes that I have some cards with patches incorrectly labelled: besides the card with a red patch and the name 'red', I have a card with a blue patch and the name 'red' on it. (This latter represents a misconception.) It is now possible, Theaetetus suggests, without any breach of the principle mentioned above, that I may unwittingly bring the wrong card. I understand the request to bring a card with a colour patch and the name 'red', and I have such a card, and I bring such a card. But the card I bring (the mislabelled one) is not the right card; it is a card that ought never to have been in my pack.

Socrates rebuts this suggestion as follows. Bringing *this* card is *not* wrong if I was asked simply to bring a card with a colour patch and the name 'red'; for this card is such a card. It is wrong only if the request was for a card with a colour patch *correctly* labelled 'red'. But then, if *that* was the request, our mere possession of 'bad' cards (misconceptions) does not explain the possibility of mistake, given the principle with which we started and which has not been challenged. For that principle was, to put it generally, that if one understands a request—the description of a card desired—one cannot fail to know which of one's cards is being asked for. Bringing a card incorrectly labelled 'red' would be wrong only if the request was for a card correctly labelled 'red'; but it follows from the principle that I could not both understand this request and fail to know which of my cards is the card correctly labelled 'red'. So I could not unwittingly bring the wrong card.

This model is the best I can do to give some sort of point to Theaetetus's suggestion, and to explain Socrates' contention that when we try to apply it to the problem of intellectual error, we discover that 'we have gone a long way round only to find ourselves confronted once more with our original difficulty' (200a11).

9. I will end by giving a brief synoptic account of Plato's whole discussion of false belief in the *Theaetetus*. In the earlier sections he claims that it is logically impossible for a man to hold a false belief which he could correctly express by saying such a thing as 'Theaetetus is identical with Theodorus', or again, 'Beauty is identical with ugliness'. In each case, knowing what the names stand for precludes the possibility of supposing them to stand for one and the same thing. In the wax tablet section Plato explains the possibility of misidentification of people or other physical continuants by giving a certain analysis of such statements, an analysis which makes out that they are not strict identity statements, and do not affirm the identity of two items referred to: believing that the man I see is the man I saw yesterday is believing that this item of experience belongs to one and the same continuant as that item of experience. This account of ordinary misidentification statements does not exploit or bring to light the notions of connotation and denotation or sense and reference. It does not reveal the confusion involved in the axiom that if you know what each of two expressions *stands for*, you cannot fail to know that they stand for different things (if they do). The wax tablet gives a Hume-like account of the identity of physical objects, which makes misidentification statements about them invulnerable to that confused axiom. A further application of the wax tablet idea (only hinted at) serves also to explain ordinary misclassification and misdescription.

Plato is now left with the problem of misidentification in the purely conceptual field. The Hume-like analysis of physical continuants does not help here. Statements like 'The sum of seven and five is eleven' are irreducibly and irresistibly assertions of identity. Plato fails to see how such mistakes can be possible. The aviary suggestion has some analogy with the wax tablet solution, but it is quickly seen to fail. The distinction between the dispositional and the actualized 'way' of knowing is unhelpful; for one who understands what he is saying must be actualizing his knowledge of the items referred to. The idea that we should like to see developed here is the idea that the same item can be referred to in different ways, and that the principle that to understand an expression involves knowing what it stands for is ambiguous and misleading. But there is no trace of this line of thought in Plato's discussion, except perhaps in the final remark. We need a better understanding of *knowing*—knowing a thing, knowing a word, knowing what an expression means, knowing what it refers to.

4

ΣΥΜΠΛΟΚΗ ΕΙΔΩΝ

It is the purpose of this short essay[1] to consider the meaning and implications of a sentence in Plato's *Sophist*. At the end of the section on κοινωνία γενῶν (the combination of kinds) the Eleatic visitor is made to speak as follows (259e4–6): τελεωτάτη πάντων λόγων ἐστὶν ἀφάνισις τὸ διαλύειν ἕκαστον ἀπὸ πάντων. διὰ γὰρ τὴν ἀλλήλων τῶν εἰδῶν συμπλοκὴν ὁ λόγος γέγονεν ἡμῖν (the isolation of everything from everything else is the total annihilation of all statements; for it is because of the interweaving of Forms with one another that we come to have discourse). I shall be mainly concerned with the second half of this remark, and shall refer to it, for brevity, as sentence or statement S.

Cornford translates sentence S thus: 'Any discourse we can have owes its existence to the weaving together of Forms.'[2] In his commentary he writes: 'All discourse depends on the "weaving together of Forms." ... It is not meant that Forms are the only elements in the meaning of all discourse. We can also make statements about individual things. But it is true that every such statement must contain at least one Form.' A few lines later Cornford says that the point made by Plato in S is 'that every statement or judgement involves the use of at least one Form'; and later he remarks that Plato 'has said that "all discourse depends on the weaving together of Forms," i.e. at least one Form enters into the meaning of any statement' (p. 314).

Cornford seems to take it for granted that Plato is saying something about Forms being 'contained in' or 'used in' statements. But he notices that not every statement does 'contain' a plurality of Forms—Plato's own examples a few pages later, the statements

[1] This is a shortened version of a paper read to a colloquium at the Classical Institute on 14 March 1955. The paper was designed to provoke discussion; this fact may help to excuse some oversimplification and some overstatement.

[2] F. M. Cornford, *Plato's Theory of Knowledge* (London: Routledge and Kegan Paul, 1935), 300; subsequent page references are given in parentheses in the text.

about Theaetetus, do not do so. So, to avoid attributing to Plato an obvious howler, he construes S as meaning not that every statement uses or contains or is about a συμπλοκὴ εἰδῶν (interweaving of Forms) but that it necessarily contains at least one Form. But this of course is just what τὴν τῶν εἰδῶν συμπλοκήν does not mean, as is particularly evident when we take account of the word ἀλλήλων (one another), which Cornford omits in his translation. 'Discourse depends on the weaving together of Forms *with one another*.' Who could suppose that this meant merely that at least one Form enters into the meaning of any statement? *If* S says something about Forms being contained in any *logos*, then what it says must be that a συμπλοκὴ εἰδῶν is contained in any *logos*. If this last is evidently false, as shown by Plato's examples a moment later, we must question the assumption that S does say something about Forms being contained in *logoi*.

It is worth noticing briefly how Ross deals with our passage. The Eleatic visitor, he says, asserts 'that all discourse depends on the weaving together of Forms by the speaker or thinker. This is in fact an over-statement, since a sentence may have a proper name for subject, and a proper name does not stand for a Form or universal. But the *predicate* of a sentence normally stands for a Form, and all subjects of statements except proper names stand either for Forms or for things described by means of Forms.'[3] Ross does not pretend that S is true; he takes it to mean that every statement involves at least two Forms, and shows this to be false. But notice how he proceeds. He does not say: since on our interpretation of S it is blatantly false, perhaps our interpretation is wrong. Instead, Ross glosses over the falsity of S (on his interpretation) by calling it an overstatement. But of course Plato is claiming to say something true of *all logoi* (259e4, 260a9). So S, on Ross's interpretation, is just false, and glaringly false. Misleading smoothness shows itself again a moment later: talking of the examples 'Theaetetus is sitting', 'Theaetetus is flying', Ross says not that they refute S (on his interpretation of S), but that they 'do not illustrate Plato's thesis'. If I asserted, rather solemnly, that all philosophers are good-tempered, and immediately went on to chat about the bad-tempered philosophers I know, you would hardly say that my examples were 'not illustrating my thesis'.

[3] W. D. Ross, *Plato's Theory of Ideas* (Oxford: Clarendon Press, 1951), 115.

Surely, then, something has gone wrong with the interpretation of S. Surely it must not be understood in such a way that the statements about Theaetetus are clear refutations of it. Surely it must not be taken to imply that every statement asserts or is about a relation between Forms (or even 'things described by means of Forms'). How, then, is it to be understood?

Let us look back at what Plato has said before about the συμπλοκή εἰδῶν; not at the section in which he investigated connections among various chosen Forms—this is, comparatively, a matter of detail—but at the passage 251d–252e, which seeks to show that there *must be* a συμπλοκή εἰδῶν. Statement S says something about the necessity of συμπλοκή εἰδῶν for all *logoi*: it is reasonable to try to elucidate this by considering the arguments by which in the first place Plato sought to demonstrate that there must be such a συμπλοκή.

Plato lists, in this earlier passage, three possibilities: (1) that every Form combines with every other; (2) that no Form combines with any other; (3) that while some pairs of Forms do, others do not, combine with one another. By ruling out the first two possibilities, he establishes the third; and it is this limited intercommunion of Forms that is subsequently spoken of as the συμπλοκή εἰδῶν. The argument for this last consists in effect of the arguments which disprove the other two possibilities.

The first possibility is ruled out on the ground that if it were true, such statements as κίνησις ἵσταται (motion rests) would follow. These we can see to be self-contradictory, logically impossible—ταῖς μεγίσταις ἀνάγκαις ἀδύνατον (to the last degree impossible). So if they are entailed by (1), then (1) must be false. To generalize: if a statement in which A is asserted of B is self-contradictory, logically impossible, then it follows that Form A does not combine with Form B. Since we are trying to understand what Plato means by his talk of 'combination', there can be no question of challenging the validity of his argument here; we have to take the argument as a clue to what 'combination' means. What emerges so far is that some restriction on the intercommunion of Forms is implied by the fact that some sentences express statements which are self-contradictory.

Plato's refutation of the second possibility—μηδεμία σύμμειξις (no intermixture)—has two parts. First, if this were true, all the theories put forward by philosophers about reality, change, the consti-

tution and behaviour of the world, would be null and void. Plural-
ists, monists, Eleatics, Heracliteans, all of them λέγοιεν ἂν οὐδέν,
εἴπερ μηδεμία ἔστι σύμμειξις (would be saying nothing, if there were
no intermixture). Secondly, the very statements of (2) involves a
contradiction. Its exponents, in stating it, must combine words into
sentences—συνάπτειν ἐν τοῖς λόγοις—and in so doing they contradict their own thesis. It does not need others to refute them: οἴκοθεν
τὸν πολέμιον καὶ ἐναντιωσόμενον ἔχουσιν (they will be opposed by a
foe within their own household).

Taking this point first, we must notice exactly how the exponents
of (2) are refuted out of their own mouths. It is not of course that
they straightforwardly both assert and deny σύμμειξις (intermixture); it is that the statement of (2) necessarily presupposes the
falsity of (2). Arguments of a somewhat similar kind are used by
Plato elsewhere. In 249c he mocks those who claim to know for
certain the truth of a thesis whose truth would in fact make it
impossible for anyone to know anything. Or compare *Sophist* 244.
The theory that only one thing exists must be false, or at any rate it
cannot be true. The statement 'Only one thing exists' would have
no meaning at all unless there were several different words with
different meanings. The meaningfulness of the statement therefore
presupposes, as a necessary condition, its own falsity.

The thesis 'No Forms combine with one another' is held to be
self-refuting because its meaningfulness presupposes that some
Forms do combine. Here, then, is another clue to an understanding
of Plato's talk about Forms combining. That some statements are
self-contradictory was taken as proof that some pairs of Forms are
irreconcilable; now the fact that a certain statement is meaningful is
taken to prove that some Forms do combine with others. Plato's
conclusion, that there are connections between Forms, but not
between every pair of Forms, rests upon the simple fact that some
sentences are meaningful and some are not. The former presuppose the existence of concept friendships or compatibilities, the
latter the existence of concept enmities or incompatibilities.

To return to the first part of Plato's refutation of (2): if there
were no σύμμειξις, all the philosophers' accounts of things would be
empty; they would not be saying anything at all, nothing significant.
This last is how I want to translate λέγοιεν οὐδέν. This expression
can of course mean simply 'to say what is false' or 'to say what is
silly'; but it can also mean 'to make no genuine statement at all',

'not to succeed in saying anything'. It seems to me that the argument here demands this last sense: if there were no σύμμειξις, then no statement of any theory could be even significant. For suppose λέγειν οὐδέν here meant just 'to say what is false'. Then (a) the argument would be evidently inconclusive. For granted that alternative (2) did entail that all those philosophers' theories were false—well, perhaps they are false. Plato himself remarks that it is hard to decide about the truth of such theories (243a2–3). To point out that (2) entailed the falsity of the theories listed would convince nobody that (2) was false unless he chanced to be a firm believer in one of those theories. (b) Again, on this interpretation of λέγειν οὐδέν, it is completely mysterious why (2)—the thesis that no Forms combine—should entail that the theories are false. For they are certainly not all theories *about* Forms. Empedocles talked about the world and its processes; he did not assert that certain Forms combined. So how would the assumption that no Forms combine make his theory necessarily false? (c) If, however, it were claimed that the philosophical theories mentioned did in fact *assert* that Forms combined, the result would be that Plato's argument was not indeed invalid, but utterly pointless. For it would amount to this: some Forms must combine; for if none did, then all philosophers who said they did would be wrong.

Taking λέγειν οὐδέν to mean 'to speak falsely', we find Plato's argument weak, obscure, or pointless. It is surrounded by arguments that are cogent, clear, and highly relevant. This is a good reason to suspect that interpretation. If we take the expression to mean 'to make no genuine statement, to convey no *logos* whatsoever', the argument falls properly into place. If there were no liaisons among concepts, the philosophers' statements (indeed, all statements) would be just meaningless. Just as it is a presupposition of there being self-contradictory statements that some pairs of concepts will not go together, so it is a necessary condition of there being significant, non-self-contradictory statements (whether true or false) that some concepts will go together. These, I suggest, are the points Plato is making in his proof that there is a συμπλοκὴ εἰδῶν. Human discourse is possible only because the meanings of general words are related in definite ways; it is essential to language that there be definite rules determining which combinations of words do, and which do not, constitute significant sentences. To map out the interrelations of concepts (inclusion, incompatibility, and so on) is the task of dialectic (cp. *Sophist* 253b–e).

I am obviously under an obligation to show that with my interpretation of *S*—as opposed to that of Cornford and Ross—there is no difficulty over the specimen *logoi* about Theaetetus. I must show that the dictum 'without a συμπλοκὴ εἰδῶν no *logos* would be possible' is *not* invalidated by the fact that many *logoi* contain only one general word, together with, for instance, a proper name. A quotation from a recent book on logical theory will help to make this clear:

One of the main purposes for which we use language is to report events and to describe things and persons. Such reports and descriptions are like answers to questions of the form: what was it like? what is it (he, she) like? We describe something, say what it is like by applying to it words that we are also prepared to apply to other things. But not to all other things. A word that we are prepared to apply to everything without exception (such as certain words in current use in popular, and especially military, speech) would be useless for the purposes of description. For when we say what a thing is like, we not only compare it with other things, we also distinguish it from other things. (These are not two activities, but two aspects of the same activity.) Somewhere, then, a boundary must be drawn, limiting the applicability of a word used in describing things.[4]

Substantially the same point is made by Aristotle in *Metaphysics* Γ. 4, where he argues for the Principle of Contradiction. He admits that it cannot be proved; for any proof would necessarily make use of the principle in question. But he says that you can explain to someone the necessity of this principle—provided he will say something significant, with a definite meaning; for you can then show him that he must intend his statement to rule out something or other, to be incompatible with at least one other statement. A statement compatible with every other statement would tell one nothing. ἀρχὴ ... τὸ ἀξιοῦν ... σημαίνειν γέ τι καὶ αὐτῷ καὶ ἄλλῳ. τοῦτο γὰρ ἀνάγκη, εἴπερ λέγοι τι. εἰ γὰρ μή, οὐκ ἂν εἴη τῷ τοιούτῳ λόγος, οὔτ' αὐτῷ πρὸς αὑτὸν οὔτε πρὸς ἄλλον. ἂν δέ τις τοῦτο διδῷ, ἔσται ἀπόδει ξις. ἤδη γάρ τι ἔσται ὡρισμένον ('The starting-point ... is the demand ... that he shall say something which is significant both for himself and for another; for this is necessary, if he really is to *say* something. Otherwise there will be no discourse, either with himself or with another. But if this is granted, there can be demonstration; for we shall already have something definite'; 1006a18–25). To return to Plato: the statement 'Theaetetus is sitting' is a genuine

---

[4] P. F. Strawson, *Introduction to Logical Theory* (London: Methuen, 1952), 5.

informative statement only because it rules something out ('Theaetetus is not sitting' or, more determinately, 'Theaetetus is standing'). To say that it rules something out is to say that there is an incompatibility (μηδεμία κοινωνία) between two concepts ('sitting' and 'not sitting' or, more determinately, 'sitting' and 'standing'). In studying the relations among concepts, a philosopher elicits the rules governing the use of language; that there are some such relations, some such rules, is a necessary condition of there being a language at all: διὰ τὴν ἀλλήλων τῶν εἰδῶν συμπλοκὴν ὁ λογος γεγονεν ἡμῖν (It is because of the interweaving of Forms with one another that we come to have discourse).

These few remarks must suffice to indicate how a συμπλοκὴ εἰδῶν is presupposed by any and every statement, including those about Theaetetus. Plato admittedly does not argue the point in connection with the Theaetetus examples, which are used in the discussion of a different topic. Still, it is a related topic, since it does involve the incompatibility of two predicates. And I think that if we had asked Plato to reconcile S with these examples, he would have done so in the way suggested in outline above. This, at any rate, seems more plausible than to suppose that he follows up S by using examples of *logoi* which he would have been totally unable to reconcile with S.

I have gradually passed from talking about Forms to talking about concepts, and I have taken these to be, in effect, the meanings of general words. Correspondingly, I have implied that the task assigned in Plato's later dialogues to the dialectician or philosopher is the investigation and plotting of the relations among concepts, a task to be pursued through a patient study of language by noticing which combinations of words in sentences do, and which do not, make sense, by eliciting ambiguities and drawing distinctions, by stating explicitly facts about the interrelations of word meanings which we normally do not trouble to state, though we all have some latent knowledge of them in so far as we know how to talk correctly. To justify all this, and to add the many sober qualifications which it evidently demands, would take a volume. I can mention, here in conclusion, only two small points.

There is a section of the *Sophist* (254b ff.) where Plato is undoubtedly *practising* the dialectic he has previously described. He first distinguishes certain εἴδη (cp. 253d1–3), and then determines their interrelations (cp. 253d9–e2). It is important to notice that what Plato does in this section is to appeal to truths too obvious to be disputed, in particular truths which anyone who knows the language must immediately admit. For instance, Being is proved to be different from Sameness by a simple substitution argument (255b8–c4): if they were *not* different, then to say of two things that they both existed would be to say that they were both the same. But this is not so. In particular, we have agreed that κίνησις (motion) and στάσις (rest) both *exist*; but it would be different, and indeed absurd, to say that they are both *the same*. The dialectician's statement that Being is different from Sameness merely makes us see clearly (or at a new level) a fact about the meanings of words which we already in a way know. The dialectician makes explicit the rules in accordance with which we all already talk.

Finally, a reference to the *Parmenides*. After his searching criticisms of Socrates, Parmenides goes on to imply that the theory of Ideas *is* capable of being salvaged, but that great skill and subtlety will be required for this. He adds (135b): 'If in view of all these and similar objections a man refuses to admit that Forms of things exist, or to distinguish (ὁρίζεσθαι) a definite Form in each case, he will have nothing on which to fix his thought, so long as he will not allow that each real thing has a character which is always the same; and thus he will completely destroy the possibility of significant talk (τὴν τοῦ διαλέγεσθαι δύναμιν).' This passage may be taken to show that, in spite of the powerful criticisms voiced by Parmenides, Plato did not propose to abandon completely his theory of Ideas. It may be that he thought of himself as maintaining a revised version of the theory, whereas we might find it more natural to say that he jettisoned the theory. Anyway, the passage quoted strongly suggests that what he is now sure of is *not* that there must be Forms as conceived in the middle dialogues, Forms as ethical ideals and as the metaphysical objects of intuitive and perhaps mystical insight; what he is now sure of is that there must be fixed things to guarantee the meaningfulness of talk, fixed concepts—the meanings of general words—whose role is to ensure τὴν τοῦ διαλέγεσθαι δύναμιν. The *Sophist* explains further that these concepts must stand in certain definite relations to one another, and gives the dialectician the task of investigating the boundaries and interrelations of concepts.

5

Plato and the Copula: *Sophist* 251–259

My purpose is not to give a full interpretation of this difficult and important passage, but to discuss one particular problem, taking up some remarks made by F. M. Cornford and by Mr. R. Robinson in his paper on Plato's *Parmenides*.[1] First it may be useful to give a very brief and unargued outline of the passage. Plato seeks to prove that concepts[2] are related in certain definite ways, that there is a συμπλοκὴ εἰδῶν (an interweaving of Forms) (251d–252e). Next (253) he assigns to philosophy the task of discovering what these relations are: the philosopher must try to get a clear view of the whole range of concepts and of how they are interconnected, whether in genus–species pyramids or in other ways. Plato now gives a sample of such philosophizing. Choosing some concepts highly relevant to problems already broached in the *Sophist*, he first (254–5) establishes that they are all different one from the other, and then (255e–258) elicits the relationships in which they stand to one another. The attempt to discover and state these relationships throws light on the puzzling notions ὄν (being) and μὴ ὄν (not being), and enables Plato to set aside with contempt certain puzzles and paradoxes propounded by superficial thinkers (259). He refers finally (259e) to the absolute necessity there is for concepts to be in definite relations to one another if there is to be discourse at all: διὰ γὰρ τὴν ἀλλήλων τῶν εἰδῶν συμπλοκὴν ὁ λόγος γέγονεν ἡμῖν (it is because of the interweaving of the Forms with

---

[1] F. M. Cornford, *Plato's Theory of Knowledge* (London: Routledge and Kegan Paul, 1935); R. Robinson, 'Plato's *Parmenides* II', *Classical Philology*, 37 (1942), 159–86. I shall refer to these two works by page numbers in the text, without repeating their titles.

[2] The use of this term may seem provocative. But whether or not the εἴδη (Forms) and γένη (kinds) of the *Sophist* are something more than 'mere' concepts, a good deal of interpretation of 251–9 can satisfactorily proceed on the assumption that they are *at least* concepts.

First published in 1957.

one another that we come to have discourse).[3] So the section ends
with a reassertion of the point with which it began (251d–252e):
that there is and must be a συμπλοκὴ εἰδῶν (an interweaving of
Forms).

The question I wish to discuss is this. Is it true to say that one of
Plato's achievements in this passage is 'the discovery of the copula',
or 'the recognition of the ambiguity of ἔστιν' as used on the one
hand in statements of identity and on the other hand in attributive
statements? The question is whether Plato made a philosophical
advance which we might describe in such phrases as those just
quoted, but no great stress is to be laid on these particular phrases.
Thus it is no doubt odd to say that Plato (or anyone else) *discovered*
the copula. But did he draw attention to it? Did he expound or
expose the various roles of the verb ἔστιν? Many of his predecessors
and contemporaries reached bizarre conclusions by confusing different uses of the word; did Plato respond by elucidating these
different uses? These are the real questions. Again, it would be a
pedantic misunderstanding to deny that Plato recognized the ambiguity of ἔστιν merely on the ground that he used no word meaning
'ambiguity', or on the ground that he nowhere says 'the word ἔστιν
sometimes means . . . and sometimes means . . .'. If he in fact
glosses or explains or analyses the meaning of a word in one way in
some contexts and in another way in others, and if this occurs in
a serious philosophical exposition, then it may well be right to
credit him with 'recognizing an ambiguity'. I mention these trivial
points only to indicate, by contrast, what the substantial question at
issue is.

It is generally agreed (e.g. Cornford, p. 296) that Plato marks off
the existential use of ἔστιν from at least some other use. How he
does this can be seen from his remark about κίνησις (change) at
256a1: ἔστι δέ γε διὰ τὸ μετέχειν τοῦ ὄντος (it is because it shares in
being). This διά ('because') does not introduce a *proof* that κίνησις
ἔστιν (change is): this was already agreed without question before,
and used to establish a connection between κίνησις and τὸ ὄν
(between change and being) (254d10). Nor, obviously, does it introduce the *cause* why κίνησις ἔστιν: it does not refer to some event

---

[3] It will be convenient to give here, once and for all, the translation of a few Greek
expressions that occur often in this essay: ἔστι (or ἔστιν) means 'is'; οὐκ ἔστι (or οὐκ
ἔστιν) means 'is not'; μετέχει means 'shares in' or 'partakes of'; μετέχειν (infinitive) and
μέθεξις (noun) mean 'sharing in'; εἶδος (plural εἴδη) means 'Form'.

or state which resulted in the further state described by κίνησις
ἔστιν. The words introduced by διά give an expansion or *analysis* of
ἔστιν as this word is used in κίνησις ἔστιν—that is, as used existen-
tially. μετέχει τοῦ ὄντος ('shares in being') is the philosopher's
equivalent of the existential ἔστιν; but, as will be seen, it is not his
analysis of ἔστιν in its other uses. So the existential meaning is
marked off.

The philosopher's formulation—κίνησις μετέχει τοῦ ὄντος (change
shares in being)—both elucidates the sense of ἔστιν in κίνησις ἔστιν
and also makes clear—what is not clear in the compressed collo-
quial formulation—the structure of the fact being stated; makes
clear that a certain connection is being asserted between two concepts. The philosopher's formulation contains not only the names
of two concepts, but also a word indicating their coherence, μετέχει,
which is not itself the name of an εἶδος, but signifies the connection
between the named εἴδη.

There remain two other meanings of ἔστιν, as copula and as
identity sign. The assimilation of these had led to a denial of the
possibility of any true non-tautological statements. What is needed
in order to deprive this paradox of its power is a clear demonstration of how the two uses of ἔστι differ. By 'demonstration' I do not
mean 'proof', but 'exhibition' or 'display'. The way to sterilize a
paradox is to expose and lay bare the confusion from which it
arises. One can draw attention to the two different uses of ἔστι,
point out how they are related, perhaps provide alternative modes
of expression so as to remove even the slightest temptation to
confuse the two.

Consider how Plato deals, in 256a10–b4, with the pair of statements κίνησίς ἔστι ταὐτόν, κίνησίς οὐκ ἔστι ταὐτόν (change is the
same, change is not the same). These look like contradictories, yet
we want to assert both. We need not really be worried (οὐ
δυσχεραντέον); for we are not in both statements speaking ὁμοίως
(in the same way). Analysis of the statements (introduced again by
διά (because of)) will show exactly what is being asserted in each,
and enable us to see that there is no contradiction between them
when properly understood. The first statement means κίνησις
μετέχει ταὐτοῦ (change shares in sameness). The second means
κίνησις μετέχει θατέρου πρὸς ταὐτόν (motion shares in difference with
respect to the same).

The essential points in Plato's analysis of the two statements are these: (1) where ἔστιν is being used as copula, it gets replaced in the philosopher's version by μετέχει; (2) the philosopher's version of οὐκ ἔστιν, when the ἔστιν is not the copula but the identity sign, is (not οὐ μετέχει, but) μετέχει θατέρου πρός (shares in difference from). By his reformulation of the two statements, Plato shows up the difference between the ἔστιν which serves merely to connect two named concepts (copula) and the ἔστιν (or οὐκ ἔστιν) which expresses the concept of Identity (or Difference) and at the same time indicates that something *falls under* the concept of Identity (or Difference).

With Plato's procedure here, one may compare a passage in Frege's paper 'Über Begriff und Gegenstand'. One can just as well assert of a thing that it is Alexander the Great, or is the number four, or is the planet Venus, as that it is green or is a mammal. But, Frege points out, one must distinguish two different usages of 'is'.

In the last two examples it serves as a copula, as a mere verbal sign of predication. (In the sense the German *ist* can sometimes be replaced by the mere personal suffix: cf. *dies Blatt ist grün* and *dies Blatt grün*.[4]) We are here saying that something falls under a concept, and the grammatical predicate stands for this concept. In the first three examples, on the other hand, 'is' is used like the 'equals' sign in arithmetic, to express an equation. . . . In the sentence 'the morning star is Venus' 'is' is obviously not the mere copula; its content is an essential part of the predicate, so that the word 'Venus' does not constitute the whole of the predicate. One might say instead: 'the morning star is no other than Venus'; what was previously implicit in the single word 'is' is here set forth in four separate words, and in 'is no other than' the word 'is' now really is the mere copula. What is predicated here is thus not *Venus* but *no other than Venus*. These words stand for a concept.[5]

Frege explains the copula by talking of something's *falling under* a concept: Plato uses for this the term μετέχειν. Frege expands the 'is' of identity into 'is no other than', in which phrase the 'is' is simply the copula ('falls under the concept'), and 'no other than' stands for a concept. Plato expands the ἔστιν of identity into μετέχει ταὐτοῦ . . . (shares in sameness) (and οὐκ ἔστιν into μετέχει θατέρου

---

[4] One is reminded of Aristotle, *Physics* 185b28.

[5] I quote Geach's translation, in Peter Geach and Max Black (eds.), *Translations from the Philosophical Writings of Gottlob Frege* (Oxford: Basil Blackwell, 1952), 43–4.

(shares in difference))), where μετέχει does the copula's job ('falls under') and ταὐτόν (or θάτερον) names a concept (sameness (or difference)). In offering the analyses that he does, it seems to me that Plato, no less clearly than Frege, is engaged in distinguishing and elucidating senses of 'is'.

The claim that one of the things Plato does in *Sophist* 251–9 is to distinguish between the copula and the identity sign would seem to be supported by the following consideration: that this distinction is just what is required to immunize us against the paradoxes of the ὀψιμαθεῖς (late learners) (251b), and Plato does suppose that his discussion puts these gentlemen in their place. Robinson, however, denies that this consideration has any force: 'Plato certainly thought of his Communion as refuting the "late learners". But it does not follow that he thought the manner of refutation was to show that they confused attribution with identity. Nor is there anything in the text to show that he thought this' (p. 174). Robinson is certainly right to say that it does not *follow*. Still, we are surely entitled—or, rather, obliged—to make some reasonable suggestion as to how exactly Plato did suppose himself to have 'refuted' the late learners. If the above interpretation of 256a10–b10 is sound, that passage exposes the error of the late learners, who construed every 'is' as an identity sign; and it would be natural to infer that Plato himself regarded the distinction drawn in that passage (and elsewhere) as the decisive counter move against the late learners. Moreover, if no *other* reasonable suggestion can be made as to how exactly Plato thought he had disposed of the late learners and their paradox, this fact will be an argument in favour of the interpretation of 256a–b which finds in it an important point which is directly relevant to, and destructive of, the paradox.

Now it might be suggested that it is by his proof that there is Communion among εἴδη (251d–252e) that Plato refutes the view that only identical statements are possible; that it is here, and not in later talk about ὄν (being) and μὴ ὄν (not being), that he supposes himself to be refuting the late learners. But what are the arguments by which he proves there is Communion?[6] The first (251e7–252b7) is this: if there were no Communion, then philosophers and 'physicists', in propounding their various views, would in fact be 'saying

---

[6] I have discussed these arguments, in another connection, in a short paper in the *Bulletin of the Institute of Classical Studies of the University of London*, 2 (1955), 31–5; repr. here as Ch. 4.

nothing' (λέγοιεν ἂν οὐδέν). It is simply *assumed* that this apodosis is false, and that Empedocles and the rest were talking sense. But, of course, this assumption is exactly what the late learners, maintaining their paradox, will deny; and an argument based on it is obviously no good against them. Plato's second argument for Communion (252b8–d1) is that the theory that there is no Communion cannot be stated without implying its own falsity. As applied to the later learners, the argument would be: you say only identity statements can be true; but this statement—'Only identity statements can be true'—is not an identity statement; so on your own theory your theory is false. Now this argument is certainly formidable, and might easily put a late learner to silence; he could hardly be expected to distinguish between first- and second-order statements. Yet, as a refutation of the thesis itself, it is surely superficial and unsatisfactory. For the thesis was put forward not only by elderly jokers, but also by serious thinkers who felt themselves obliged to maintain it for what seemed to them compelling theoretical reasons. Robinson writes as follows:

To such more responsible thinkers it is folly to say: 'But you obviously can say "man is good"; and if you could not, all discourse whatever would be impossible, including the paradox that you cannot say "man is good".' For these thinkers already know that you can say that 'man is good', and that the supposition that you cannot immediately destroys all thought and speech. Their trouble is that, nevertheless, they seem to see a good reason for denying that you can say that 'man is good'. What they want is to be shown the fallacy in the argument which troubles them. They know it must be a fallacy; but they want to see what it is. Now for such thinkers Plato's exposition of his doctrine of Communion is no help whatever. For he merely points to the fact that we *must* be able to say 'man is good,' because otherwise no thought or communication would be possible. He does not even notice any argument to the contrary, much less show us where they go wrong. (p. 175)

I agree with Robinson that, for the reason he gives, Plato's proof of Communion cannot be said to dispose satisfactorily of the paradoxical thesis (even though the second argument in the proof is valid against the thesis); for nothing is done to expose the error or confusion which led quite serious persons to embrace the paradox. Surely this passage (251d–252e) cannot be the whole of what Plato has to say in rebuttal of the late learners and their paradox. Surely he somewhere exposes the underlying error, the rotten foundations on which the paradox was built. And he does this, I suggest, for instance in the passage previously discussed, by clearly distinguishing two different uses of ἔστιν, as copula and as identity sign, and by showing how the two uses are related.

Let us turn now to Cornford. He says that the copula 'has no place anywhere in Plato's scheme of the relations of Forms' (p. 279). The relation between Forms that combine—'blending'—is a symmetrical relation; so it cannot be the same as the relation of subject to predicate in an attributive statement—that is, the relation indicated by the copula (pp. 256–7, 266).

First a very general point. The relation 'being connected with' or 'being associated with' is a symmetrical relation. But there are, of course, many different *ways* in which things or persons may be associated or connected; and many of these ways involve non-symmetrical relationships. One may say of a group of people, members of one family, that they are all connected. But if one wishes to say *how* they are connected each with the other, one must employ such expressions as 'father of', 'niece of', which do not stand for symmetrical relationships. Now it is agreed by Cornford that the philosopher's task, according to Plato, is to 'discern clearly the hierarchy of Forms . . . and make out its articulate structure' (pp. 263–4). Every statement the philosopher makes in performing this task may be expected to assert some connection or association between Forms. And 'association' is indeed a symmetrical relation. But surely the philosopher could not possibly achieve his purpose without specifying the *kind* of association there is in each case. And he could not do this without bringing in some non-symmetrical relations. Consider the small extract from a possible 'map of the Forms' shown below. The structure exhibited here must be described by the philosopher; and to do this he *must* advert to a non-symmetrical relationship. In the figure, the words 'Virtue' and 'Justice' are not merely close together; one is *under* the other. Similarly, Virtue and Justice are not merely

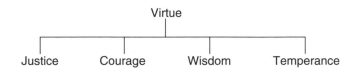

connected; they are connected in a particular way: Justice is *a species of* Virtue.

Non-symmetrical relations must then be invoked if the complex structure of the 'world of Forms' is to be described; nor is this something Plato could easily have overlooked. Certainly the analogy he draws with letters and musical notes (253a–b) does not support the idea that the dialectician would, according to him, be satisfied with asserting *symmetrical* relations between εἴδη. If we are to say whether 'f' and 'g' fit together, with the aid of 'i', to make an English word, we must obviously specify the *order* in which the letters are to be taken: 'gif' is not a word, 'fig' is. The scale of C major is not just such-and-such notes, but these notes in a certain order. Whatever terminology one uses to state the facts about spelling or scales or Forms, some non-symmetrical relation must come in. But if Cornford's view were right and every philosopher's statement told of a symmetrical 'blending' of Forms, the philosopher would never be able to express irreducibly non-symmetrical truths, such as that Justice is a species of Virtue. So we may suspect that Cornford's view is not right.

To this it will be objected that the *Sophist*, though it implies that the philosopher will have to study relations between genera and species, does not itself explore such relations; so a proper interpretation of the *Sophist* should leave them aside, and concentrate on how Plato proceeds in exhibiting the relations which he does in fact consider. Let us then look at some of the statements of Communion which Plato makes.

Firstly, 'Motion exists' (I retain Cornford's translation; 'Change' would be better). Cornford says: ' "Motion exists" means that the Form Motion blends with the Form Existence' (p. 256); and ' "Motion blends with Existence" is taken as equivalent to "Motion exists" ' (p. 279). He also says: 'The relation intended (*sc.* by "blending") is not the meaning of the "copula" . . . ; for we can equally say "Existence blends with Motion" ' (p. 278). Taken together, these remarks lead to absurdity. For if 'Motion blends with Existence' means 'Motion exists', then 'Existence blends with Motion' must mean 'Existence moves'. And then, if 'Motion blends with Existence' is equivalent to 'Existence blends with Motion', 'Motion exists' must be equivalent to 'Existence moves'. Plato obviously did not intend this. The trouble lies in Cornford's insistence on the 'blending' metaphor, which suggests a symmetrical relation, to the exclusion of others which do not. What 'Motion exists' is equivalent to is not 'Motion blends with Existence' ('blending' being symmetrical), but 'Motion shares in, partakes of Existence' ('partaking of' being non-symmetrical). Cornford's remarks lead to absurdity because he will not let into his exposition any non-symmetrical expression like 'partakes of' (even though Plato's exposition bristles with this metaphor).

Secondly, 'Motion is different from Rest.' Now this is indeed equivalent to 'Rest is different from Motion'. But before drawing any inference concerning 'Communion', we must put the statement into its 'analysed' form, into dialectician's terminology. We get: 'Motion communicates with Difference from Rest'. The question is whether 'communicates with' in this formulation can be taken to stand for a symmetrical relation. But if it is so taken, we must be prepared to say that 'Motion communicates with Difference from Rest' is equivalent to 'Difference from Rest communicates with Motion'; for the 'Communion' asserted in the first statement is evidently between Motion on the one hand and Difference from Rest on the other. But then, since 'Motion communicates with Difference from Rest' is the technical way of saying that Motion is different from Rest, we must suppose that 'Difference from Rest communicates with Motion' is the technical way of saying that Difference from Rest moves. So we shall find ourselves claiming that 'Motion is different from Rest' means the same as 'Difference from Rest moves'. As before, the absurdity results from taking 'communicates with' as standing for a symmetrical relation. If 'Motion communicates with Difference from Rest' means that Motion is different from Rest (as it clearly does), then 'communicates with' must here stand not for 'blending', but for a non-symmetrical relation ('partaking of', 'falling under').

These considerations, it may be said, are still very general, and involve too much extrapolation and 'interpretation'. I am not sure how much weight to attach to this criticism. For one must suppose that Plato had something reasonable and consistent in his mind when writing the very taut piece of exposition in *Sophist* 251–9; and if Cornford's account leads, on reflection, to grave difficulties or absurdities, this is a sound prima-facie argument against it. (Even if, in the end, Cornford's account were to be accepted, it would be desirable that the defects in Plato's discussion—as interpreted by Cornford—should be candidly exposed.) However, it is·certainly necessary to turn to a closer examination of Plato's actual terminology.

Plato uses a great variety of terms in speaking of relations among εἴδη. While some of them (e.g. *συμμείγνυσθαι*) seem naturally to stand for the rather indeterminate symmetrical relation 'being connected with', there are others, like *μετέχειν*, which we expect to be standing for some more determinate, non-symmetrical relation. Cornford denies that this expectation is fulfilled, and says that Plato does not distinguish 'partaking' from the mutual relation called 'blending' or 'combining' (pp. 296–7). He does not support this by a detailed study of all the relevant passages. His explicit argument that 'participation' as between Forms is a symmetrical relation (like 'blending', hence nothing to do with the copula) rests on the one passage 255d, in which Existence is said to *partake of* both τὸ καθ' αὐτό and τὸ πρὸς ἄλλο (roughly 'the absolute' and 'the relative'). Cornford writes: 'So the generic Form partakes of (blends with) the specific Form no less than the specific partakes of the generic' (p. 256). And in his footnote on 255d4 he says: 'Note that Existence, which *includes* both these Forms (*sc.* τὸ καθ' αὐτό and τὸ πρὸς ἄλλο), is said to *partake of* both. This is one of the places which show that "partaking" is symmetrical in the case of Forms.' I do not know which are the other places Cornford here alludes to; yet the reference to 255d is by itself a very inadequate justification of Cornford's sweeping remarks about 'participation', ˙ and of his insistence on symmetrical 'blending' as the one and only relation holding between Forms.

Professor Karl Dürr, in his paper 'Moderne Darstellung der platonischen Logik',[7] assigned precise and distinct meanings to various terms used by Plato in *Sophist* 251–9, but did not attempt anything like a full justification. More useful for us is the following observation by Sir David Ross: 'Plato uses κοινωνία, κοινωνεῖν, ἐπικοινωνία, προσκοινωνεῖν in two different constructions—with the genitive (250b9, 252a2, b9, 254c5, 256b2, 260e2) and with the dative (251d9, e8, 252d3, 253a8, 254b8, c1, 257a9, 260e5). In the former usage the verbs mean "share in"; in the latter they mean "combine with" or "communicate with"'.[8] I do not think Ross should have

---

[7] In *Museum Helveticum*, 2 (1945), esp. 171–5.

[8] W. D. Ross, *Plato's Theory of Ideas* (Oxford: Clarendon Press, 1951), 111. n. 6.

added that 'though Plato uses the two different constructions, he does not seem to attach any importance to the difference between them'. For Plato does not use the two constructions indiscriminately or interchangeably. A comparison between the two groups of passages yields a clear result (I leave out of account 250b9 and 260e2 and e5, which are not in the main section on κοινωνία γενῶν (the combination of kinds)). κοινωνεῖν followed by the genitive (e.g. θατέρου) is used where the fact being asserted is that some εἶδος is (copula) such-and-such (e.g. different from . . .); that is, it is used to express the fact that one concept *falls under* another. The dative construction, on the other hand, occurs in highly general remarks about the connectedness of εἴδη, where no definite fact as to any particular pair of εἴδη is being stated. Surely this confirms— what ordinary Greek usage would suggest—that Plato consciously uses κοινωνεῖν in two different ways. Sometimes it stands for the general symmetrical notion of 'connectedness', sometimes it stands for a determinate non-symmetrical notion, 'sharing in'.

There are thirteen occurrences of the verb μετέχειν or noun μέθεξις in *Sophist* 251–9. One of these is at 255d4, in the passage used by Cornford in his argument quoted above. But in all the other twelve cases it is clear that the truth expressed by 'A-ness μετέχει B-ness' is that A-ness is (copula) B, and never that B-ness is (copula) A. For instance, τὸ ὂν μετέχει θατέρου (*Being* shares in *Difference*) . . . formulates the fact that Existence is different from . . . ; it does not serve equally to express the fact that Difference exists—that is expressed by τὸ ἕτερον μετέχει τοῦ ὄντος (*Difference* shares in *Being*). The way Plato uses μετέχειν in all these cases makes it very hard to believe that he intended by it a symmetrical relation.

It is worth attending specially to the passage officially devoted to the statement of certain relations among the five chosen γένη (kinds), 255e8–257a11. Here the objective is to state definite truths in careful, philosophical terminology; not merely to allude to the fact that there are connections among γένη, but to say precisely what some of them are. Now in this passage Cornford's favourite metaphor occurs once (256b9), in a purely general reference to the connectedness of concepts (εἴπερ τῶν γενῶν συγχωρησόμεθα τὰ μὲν ἀλλήλοις ἐθέλειν μείγνυσθαι, τὰ δὲ μή (if we are to agree that some of the kinds will blend with one another, some will not)). And κοινωνία with the dative occurs once (257a9), in an equally unspecific context (εἴπεϱ ἔχει κοινωνίαν ἀλλήλοις ἡ τῶν γενῶν φύσις (if kinds are of a nature to admit combination with one another)). The other terms used are as follows. κοινωνία with the genitive occurs once (256b2), and is used to state the definite relation holding between two named εἴδη (κίνησις and θάτεϱον); the fact stated is that Motion is different from . . . , not that Difference moves. μεταλαμβάνειν occurs once (256b6), in a passage whose interpretation is controversial. But the significance of the verb is clear. If it were true to say κίνησις μεταλαμβάνει στάσεως (Change participates in Unchangingness), then one could rightly say κίνησίς ἐστι στάσιμος (Change is unchanging). μετέχειν (or μέθεξις) occurs five times (256a1, a7, b1, d9, e3), in each case expressing the relation between two named εἴδη the first of which falls under the second. Thus all the real work of the section 255e8–257a11, all the exposition of actual connections between particular εἴδη, is done by the terms μετέχειν, μεταλαμβάνειν, and κοινωνεῖν (with genitive)—that is, by the non-symmetrical metaphor 'partaking of', which Cornford is so determined to exclude. And the role of 'partakes of' in Plato's terminology is clear: 'partakes of' followed by an abstract noun, the name of a concept, is equivalent to the ordinary language expression consisting of 'is' (copula) followed by the adjective corresponding to that abstract noun.

This examination of Plato's use of some terms, though far from exhaustive, is, I think, sufficient to discredit Cornford's claim that the 'blending' metaphor is the one safe clue to Plato's meaning, and to establish that μετέχειν and its variants, μεταλαμβάνειν and κοινωνεῖν (with genitive), are not used by Plato as mere alternatives for μείγνυσθαι (blending). It may be admitted that in 255d, the passage Cornford exploits, μετέχειν is used in an exceptional way; but one passage cannot be allowed to outweigh a dozen others.[9]

To sum up: I have tried to argue, firstly, that the verb μετέχειν, with its variants, has a role in Plato's philosophical language corresponding to the role of the copula in ordinary language; and

[9] This is rather a cavalier dismissal of the passage on which Cornford relies so heavily. But it is not possible in the space available to attempt a full study of the perplexing argument of 255c12–e1, and without such a study no statement as to the exact force of μετέχειν in 255d4 is worth much. My own conviction is that even in this passage μετέχειν does not stand for the symmetrical relation 'blending'; but it is certainly not used in quite the same way as in the other places where it occurs in 251–9.

secondly, that by his analysis of various statements Plato brings out—and means to bring out—the difference between the copula (μετέχει (shares in) . . .), the identity-sign (μετέχει ταὐτοῦ (shares in sameness) . . .), and the existential ἔστιν (μετέχει τοῦ ὄντος (shares in being))).

6

In Defence of Platonic Division

INTRODUCTION

Expositors of Plato have sometimes identified Plato's later dialectic with *diairesis*, the method of division recommended and exemplified in well-known parts of the *Phaedrus, Sophist, Politicus*, and *Philebus*. In his *Mind* paper of 1939[1] and again in the chapter on dialectic in *Plato's Progress*,[2] Professor Ryle has made scathing remarks about this 'method', and has drawn a sharp contrast between it and genuine dialectic or philosophy: the construction of Linnaeus-type genus–species trees has nothing to do with the philosophical activity of hard reasoning which leads to truths about the powers and interrelations of topic-neutral concepts. While allowing that Plato may on occasion have attached some (improper) importance to division, Ryle holds that the philosopher who wrote the central part of the *Sophist* and the *Parmenides* could not (then, or seriously, or for long) have supposed division to be a significant part or instrument of philosophy.

I think that Ryle has exaggerated the contrast between Platonic division and genuine dialectic or philosophy—both in Plato's thought and in fact—and I want to mitigate the sharpness of his contrast by suggesting a more generous interpretation of division. I shall not attempt a close study of the relevant texts, but I shall try to say enough to show that it is bad history of ideas to write off Platonic division as a minor aberration, and that a less severe appraisal of it may discover in it material worthy of a philosopher's consideration.

---

[1] G. Ryle, 'Plato's *Parmenides* II', *Mind*, 48 (1939), 302–25; repr. in R. E. Allen (ed.), *Studies in Plato's Metaphysics* (London: Routledge and Kegan Paul, 1965), 97–147.
[2] G. Ryle, *Plato's Progress* (Cambridge: Cambridge University Press, 1966), hereafter *PP*, with page references given in parentheses in the text.

First published in 1970.

I

A brief survey of four dialogues will serve to make clear what difficulties stand in the way of one who seeks to excise division from the serious development of Plato's thought.

Phaedrus

Socrates' speeches have been dominated by the necessity to define love and to distinguish different varieties of irrationality or madness; at 265c Socrates says that, whatever may have been light-hearted in the speeches, two procedures were used which deserve serious attention.

The first is that in which we bring a dispersed plurality under a single form, seeing it all together; the purpose being to define so-and-so, and thus to make plain whatever may be chosen as the topic for exposition. For example, take the definition given just now of love: whether it was right or wrong, at all events it was that which enabled our discourse to achieve lucidity and consistency. [The second procedure] is the reverse of the other, whereby we are enabled to divide into forms, following the objective articulation; we are not to attempt to hack off parts like a clumsy butcher, but to take example from our two recent speeches. (265d–e, Hackforth's translation[3])

After giving a (not quite accurate) account of how in those speeches the single form of madness or irrationality had been divided, Socrates continues:

Believe me, Phaedrus, I am myself a lover of these divisions and collections, that I may gain the power to speak and to think; and whenever I deem another man able to discern an objective unity and plurality, I follow 'in his footsteps where he leadeth as a god.' Furthermore—whether I am right or wrong in doing so, God alone knows—it is those that have this ability whom for the present I call dialecticians.

Ryle does not deny that the natural interpretation of this passage makes Plato assimilate division to dialectic (like Ryle, I omit special reference to the reverse operation, 'collection'). But he argues—using arguments to be examined below—that certain considerations 'require us to suppose that in the *Phaedrus* he means but omits to say explicitly that division is only a preparation

---

[3] R. Hackforth, *Plato's* Phaedrus (Cambridge: Cambridge University Press, 1952).

for dialectic' (*PP* 141). The last sentence in the *Phaedrus* passage quoted above certainly allows us some leeway, and if Ryle had suggested that Plato felt some qualms about *identifying* division with dialectic, one would not have to disagree. But it is surely implausible to say that the writer of that warm testimonial to collection and division really meant that they are only 'a preparation for dialectic'—a philosophically quite unrewarding propaedeutic for 18-year-olds, a Pass Mods. subject for freshmen. Nor can the testimonial be treated as a rather silly aside: the account of division picks up points about the method and motive of Socrates' earlier speeches, and is echoed in later discussions of 'scientific rhetoric' at 270–1.

Sophist

This dialogue 'consists queerly of a stretch of highly abstract and sophisticated philosophical reasoning sandwiched between some division-operations which presuppose no philosophical sophistication whatsoever' (*PP* 139). It is difficult to dissent from this verdict, but the queerness demands explanation. Why did Plato make up this 'clumsily assembled sandwich'? The sharper one draws the contrast between division and genuine philosophy, the more baffling the problem. That Plato did not find the contrast so sharp is shown by a passage (which Ryle refers to) within the central, sophisticated section. For, having brought out the need for a 'science' to determine which Forms (or 'Kinds') blend with one another and which do not, and to detect any all-pervasive forms that serve to connect or disconnect others, the Eleatic Stranger continues:

And what name shall we give to this science? . . . Have we stumbled unawares upon the free man's knowledge and, in seeking for the Sophist, chanced to find the Philosopher first?

THEAETETUS. How do you mean?

STRANGER. Dividing according to Kinds, not taking the same Form for a different one or a different one for the same—is not that the business of Dialectic? . . . And the man who can do that discerns clearly *one* Form everywhere extended through many, where each one lies apart, and *many* Forms, different from one another, embraced from without by one Form; and again *one* Form connected in a unity through many wholes, and *many* Forms, entirely marked off apart. That means knowing how to distinguish,

Kind by Kind, in what ways the several Kinds can or cannot combine. (253c–e, Cornford's translation[4])

The Stranger then repeats that this is dialectic and its practitioner is the philosopher.

Ryle says that it is 'tempting, though not compulsory, to infer that Plato thought that the task of constructing kind-ladders was not only a propaedeutic to the philosopher's or dialectician's task; it was a part of it or else the whole of it' (*PP* 140). Rather, it is compulsory, however unwelcome, to infer that Plato saw at least a close connection between division and the philosophical task of mapping the interrelations of concepts. Perhaps he was quite wrong to think so; in this case we have to recognize and try to understand his mistake. Perhaps, however, we load the dice un-fairly against him if we give the most trivial possible interpretation of his 'division' and the most limited and rarefied interpretation of 'dialectic' or 'philosophy'.

Politicus

Like the *Sophist*, this dialogue contains numerous division opera-tions and explicit recommendation of the procedure of division. There is little hard argument of the kind so excitingly exemplified in the central part of the *Sophist*. Ryle concludes that the *Politicus* was designed for beginners only (*PP* 285), 'for the special benefit of the philosophically innocent novices who were at that moment getting their freshmen's training in the ABC of thinking' (*PP* 139). It is easy to share Ryle's evident distaste for 'this weary dialogue'; it is less easy to brush aside, as he does, the evidence that when Plato wrote it, he attached great importance to division as an essential instrument or part of dialectic. Ryle writes: 'Dialectic is alluded to only twice, at 285d and 287a, and then only in the Stranger's explanation of the preparatory role of the intellectual exercises that he is giving' (*PP* 139). This is a rather misleading comment. It suggests that the Stranger contrasts dialectic with the kind of operations of division and definition he is engaged in, and that (like Ryle) he regards such operations as merely preliminary to the quite different tasks of dialectic proper. In fact, however, the Stranger contrasts simple division operations on easy concepts with

---

[4] F. M. Cornford, *Plato's Theory of Knowledge* (London: Routledge and Kegan Paul, 1935).

more difficult ones; and the implication is not that dialectic has nothing to do with division, but that it has very much to do with it. Nor are the two 'allusions' to dialectic mere passing allusions: they are embedded in long theoretical discussions of procedure.

The thought that his trivial and lengthy divisions, culminating in a definition of weaving, may be criticized as excessive leads the Stranger to distinguish two types of measurement. One is concerned with the relative length or magnitude etc., of different things; the other is concerned with whether a thing is *too* long or large, etc., with reference to a certain standard. Having made this division of measurement into two 'parts', the Stranger develops a generalized criticism of those who fail to follow correct procedure.

Because they are not accustomed to conduct their enquiries by dividing into sorts, they straight off jumble these very different things together, thinking them similar; and then again they do the opposite, dividing other things but not into their parts. Whenever one starts by perceiving the common nature of the many things, one ought not to give up until one has seen in it all the differences that constitute sorts. Whenever, on the other hand, one has seen the multifarious differences in pluralities, one ought not to be able to be discouraged and stop until one has brought all the related things within one similarity and confined them all within the being of some kind. (285a–b)

The Stranger now turns to the motive and purpose of the discussion of the statesman and of the attempt to define weaving. A pupil learning to spell a given word is not so much interested in how to spell that particular word as in increasing his proficiency in orthography in general.

Now what of our present question about the statesman? Has it been raised for its own sake, or rather so that we may become better dialecticians about everything? Clearly the latter. No man of sense would want to chase after a definition of weaving for its own sake. But what most people, I think, fail to realize is this: some of the things there are have sensible likenesses, easy to recognize, and these can be indicated without difficulty when anyone wishes in reply to a request for a *logos* of such a thing to avoid trouble and indicate them easily without a *logos*. But the greatest and most important things have no images fashioned with clarity for men; to content the enquirer's mind there is nothing to show which can be fitted to a sense perception so as to give adequate satisfaction. This is why we must practise the ability to give and receive a *logos* of each thing. The incorporeals, the finest and greatest of things, are clearly shown only by a *logos* and in no other way; and it is for the sake of them that all our present discussions are taking place. Practice in anything is easier with relatively minor examples than with more important ones. (285d–286b)

There is room for discussion as to the precise contrast Plato intends between Forms or concepts which can be illustrated by sensible instances and those which can only be made clear in a definition. One thing, however, is obvious. The notion of practising on easy cases like weaving, in order to acquire greater skill to handle other cases, would be entirely out of place unless the envisaged operations on or about the difficult concepts were taken to be similar in kind to those we practise on easy ones; and these are indisputably division operations. Again, when the Stranger says that we study the particular case not out of special interest in it, but in order to increase our capacity to do dialectic about anything, he certainly implies that exercises in the general dialectical skill we seek will be of the same kind as the particular exercises we do to acquire the skill. Thus the fact that there is only one explicit reference to dialectic in the section 284e–286b does not prevent us drawing from the whole section the clear conclusion that dialectic is, or at least essentially involves, division.

The other use of the term 'dialectic' (287a) is embedded in a context which leads to the same conclusion. The Stranger says that if our discussion is criticized for being terribly long, we shall defend ourselves by referring to its purpose, and we shall try to show that, even if it is very long, it is not *too* long—judged by the standard of what is appropriate for our purpose. We are not out to give pleasure or, primarily, to get a quick answer to the particular question before us. What we value most is 'the method itself, which consists in the ability to divide into sorts'. A discourse will be acceptable, however long, if it 'makes its hearer better able to find things out'. It is no good for a critic to complain that our discussion is long. He must show that if it had been shorter it would have done more 'to make its participants good at dialectic and at finding out how to make clear in a *logos* the things there are' (286b–287a).

The method of division is here identified with skill at dialectic and with getting clear about 'the things there are'. These are alternative ways of describing the ulterior object of our particular discussion. Thus the whole section from 284e to 287a assimilates division to dialectic, and in doing so offers to justify the tedious divisions in the surrounding parts of the dialogue. So, however tedious or even pointless we may find these divisions, we cannot say that Plato thought them unrelated to genuine dialectic or philosophy. Nor can we say that he thought them related to dialectic merely as elementary formal logic is related to philosophical investigations. He clearly takes the operations of dialectic in general to be the same in kind as the division operations he himself conducts. If these are preparations for more important and difficult operations, they are so not in the way in which cleaning saucepans is a preparation for making cakes, but in the way in which making scones is a preparation for making cakes and other more elaborate confections.

Philebus

Ryle says that 'in the *Phaedrus*, the *Politicus* and, debatably, the *Philebus* Plato seems closely to connect the task of dialectic with the tasks of Definition and especially Division' (*PP* 135). He does not explain his 'debatably' or revert to the *Philebus* in connection with his thesis that division is a philosophically worthless procedure that plays no part in dialectic. It is true that, as in the *Politicus*, there are only two explicit references to the practice of dialectic. But, as in the *Politicus*, consideration of the contexts forces the conclusion that Plato is advancing a method of division as characteristic of dialectic, which is itself identified as the noblest science of all, which seeks truth about unchanging realities.

Socrates outlines a method which, he says, is easy to describe but very difficult to practise. He says he has always been a lover of this method, though it has often eluded him and left him desolate and perplexed.

We ought, whatever it be that we are dealing with, to assume a single form and search for it, for we shall find it there contained; then if we have laid hold of that, we must go on from one form to look for two, if the case admits of there being two, otherwise for three or some other number of forms: and we must do the same again with each of the 'ones' thus reached, until we come to see not merely that the one that we started with is a one and an unlimited many, but also just how many it is. (16d, Hackforth's translation).

This is the method the gods have given us 'for enquiring and learning and teaching one another'. The careful use of this method and the noticing of all the forms intermediate between the original one and the unlimited plurality is what distinguishes the dialectical from the eristic mode of discussion (16b–17b).

The examples Socrates proceeds to give are interestingly different from others so far mentioned: the division of language into its elements is not a simple case of genus–species articulation. This, however, need not prevent our insisting against Ryle that Plato is here recommending some sort of division procedure as of the highest importance. Moreover, there is appeal to it later in the dialogue, when the participants come to examine pleasure on the one hand and knowledge on the other. That the method just explained is to be applied to these is explicitly stated at 18e, 19b, and 20a; and, though the task is postponed, the detailed discussion of pleasure and knowledge from 31b to 59c takes the form of an analysis of each into its different types. One can indeed contrast the official statement of the method with the loose structure of the later discussion. But Plato evidently regards the latter as somehow exemplifying the former.

The other reference to dialectic is at 57e, where Socrates picks it out as the truest, most accurate, and purest form of knowledge. Its objects are the truest entities, unchanging and divine. Socrates allows that a man needs more than this knowledge in order to live.

Imagine a man who understands what justice itself is, and can give a *logos* conformable to his knowledge, and who moreover has a like understanding of all the other things there are. Will such a man be adequately possessed of knowledge, if he can give the *logos* of the divine circle and divine sphere themselves, but knows nothing of these human spheres and circles of ours? (62a)

Evidently not. But the important point for us is that the kind of knowledge here attributed to the dialectician is knowledge of what so-and-so *is*, expressed in the appropriate *logos* of the thing. While there is here no reference to division, the assimilation of dialectic to definition is clear, and the inference that the way to get the desired definitions is the method recommended earlier in the dialogue is an obvious one. *That* is how the gods told us to conduct our investigations and to learn and to teach one another; understanding of the essential nature of each form is the objective and outcome.

This cursory survey is, I hope, sufficient to establish the following points. (a) In all these dialogues Plato regards division as the method of dialectic, which is itself directed to clarifying the nature

of forms of all kinds. The differences between different accounts
and examples of division are of great interest and importance, but
not for present purposes, since we are concerned with a broad
contrast between two general views of dialectic. In all the dialogues
considered, dialectic is explicitly associated with some kind of division procedure; in none is it identified with the type of argument
about topic-neutral concepts that Ryle exclusively commends. (b)
The references to division in these dialogues cannot be dismissed as
obiter dicta representing temporary silliness, or as the result of a
senile patching together of passages originally distinct. For they are
not just passing allusions: they are closely integrated into the whole
flow and argument of each dialogue. (c) Instead of arguing that the
writer of these dialogues was a good philosopher, and could not
therefore seriously have proposed to do philosophy by the method
of division, we must ask: since the writer of these dialogues was a
good philosopher, and did seriously recommend division, is there
perhaps some way of understanding his recommendation which
will make it seem perfectly reasonable? We may need to allow that
he waxed over-enthusiastic about a certain approach he thought
important, and that he exaggerated its utility or role in philosophy
(including his own philosophy); but the mass of evidence requires
that we should try to find some element of serious philosophical
worth in the method Ryle so firmly rejects.

III

Some of Ryle's reasons for rejecting the method of division as
useless for the resolution of any serious philosophical problem are
contained in the following passages.

First of all it can only be applied to concepts of the genus–species or
determinable–determinate sort, and it is not concepts of this sort that in
general, if ever, engender philosophical problems. And, next, most generic
concepts do not subdivide into just two polarly opposed species; usually
there are numerous species of a genus or subspecies of a species. And the
question whether a sort divides into two or seventeen sub-sorts is, in
general, a purely empirical question. So nearly any case of a philosopher's
operation by division could be upset by the subsequent empirical discovery
of sorts lying on neither side of the philosopher's boundary lines. And, finally, there is room for almost any amount of arbitrariness in the

selection from the ladders of sorts *en route* for the definition of a given concept. . . . There are many tolerable and no perfect ways of defining most of the sort-concepts that we employ.[5]

A chain of *summa genera, genera, species, sub-species* and *varieties* is not itself a chain of premises and conclusions. But what is more, it cannot in general be deductively established or established by *reductio ad absurdum*. The work of a Linnaeus cannot be done *a priori*. How could Plato who knew exactly what question–answer arguments were really like bring himself to say, if he did say, that the philosophically valuable results of such arguments are kind-ladders? (*PP* 136)

In this section I propose to consider these points in turn, and first the objection that most generic concepts do not subdivide dichotomously. Ryle half-withdraws this complaint in *Plato's Progress*, but he still says that Plato 'is tempted to treat this articulation as being necessarily dichotomous, though he prudently resists this temptation some of the time' (p. 135). There is, in fact, abundant evidence that Platonic division into kinds is not, and is not thought of as being, necessarily dichotomous. In the *Philebus* passage already quoted, Plato recommends looking for a division into two, 'if the case admits of there being two, otherwise for three or some other number' (16d). None of the subsequent examples is dichotomous; nor does the later discussion of types of pleasure and knowledge seek dichotomous kind-ladders. The *Phaedrus* account stresses the crucial importance of following the *natural* articulation of the item under examination (265e); and though the illustrative description of the division of madness refers to left-hand and right-hand lines of division, the actual practice followed was not dichotomous (e.g. 238a–c, 244–5). Later on (270c) Socrates says that the way to think about the nature of anything is to ask whether it is simple or multiform, and if it is multiform, to enumerate the forms. The principle is then applied to types of speech and types of soul, in which discussion there is no suggestion of dichotomous division. The Stranger's recommendation of division in the *Politicus* makes no reference to dichotomy, and it is immediately followed by an enquiry into kinds of productive skill which is explicitly non-dichotomous. 'It is difficult to cut them into two. . . . So since we cannot bisect, let us divide them as we should carve a sacrificial victim into limbs. For we ought always to cut into the number as

[5] Ryle, 'Plato's *Parmenides II*', 322, repr. in Allen (ed.), *Studies*, 141–2.

near as possible to two' (287c). The metaphor of the natural carving of a joint is that of the *Phaedrus*; the principle of minimizing the cuts is that of the *Philebus*.

It is not difficult to understand why Plato should advise the enquirer to try for two or very few cuts at each stage: a slapdash division into a lot of species will very probably cause important similarities and groupings to escape notice. The advice is, however, subordinate to the basic requirement that divisions must correspond to the natural or real structure of the subject-matter. That Plato's practice is not in general dichotomous has been sufficiently indicated above. That it is dichotomous in large parts of the *Sophist* and *Politicus* is not surprising. For he is not here seeking to bring to light the structure of a whole genus, but to achieve a definition of a particular species. For this purpose the important thing is at each stage to hit on the *relevant* subgenus of the superior genus; the irrelevant subgenus can be thrown away—and it doesn't *matter* if there are some other (irrelevant) subgenera we have not mentioned.

Ryle complains that the method of division is not a method of demonstration or argument, and that since it is an empirical question into how many sub-sorts a sort divides, division cannot be done a priori. To take these points as showing that Plato's advocacy and practice of division have nothing to do with real philosophy is to take a narrow view of both philosophy and division. A reasonably sympathetic interpretation of the latter will see in it a method aimed either at defining a specific term or at clarifying and analysing a general concept. Of course, the steps by which a definition is reached or tested are not deductive—as Aristotle was often to insist; and of course, the recognition that (say) 'enjoyment' covers many diverse types and the bringing to light of the diversity are not exercises in pure a priori thought. Yet both these projects seem capable of being distinctly and importantly philosophical. Certainly Aristotle gave much fruitful attention to both, and his efforts in these directions are as much admired as his efforts to clear up problems involving topic-neutral concepts.

That one of the aims of Platonic division was to get a clear and correct definition of particular terms hardly needs proof. Introducing his divisions in the *Sophist*, the visitor remarks that the use of the same name does not prove that people have the same 'thing' in mind, so it is always desirable to make clear by a definition the meaning of the term (218b–c). The same point is made in the *Phaedrus*:

> If anyone means to deliberate successfully about anything, there is one thing he must do at the outset: he must know what he is deliberating about; otherwise he is bound to go utterly astray. Now most people fail to realize that they don't know what this or that really is: consequently when they start discussing something, they dispense with any agreed definition, assuming that they know the thing; then later on they naturally find, to their cost, that they agree neither with each other nor with themselves. . . . So we ought to agree upon a definition of love which shows its nature and its effects, so that we may have it before our minds as something to refer to while we discuss whether love is beneficial or injurious. (237b–d)

Interest in the 'What is it?' question and the search for definition are of course as characteristic of earlier Socratic dialogues as of these later dialogues; and indeed, most of the vocabulary used in later expositions of methodology is already found casually employed in earlier dialogues. It is not of present concern to ask how far the later expositions reflect or modify earlier practice, or even how useful they are as guides to reaching good definitions. What is clear (and relevant) is that Plato sees the definition of terms as one of the aims of division, and that from Socrates to Aristotle such definition—elucidating the meaning of interesting terms—is regarded as an important task of philosophy. No doubt not all terms are of interest to the philosopher, and no doubt there are important types of definition or elucidation which Platonic division does not cater for. But it would seem altogether too restrictive to exclude from philosophy the attempts so many philosophers have made to clarify particular concepts—even though such attempts are not exercises in deductive reasoning, and cannot be conducted a priori.

Often, though, Platonic division is concerned not to elucidate a particular term, but to illuminate a whole area, to lay bare the structure of some 'genus'. A hostile characterization of the method can make it seem very silly: what philosopher spends his time constructing kind-ladders? Consideration of the diverse examples of the method permits a more generous construal. Distinguishing different kinds or types of so-and-so need not be (if the so-and-so is well chosen) a philosophically barren activity; and distinguishing the different senses of a word (though not of course any word) can surely be a significant philosophical achievement. Certainly Aristotle (not to mention Ryle) devotes much effort to these tasks. It may be admitted that neither Plato nor Aristotle is absolutely clear about the difference between distinguishing types of X and distinguishing senses of 'X' (nor indeed is the difference always easy to maintain). But either activity can be philosophically rewarding; and it is difficult to deny that Platonic division concerns itself with such activities.

Some of the passages already referred to show that Plato regards himself as applying division in such non-futile exercises as distinguishing purely quantitative measurement from measurement against a norm or standard, mapping the complexities of the concept of enjoyment, recognizing the diversity of types of *technē* (a word that covers crafts, arts, and sciences), and investigating the forms that irrationality or 'madness' can take. No doubt these actual exercises—and many others that could be added—fall short of the complete and systematic analysis of a general concept which the *Philebus* account recommends us to seek. But they are essays in that direction, fragmentary contributions towards the full understanding the philosopher seeks. Though argument is often involved in establishing conceptual distinctions, these are not themselves conclusions of deductive reasoning; they demand insight, and produce clarification—visual metaphors that abound in Plato's accounts of, and efforts in, division. That they cannot be conducted a priori does not mean that they are a matter for empirical research as opposed to philosophical reflection. Ryle's sweeping dismissal of Plato's hopes for division and his tries at it amounts to a denial that conceptual analysis is a proper part of the philosopher's task.

How important was Platonic division in advancing the study of ambiguity? Only two small points can here be made. First, the terms 'division' and 'divide' repeatedly turn up in reports of the work of the Sophist Prodicus, who was noted for his interest in drawing verbal distinctions. Socrates very often refers to him, and several times professes himself his pupil (e.g. *Meno* 96d, *Protagoras*, 341a, *Charmides* 163d). Some of his distinctions find important echoes in Plato and Aristotle—for example, that between 'wish' and 'desire' (*Protagoras* 340a) and that between different types of enjoyment (*Protagoras* 337c). At *Phaedrus* 267b Socrates attributes to him the recognition that what is required in speeches is not that they be long or short, but that they be of the right length—the distinction generalized by Plato in the *Politicus*. If Zeno is the father of the method of reasoning found in the *Parmenides*, Prodicus with his concern for the precise meanings of words and the drawing of distinctions is surely an important precursor of Platonic division. Secondly, a word about Aristotle. He reaches new sophistication in the study of ambiguity, and is rightly praised for noticing and exploiting the fact that different uses of a word may be overlapping or interrelated in various ways, and that one use or sense may be primary and others secondary or parasitic. Many of Plato's divisions exhibit such features, and it would be surprising if they were not part of the material and impetus for Aristotle's enquiries. Among the divisions I have in mind are those in which one side is defined by reference to what is genuine or real or original or pure or perfect, while the other side is defined by reference to the bogus, the apparent, the imitative, the impure, the defective (e.g. *Sophist* 236, 265–6; *Politicus* 293; *Philebus* 55–7).

Ryle complains that the method of division can only be applied to concepts of the genus–species or determinable–determinate sort, and that such concepts do not normally engender philosophical problems. Dialectic proper, on the other hand, as practised in the central part of the *Sophist* and in the *Parmenides*, is concerned to resolve *aporiai* ('puzzles') by investigating the topic-neutral concepts which are 'the hinges on which turn both confutations and philosophical discoveries' (*PP* 144).

The complaint that Platonic division cannot get to work on philosophically interesting concepts could be made even by one who resisted Ryle's too narrow view of dialectic or philosophy as the attempt to solve *aporiai* through logical enquiries about topic-neutral concepts. But the complaint depends upon a strikingly unsympathetic construal of Plato's theory and practice of division. Consider, for example, Ryle's remarks on page 140 of *Plato's Progress*. He has over several pages been making scathing comments on the philosophical inutility of constructing kind-ladders after the manner of Linnaeus. He contrasts it unfavourably with the Stranger's exploration in the middle of the *Sophist* of the mutual dependences and independences of the Greatest Kinds (like Existence, Identity, Otherness), an exploration that does not yield one kind-ladder, however short. 'For the Greatest Kinds are not related to one another as genus to species or as species to co-species.' Ryle continues: 'Even to render "γένη" by "kinds," and *a fortiori* by

"classes," is to prejudice the interpretation of the Stranger's operations. *Existence, identity* and *otherness* are not sorts or sets of things,
embracing subsorts or subsets of things.' I do not want to claim that
this bit of the *Sophist* is an exercise in division (and it is not
immediately germane to enquire how Plato thought it was related
to division, as the evidence quoted above shows that he did); I am
only claiming *an* important place for division in Plato's thought and
practice (and in philosophy). The point I draw attention to is that
Ryle rejects as prejudicial the translation of γένη as 'kinds' in the
passage he admires, because the items under investigation are evidently not sorts or sets of things. Yet his talk about the passages he
does not admire gains much of its effect by its use of a hard-edged
terminology which attaches to Platonic division all the scholastic
precision and philosophical futility of a traditional genus–species
tree. Might one not adopt a more sympathetic approach? It is not
only in the arguments about existence, etc., that the terms γένη and
εἴδη do not carry the fixed associations of 'genus' and 'species'. They
are regularly used, before and after Plato, in a much freer way; and
Plato himself, conspicuously untied by technical terms, constantly
uses them interchangeably. That Platonic division has something to
do with dividing will not be denied. But what sort of dividing Plato
takes it to cover, and what sorts of terms are capable of being
divided, can be determined only by consideration of all the texts.
The outcome of such consideration is not, I suggest, that Platonic
division is to be rejected as a very narrowly defined procedure of no
philosophical interest. The appropriate criticism is quite the reverse. Platonic division covers a variety of types of analysis, and gets
applied to a variety of types of term. No less than the word 'analysis'
itself, which has been a modern slogan in philosophy, 'division' is
dangerously imprecise but philosophically suggestive. Commenda-
tion of it is not a brief stupidity or senility on Plato's part, for it
represents a continuing strand in his philosophical activity—and
also in Aristotle's. Aristotle does indeed have, as Plato does not, a
rather closely worked-out account of strict genus–species kind-
ladders. But he continually speaks of divisions and of kinds and
sorts ('genera' and 'species') in contexts where nobody supposes
that he is, or thinks he is, doing the work of a Linnaeus. When he
speaks of his categories as 'divisions' of being, or distinguishes
movement, alteration, and growth as different 'sorts' of change,
nobody complains that he is performing absurd Linnaean opera-

tions upon the concepts of being and change. May not Plato's efforts be accorded a like charity?

IV

It is compatible with this defence of Platonic division to allow that his formal accounts of it are variously defective or even misleading, and to admit a contrast between the systematic and comprehensive procedure set up as an ideal and the fragments of useful analysis actually achieved. Let us grant too that something quite different is afoot in the examination of some topic-neutral concepts in the middle part of the *Sophist*. There is, however, the question how division is related (in fact or in Plato's mind) to the *Sophist* investigation. For Ryle there is an absolute contrast: division is futile, the *Sophist* investigation is philosophy. No question arises as to how they are related, even though Plato himself clearly implies that they are. I think that the relation can be made out if, having adopted a more generous interpretation of division than Ryle's, we now give a rather wider scope to the enquiries made or advertised in the central part of the *Sophist*.

Plato does not say that the concepts to be investigated here are 'the Greatest Kinds', only that they are *some* of the greatest kinds. He does not explain the term 'greatest', but it will not be too risky to think with Ryle of formal or 'common' concepts, bearing in mind such passages as *Theaetetus* 185–6 and *Parmenides* 136. This does not yet show that Plato in the *Sophist* takes dialectic or philosophy to consist in the exploration of 'the mutual dependences and independences of the Greatest Kinds' (*PP* 142). Plato justifies selecting a few of the greatest kinds for investigation by saying: 'we will not take all the forms, for fear of getting confused in such a multitude' (254c). Of course, he has a positive reason for dwelling on the forms he does proceed to discuss. But the clear implication of his remark is that the full-scale study of the interrelations of forms would require study of all forms. This is indeed quite explicit in the account of dialectic at 253b–e, partly quoted above (p. 95). For the task of discovering 'pervasive' forms which serve to 'connect' or 'divide' other forms is set alongside, and not contrasted with, the task of systematically determining the mutual concordances and discordances of forms in general. To put the point in a nutshell (and in non-Platonic idiom), the dialectician or philosopher is invited not only to examine such concepts as compatibility and entailment, but also to determine *what* compatibility and entailment relations hold among concepts in general. Ryle says that 'dialectic, here equated with philosophy, is described at 253c–d as the science which discovers how the "Greatest Kinds" are "joined" with and "disjoined" from one another' (*PP* 140). Rather, it is described as the science which discovers how forms in general are related to one another *and* notices and studies the relational forms themselves. The dialectician will get clear the whole structure of the conceptual scheme he investigates, *and* be clear about the formal or structural concepts themselves.

Dialectic as the study of the interrelations of forms (not just 'Greatest Kinds'), still looks a good deal richer than division into kinds. But the gap is no longer unbridgeable, and Plato's association of dividing by kinds with knowing how kinds can and cannot combine (*Sophist* 253d–e) is not unintelligible. Division certainly exhibits *some* important interrelationships of concepts and reveals *some* possibilities and impossibilities of combining. The discovery of *other* interrelationships, and the study of the relational concepts themselves, may easily be seen as natural extensions to the task of division. Plato need not feel, as clearly he does not feel, that in recognizing additional requirements for an adequate understanding of 'the world of forms' he is setting division aside as irrelevant.

V

I do not wish to claim too much for this brief attempt to rehabilitate Platonic division in face of Ryle's censures. It seems to me certain that Plato took division seriously, and that we should therefore give serious and sympathetic attention to it, seeking to extract from his theorizing and practice something of philosophical significance. To say this is not to deny the outstanding excitement and importance of his investigations into topic-neutral concepts. And to oppose Ryle's verdict on division is not to deny the outstanding excitement and importance of his work on Plato in general, which has been a guide or a goad to so many of us over several decades.

7

Aristotle's Theory of Definition: Some Questions on *Posterior Analytics* II. 8–10

In working on Aristotle's theory of definition in *An. post.* II I have been impressed by the difficulty and complexity of the problems, both philosophical and philological. I have been equally impressed by the excellence of the commentators, ancient and modern, who have examined the problems with tremendous thoroughness and brilliance. In what follows I do not claim to ask any novel questions or to offer any novel answers. I simply try to open up a few of the philosophically interesting issues with a view to provoking further discussion of them.[1]

I

Some of the most difficult passages in *An. post.* II. 8–10 involve the notion of investigation or enquiry (ζήτησις), and raise questions as to how definitions are supposed to be *discovered*. But it is clear from the sentences that begin and end the section that Aristotle's primary and essential aim is to explain the nature and structure of definitions and the relation of definition to demonstration; and I should like first, therefore, to make some remarks about a question in this area.

Whatever else Aristotle may be saying, he is certainly claiming in these chapters that the definitions of some items may be expressed or made clear in appropriate demonstrative syllogisms, even though they are not demonstrated in or by them. The items in

---

[1] I am grateful for valuable comments and criticisms made by colleagues at the Symposium Aristotelicum. The present revision of the paper given there does not incorporate any substantial changes to the original version, but I have made a few minor alterations for the sake of clarity.

First published in 1981.

question are those which have a cause or explanation (αἴτιον)[2] different from themselves, and whose nature therefore can be fully revealed only when the cause is indicated. The closer characterization of this class may be left on one side: enough problems arise if we concentrate on the two examples Aristotle dwells on, eclipse and thunder. And the problem I wish to raise briefly is this: *what* syllogism exactly does Aristotle have in mind as the syllogism that corresponds to the definition of either of these? He provides many fragments of syllogisms, but is not concerned to write them out fully and carefully.

The two obvious alternatives may be roughly formulated as follows:[3]

I	II
Thunder is quenching of fire in clouds.	A noise is quenching of fire.
Quenching of fire in clouds is a noise in clouds.	Quenching of fire is (occurs) in clouds.
Thunder is a noise in clouds.	A noise is (occurs) in clouds.

There are conspicuous differences between these syllogisms. The first mentions thunder (uses the word 'thunder'), and its conclusion looks exactly like what Aristotle has in mind at II. 10, 94a7–9: 'Further, a definition of thunder is noise in clouds; and this is the conclusion of the demonstration of what it is' (ἔτι ἐστὶν ὅρος βροντῆς ψόφος ἐν νέφεσι· τοῦτο δ' ἐστὶ τῆς τοῦ τί ἐστιν ἀποδείξεως συμπέρασμα). To know the conclusion of syllogism I is to know part (only part) of the full definition (a noise in clouds due to quenching of fire). So this syllogism seems just what Aristotle needs. It does not demonstrate the full definition, but it shows what it must be: the partial

---

[2] Aristotle's 'doctrine of the four causes' might better be called his doctrine of the four 'becauses'. Neither 'cause' nor 'explanation' is an exact equivalent of αἰτία, but neither will be misleading to those who know the background.

[3] Less rough formulations would be:

I (Barbara)
Noise in clouds applies to every quenching of fire in clouds.
Quenching of fire in clouds applies to every thunder.

Noise in clouds applies to every thunder.

II (Darii)
Noise applies to every quenching of fire.
Quenching of fire applies to some clouds.

Noise applies to some clouds.

definition given in the conclusion must be supplemented by the addition of the middle term. On the other hand, syllogism I does not appear to prove the *existence* of anything, nor to show *why* that thing exists. So it does not seem to be a satisfactory example of the kind of demonstration Aristotle desiderates for non-primitive items in I. 10, 76a31–6 and 76b11–22 (cp. II. 7, 92b15–16 and II. 9).

The second syllogism (suggested by such passages as II. 8, 93b10–12; II. 12, 95a17–19; I. 13, 78a39–b3 and 78b10–11) meets these last requirements easily. It proves that something exists by appealing to its cause—it is a συλλογισμὸς τοῦ διότι (a syllogism of the because). To know only its conclusion is to know that there is a noise in clouds, but not why. On the other hand, there is no mention in syllogism II of *thunder*, nor does its conclusion look like any sort of definition. Thus, while it may be a satisfactory example of one kind of demonstrative syllogism, it does not seem to fill Aristotle's bill as a syllogism in which a definition is revealed, and whose conclusion is itself a (partial) definition.

It is possible to defend each syllogism from the criticism levelled at it. As regards syllogism I it may be held that the conclusion does in fact have existential force, and that to suppose otherwise is to treat it as merely giving 'what the word signifies'—and *that*, as we know, is something presupposed and not proved in demonstration (I. 1, 71a15; I. 2, 71b32; I. 10, 76a32, b37). If there were no such thing as thunder, there would be nothing that thunder was, though the word 'thunder' could still signify something. The conclusion of syllogism I may, in short, be thought of as a sort of combination of the verbal definition ' "Thunder" signifies noise in clouds' and the assertion that there actually is something satisfying that definition. If Aristotle fails to make this distinction absolutely clear, that is no doubt due to his lack of apparatus (inverted commas)—and still more of concern. For he is notoriously willing to talk of 'what *x* signifies or is' even in contexts in which he is quite sharply contrasting names and their significance with things and their nature.

(I omit consideration of two related points. First, a distinction may be drawn between (i) 'thunder' means the same as 'noise in clouds', and (ii) 'thunder' means noise in clouds; to know (i) is not necessarily to know what 'thunder' means. Secondly, a distinction may be drawn between two senses in which a word like 'thunder' may be said to signify something; in one sense, but not in the other, the existence of the something is implied).

As for syllogism II, it may be allowed to count as expressing the definition of thunder—even though it does not use the word 'thunder'—for either of two reasons. First, we may suppose it taken for granted that anyone, or any hearer of the syllogism, already knows the verbal definition of the word 'thunder'. He knows, therefore, that the conclusion of syllogism II asserts that there is thunder; and from the syllogism as a whole he learns why there is thunder—what exactly thunder is. (If I say 'Some men are unmarried', I am claiming that there are bachelors, and you know that I am claiming this if you know what 'bachelor' means.) Secondly, it may be held that anyone who heard syllogism II and understood and believed what he heard would have learned what thunder is, and so know the definition of thunder, even if he had never heard the word 'thunder' (or, let us add, any synonymous word). For he would know of the existence and the nature of a certain phenomenon—noise in clouds due to quenching of fire; and that phenomenon is thunder.[4]

I conclude that although the two syllogisms are very different, they can both serve Aristotle's purpose. The first is explicitly about *what* something is, but it implies that it is, and it provides all the materials for a syllogism of the other type. The second syllogism is explicitly a proof *that* something *is*; but it also makes it clear that this something is a scientifically intelligible item (whether or not the hearer or the language has a word for it), and what its definition is. So against an appropriate background either syllogism can be used in illustration of Aristotle's theory about the relation of definition to demonstration.

II

If Aristotle is concerned in II. 8–10 to show what a definition (of a certain type of things) is like, and how it is related to a corresponding demonstrative syllogism, it may seem surprising that he should have so much to say about searching and finding (93a17, 26, 27, 30,

---

[4] Note the move from 'thunder' to 'noise' at II. 8, 93b9–12.

31, 32, b4, 32; 93a35; 93b15, 33). For the question how one *gets* appropriate propositions or items of knowledge, and in what order, seems irrelevant to his present purpose; and the topic how one should hunt out definitions (πῶς δεῖ θηρεύειν) is to be treated later (II. 13, 96a22–3). However, his references to enquiry (ζήτησις) in II. 8–10 are designed primarily to make very general points about the types of item of knowledge and their interrelations, points which he does need in order to clarify the structure of the syllogism of the 'because' (συλλογισμὸς τοῦ διότι) and that of the definition corresponding to it. He is not here offering advice how to proceed in order to achieve such a definition, but he is bringing out its elements and their interconnection along the lines developed in II. 1–2. Just as a question can be identified by reference to the answer that would satisfy it (89b27), so the components and organization of a structure of knowledge can be discerned if one separates out the various questions answered in it and notes their different types and levels (89b23).

The key points made in II. 1–2 and exploited in II. 8–10 are the following. You can know whether X is, what X is, that p, why p; and there are four corresponding questions (89b24, 36). To ask 'What is X?' presupposes that X is; and to ask 'Why p?' presupposes that p (89b29–32, 34–5). In each of the four questions what is at issue is a cause or explanation, a 'middle term' (μέσον) (89b37–90a1). To ask whether S is P is to ask whether there is a term M such that S is P because it is M; to go on to ask *why* S is P is to ask what that term M is. Similarly—though this will require further elucidation—with the questions whether X is, and (if so) what X is. So there is a strict parallelism, if not identity, between asking or knowing what X is and asking or knowing why S is P: 'to know what it is is the same as knowing why it is' (τὸ τί ἐστιν εἰδέναι ταὐτό ἐστι καὶ διὰ τί ἔστιν; 90a31; cp. 93a4).

I should like to discuss in a very general way three of the questions that suggest themselves here. (1) Why must knowing *that* precede enquiry into *why*—and how can it, since knowing p if p is demonstrable involves knowing the demonstration? (2) Why must knowledge that there is X precede enquiry into what X is—and how can it, since one has to know what one is looking for in order to look for it? (3) How is the initial knowledge that p (or that there is X) obtainable, and how is the advance to knowledge why p (or what X is) achieved?

(1) Passages which make knowledge *that* precede enquiry into *why* include: 'when we know the *that* we seek the *because*' (ὅταν δὲ εἰδῶμεν τὸ ὅτι, τὸ διότι ζητοῦμεν; II. 1, 89b29); 'we seek the *because* when we grasp the *that*' (τὸ διότι ζητοῦμεν ἔχοντες τὸ ὅτι; II. 8, 93a17); 'grasping that it is, we enquire why it is' (ὅπερ ἔχοντες ὅτι ἔστι, ζητοῦμεν διὰ τί ἔστιν; II, 10, 93b32).

On the other hand, it is the settled doctrine of I. 1–3 that, in the case of what is demonstrable, to know it is to be in possession of the demonstration (τὸ ἐπίστασθαι ὧν ἀπόδειξίς ἔστι . . . τὸ ἔχειν ἀπόδειξίν ἐστιν; 71b28; cp. 71b9–12); and this is repeated at II. 3, 90b9–10 (. . . τὸ ἐπίστασθαί ἐστι τὸ ἀπόδειξιν ἔχειν; cp. 90b21–2), and in a different form at II. 11, 94a20 (. . . ἐπίστασθαι οἰόμεθα ὅταν εἰδῶμεν τὴν αἰτίαν).

Since the truths for which there is a cause (i.e. a *because*, a *why*) are presumably those capable of being demonstrated, there seems to be a sheer contradiction between the statement that knowing a truth precedes discovery of its cause and the statement that a demonstrable truth is known only when its demonstration is known. One obvious solution would no doubt be to distinguish two types of knowledge or two senses in which one and the same proposition may be known: the knowledge presupposed by enquiry into the cause is only knowledge in a weak sense; the knowledge achieved by discovery of the cause is knowledge in a strong sense ('scientific knowledge'). An alternative suggestion would be to deny that the proposition known by one ignorant of the cause is in fact the very same as the proposition known by one aware of it. Are signs of these solutions to be found in Aristotle?

The most general points underlying the first group of passages quoted above are these: *p*-because-*q* entails *p*, but not vice versa; and knowing that *p*-because-*q* entails knowing that *p*, but not vice versa. But more closely relevant to the situation of an enquirer is this: that to raise the question '*p* because of what?' (or 'Why *p*?') is to take for granted that *p*. Moreover, it is clear that if an enquiry '*p* because of what?' is to have a chance of success, it must be the case that *p*—otherwise there can be no answer to the question. Thus if an enquiry of the form '*p* because of what?' is to be made, and made with a chance of success, it is a prerequisite that the enquirer should suppose that *p*, and that he should be correct in supposing that *p*. Now this combination of requirements is not inaptly expressed by the verbs among which Aristotle moves in the relevant passages: εἰδέναι, γνῶναι, λαβεῖν, ἔχειν. The last two stress the taking for granted or supposition, the first two the truth or correctness. And I am inclined to think that this choice of verbs reflects a recognition on Aristotle's part that the prerequisite for a successful enquiry 'Why *p*?' is not strictly knowledge that *p*, but rather a belief that is true—or, not full-strength knowledge, but only knowledge in a diluted sense.

The term ἐπίστασθαι is not used in II. 1–2 after the introductory sentence; nor does it occur in II. 8–10. It occurs in II. 3 and II. 11 (the passages quoted above), where apodeictic knowledge[5] is in question; and it is, of course, the word used for apodeictic knowledge in I. 1–2, alternative verbs such as εἰδέναι, γιγνώσκειν, γνωρίζειν being applied to the grasp or understanding which is not apodeictic knowledge. Nobody will claim that Aristotle in general makes a firm distinction between εἰδέναι and ἐπίστασθαι. Nevertheless, the two terms do have different resonances, ἐπίστασθαι being more suggestive of systematic knowledge, εἰδέναι hinting at immediate experience. I think, therefore, that Aristotle's choice of terminology in the two apparently contradictory sets of passages which we are considering suggests that he would accept the following solution: one must truly believe (or 'weakly know') that *p* if one is to make and bring to a successful conclusion the enquiry '*p* because of what?'; one must be in possession of the answer to this enquiry if one is to count as knowing (or 'strongly knowing' or 'having scientific knowledge') that *p*.

But is it clear—and does Aristotle think it clear?—that the proposition originally believed and the proposition finally known are really one and the same proposition? Aristotle discusses a related question in I. 33. Part, at least, of his thought seems to be that if I say that I believe something, I am simply claiming that it is true; whereas if I say that I know something, I am claiming that it is necessarily true. (On the necessity of what is scientifically known cp. I. 4, 73a21–4; I. 6, 75a12–17.) Would he then suggest that our scientific enquirer who starts with the belief that *p* ends with a

---

[5] I am not convinced by Myles Burnyeat's contention that 'understanding' is a better translation of ἐπιστήμη in *An. post.* than 'scientific knowledge' (or 'apodeictic knowledge' or 'demonstrative knowledge'), though he is of course right to insist that Aristotle is not propounding any kind of scepticism about 'ordinary knowledge': M. F. Burnyeat, 'Aristotle on Understanding Knowledge', in E. Berti (ed.), *Aristotle on Science: The* Posterior Analytics (Padua: Editrice Antenore, 1981), 97–139.

higher grade of apprehension (ἐπιστήμη), not of *p* but of the different proposition, necessarily-*p*?

Uncertainty on this point persists in Aristotle's talk about knowledge *that* (ὅτι) and knowledge *why* (διότι). For sometimes he seems concerned to insist that ἐπιστήμη ('demonstrative knowledge', or 'd-knowledge' for short) ὅτι *p* requires knowledge of the διότι. If we use '*q*' to stand for the premisses of a demonstrative syllogism, Aristotle is requiring that a man should know both that *q* and that *q* entails *p* if it is to be true that he has d-knowledge of *p*. So *what* he d-knows is *p*, but he counts as d-knowing it if and only if his knowledge of it is based on the knowledge that *q* and that *q* entails *p*. At other times, however, Aristotle contrasts knowing that *p* with knowing that *p*-because-*q*, and insists that only the latter qualifies as demonstrative knowledge. The proposition which the man with demonstrative knowledge d-knows may now seem to be *p*-because-*q* (while the non-scientist's 'knowledge' is of *p*).

It is easy to see why Aristotle should be willing to adopt either of these ways of speaking, according to one of which the scientist's advance is from a weak grasp of *p* to a strong grasp of *p* (based on recognition of *why p*), and according to the other of which it is from a grasp of *p* to a grasp of *p*-because-*q*. It is, however, dangerously misleading to speak as though *p*-because-*q* is the object of ἐπιστήμη in the technical sense of 'demonstrative knowledge'. For neither *q* nor *p* → *p* are themselves demonstrable propositions (on pain of a regress). The learner learns that *p*-because-*q*, but he does not acquire a proof of *p*-because-*q*, but of *p*. Just as in discussion of definition Aristotle will distinguish sharply between the partial definition that is demonstrated and the complete definition that is shown, revealed, or expressed in the demonstrative syllogism, but is not itself demonstrated, so in discussing demonstration itself, he should keep clear the distinction between the conclusion that is demonstrated and the whole explanatory structure, which is not itself demonstrated, but expressed and conveyed in the demonstrative syllogism.

(2) Passages which imply that knowledge that *X* is precedes knowledge of what *X* is include II. 1, 89b34 ('knowing that it is, we enquire what it is' (γνόντες δὲ ὅτι ἔστι, τί ἐστι ζητοῦμεν)); II. 2, 89b38–90a1; II. 2, 90a22–3; and II. 7, 92b4–8 (ἀνάγκη γὰρ τὸν εἰδότα τὸ τί ἐστιν ἄνθρωπος ἢ ἄλλο ὁτιοῦν, εἰδέναι καὶ ὅτι ἔστιν. τὸ γὰρ μὴ ὂν οὐδεὶς

οἶδεν ὅ τι ἐστίν, ἀλλὰ τί μὲν σημαίνει ὁ λόγος ἢ τὸ ὄνομα, ὅταν εἴπω τραγέλαφος, τί δ᾽ ἐστὶ τραγέλαφος ἀδύνατον εἰδέναι (For one who knows *what* man—or anything else—is, necessarily knows *that* it is [exists]. For no one knows what that which is non-existent is. What the expression or name means, when I say 'goat-stag', you may know; but what a goat-stag is, it is impossible to know)). On the other hand, one must surely know what *X* is if one is to be certain that there are any *X*'s; and Aristotle himself says that the *what it is* (τί ἐστιν) is settled first, and the *being* (εἶναι) is then (in the case of non-primitive items) demonstrated: I. 2, 72a23 ('For what a unit is and that a unit is are not the same' (τὸ γὰρ τί ἐστι μονὰς καὶ τὸ εἶναι μονάδα οὐ ταὐτόν)); I. 10, 76a34–6 ('e.g. we must assume what a unit or what straight and triangle are, and that the unit and magnitude are, but we must prove that the others are' (οἷον τί μονὰς ἢ τί τὸ εὐθὺ καὶ τρίγωνον, εἶναι δὲ τὴν μονάδα λαβεῖν καὶ μέγεθος, τὰ δ᾽ ἕτερα δεικνύναι)); II. 3, 90b30–3; II. 9, 93b24–5.

As with the previous question, a distinction between two types or grades of knowledge of what *X* is would remove the appearance of contradiction. Perhaps, however, it is more illuminating to consider what may be meant by 'what *X* is'. We need one idea of 'what *X* is' that makes knowledge of it a pre-condition for the acquisition of scientific knowledge. One obvious suggestion is that the requisite initial knowledge is really knowledge of what the word '*X*' signifies; and key passages in I. 1, 2, and 10 do indeed show Aristotle moving freely between 'what . . . signifies' (τί σημαίνει) and 'what . . . is' (τί ἐστι), though in some places he sharply contrasts them. So it is plausible to attribute to him the view that it is knowledge of what '*X*' signifies that precedes knowledge that *X* is, and knowledge of what *X* is that follows it.

This suggestion may be met by the complaint that knowledge of a purely verbal kind is no sufficient basis for a scientific enquiry into a real nature or essence; and this complaint may itself be met by the claim that when Aristotle refers to knowing what a word 'signifies', he is not referring to purely verbal knowledge, but to knowledge of actual items to which the word applies. Both the complaint and the counter-claim would seem, however, to overlook the crucial distinction between the condition of the learner being taught a science and that of the investigator trying to discover one. As far as the book I passages are concerned, where teaching and learning are under discussion, the suggestion that only the verbal definition of non-primitive terms has to be given to the learner and known by him prior to the demonstration of existence does not seem absurd. (There is no question of such a definition being a sufficient basis for an *enquiry*). Such a definition must of course be in terms the hearer understands and in terms that can occur in the demonstration. If it is to be possible to demonstrate that there are *X*s, an *X* must be some such complex item as *Y* in *Z* (say, noise in clouds), where there is a *μέσον* (a middle term) *M* such that *Y–M* and *M–Z* are 'immediate' premisses. (This is of course to simplify.) So the learner is told that '*X*' signifies *Y* in *Z*; and he must also already know that there are *Y*s and *Z*s, since if *Y* and *Z* are primitive terms in the science, it is necessary to 'lay down' and 'know before' both what they signify *and* that they are. But it is the subsequent demonstration that shows, and shows him, that there actually are *Y*s in *Z*s, and why.[6]

If we turn from questions about the structure and transmission of an existing science to questions about the discovery and development of a science (from *δίδαξις* and *μάθησις* to *ζήτησις*), things are different. Suppositions of actual existence must be made with regard to items later to be proved to exist. If an investigator is to come to the knowledge expressed by the demonstration *Y–M–Z*[7] (the demonstrative knowledge *that* there is *X* and the knowledge that what *X* is, is *Y* in *Z* because of *M*), he must to start with suppose, and correctly, that such a thing as *Y* in *Z* occurs. The position is inevitably exactly parallel to that described earlier in discussion of question (1). One must truly believe that *Y* is in *Z* if one is to bring to a successful conclusion the enquiry 'Why is *Y* in *Z*?'; and one must have come to a grasp of '*Y* is in *Z* because of *M*' if one is to count as having demonstrative knowledge that *Y* is in *Z*. If we transform these propositions into definitions, we have '*Y* in *Z*' as the investigator's initial account of what *X* is, and '*Y* in *Z* because of *M*' as his final account.

I have said that if the correct complete definition of *X* is '*Y* in *Z* because of *M*', the successful investigator must have started off

<hr>

[6] This helps to explain why a verbal definition is mentioned at 93b30–2, but not referred to in the summary at 94a11–14. What is first provided to the learner as a merely verbal definition will normally reappear as the conclusion of the demonstrative syllogism.

[7] e.g. since *Y* belongs to every *M*, and *M* belongs to some *Z*, *Y* belongs to some *Z*.

supposing (correctly) that such a thing as *Y* in *Z* occurs, and that his initial account of what *X* is would have been '*Y* in *Z*'. Is this what Aristotle has in mind when he speaks of the people who are aware that *X* is 'when they grasp something of the object itself' (ἔχοντές τι αὐτοῦ τοῦ πράγματος; II. 8, 93a22)? Is he saying that the successful investigator's initial grasp of what *X* is must be a grasp of *part* of the final definition? This passage and the related passage in II. 10 deserve some scrutiny.

In II. 8, 93a21–2 Aristotle distinguishes two possibilities: 'but as to whether a thing is, sometimes we grasp this incidentally, sometimes when grasping something of the object itself' (τὸ δ' εἰ ἔστιν ὁτὲ μὲν κατὰ συμβεβηκὸς ἔχομεν, ὁτὲ δ' ἔχοντές τι αὐτοῦ τοῦ πράγματος). He then gives some examples: 'e.g. of thunder, that it is a sort of noise of the clouds; and of eclipse, that it is a sort of privation of light' (οἷον βροντήν, ὅτι ψόφος τις νεφῶν, καὶ ἔκλειψιν, ὅτι στέρησίς τις φωτός). Which of the two possibilities are the examples meant to exemplify?

On one interpretation, they are examples of our knowing only incidentally, *per accidens*, that there is thunder. In such cases, Aristotle is saying, we do not really know *that X* is, and so we are in no position to get *what* it is (93a24–7). In contrast, when we have 'something of the object itself' (93a22, 28), it is easier. By 'something of the object itself' is meant *the cause*—for example, the screening by the earth in the case of an eclipse (93a30–2). Having this, we can really know that there are eclipses, and from this knowledge as expressed in a demonstrative syllogism, it is easy to derive or extract the full correct definition. The idea is that only if a person has the demonstrative knowledge given by such a syllogism as:

(i) noise is (caused by) quenching of fire,
(ii) quenching of fire occurs in clouds,
so, (iii) noise occurs in clouds,

does he *know* that there is thunder, and *this* person can easily formulate the definition of thunder—noise due to quenching of fire in clouds.

When such a conclusion as (iii) is derived not from the true cause (93a36–b3), Aristotle says that we know that *X* is (ὅτι ἔστι *X*), though not what it is; but this must be taken loosely. For the position is similar to that described earlier as knowledge *per accidens*, and hence not really knowledge (93a22–6). To 'know' that there is eclipse through the middle term failure of moon to cast shadows (93a37–8), which is not the real middle term or cause, is just like 'knowing' that there is eclipse when we take an eclipse to be simply a deprivation of light (93a23). Only if 'knowledge' that there is thunder is based on knowledge that thunder is due to the quenching of fire is it real knowledge that there is thunder; and the person with this real knowledge can easily put together the definition of what thunder is. If 'knowledge' that there is thunder is based on the 'knowledge' that thunder is a noise in the clouds, it is not real knowledge that there is thunder, but only *per accidens* 'knowledge'; and a person with it is in no position to produce the full definition of thunder.

There is something to be said for this interpretation, which Zabarella gives,[8] following Averroës, is opposition to other commentators. For it concentrates on what is germane to Aristotle's central purpose, the explanation of the relation between a demonstration and a definition and of the manner in which a definition is expressed in a demonstration, and it does not attribute to him extraneous ideas about how one can get into possession of a demonstration. But, apart from any other objection, Zabarella's account has to give an incredibly forced sense to 'something of the object itself'. It has to understand it as referring to the cause, or the causal part of the what-*X*-is; and as not applicable to the rest, the non-causal part (e.g. *noise in clouds*). It is very hard to see how in a context where a complex definition is in prospect (e.g. noise due to quenching of fire in clouds) Aristotle could say that a person 'knowing' that thunder is noise in clouds had *not* got *something* 'of the object itself'. After all, if the object itself were to be actually *identified* with the cause—so that 'noise in clouds' failed to count as giving even a part of the object—a grasp of the cause could hardly be described as a grasp of only 'something of' the object itself.

The alternative—and usual—interpretation takes the examples in 93a22 ff. to be examples not of *per accidens* 'knowledge' but of the *favourable* case, when we grasp something of the object itself. A person aware that thunder is a noise in the clouds is in a position to advance by investigation to the discovery of its cause, and thus to a full knowledge of what it is, unlike a person whose belief that

---

[8] Jacobi Zabarellae, *Opera logica*, ed. W. Risse (Hildesheim: Olms, 1966), 1120.

thunder occurs is based on a notion of thunder that does not include any part of the nature of thunder. The former knows that there is thunder (though not yet why), but the latter does not, and is therefore in no position to seek out what it is (93a25–6).

Within this general interpretation opinions may differ as to what exactly Aristotle counts as 'something of the object itself', and hence what cases fall under the disparaging heading of incidental or *per accidens* (κατὰ συμβεβηκός) knowledge. The examples themselves suggest that 'having something of the thing itself' is knowing part of the definition: to advance to the complete definition, Y in Z because of M, one must start from the partial definition, Y in Z. Yet this may well seem an unnecessarily stringent requirement. Surely an investigator into X may work successfully towards knowledge of what X is even if he initially identifies Xs by means of a specification or description that will *not* enter into the real definition of X—provided only that his specification or description does pick out Xs.

Let 'Q' stand for an investigator's initial idea of X. The stringent requirement is that only where Q is part of the real definition of X can the investigator hope to achieve knowledge of the real definition of X. But there are surely many other cases where success may reasonably be hoped for: where Q is (a) a property peculiar to X (ἴδιον), or (b) otherwise necessarily connected with X, or (c) not necessarily but in fact universally connected with X, or (d) not universally but nearly always connected with X. In every one of these cases the investigator is in some sort of position to investigate the right items and learn more about them, though much could of course be said about the ways in which the cases differ from one another and about the various steps by which the investigator might move in each case to a final grasp of the correct complete real definition of the thing he is investigating.

According to Zabarella, then, the II. 8 passage has nothing to do with the conditions under which investigation may lead to discovery of the διότι. It is concerned simply to insist that one can formulate a complete definition if and only if one possesses the relevant demonstrative syllogism. According to the usual interpretation, the passage does concern the necessary starting-point for the enquiry διὰ τί. It may be making the strong claim that the starting-point must be a grasp of part of the real definition of X must in fact be knowledge of the conclusion that will be demonstrated eventually in the demonstrative syllogism corresponding to the complete definition. It may, on the other hand, be making some less strong claim, perhaps even the rather weak claim that the starting-point must be a grasp of X via some feature or features of X that are sufficient in practice to distinguish Xs, and hence to enable the investigator to study the right items and advance to a better understanding of what X really is.

We might hope to derive some help from the first paragraph of II. 10, since here again the notion of *per accidens* knowledge is used, with a direct reference back to II. 8 (93b33–5 referring to 93a24–7). The context (93b29–33) suggests that *per accidens* knowledge 'that it is' (ὅτι ἔστιν) has something to do with knowing 'what the name signifies' (τί σημαίνει τὸ ὄνομα). Having just referred to 'an account of what the name signifies . . . , e.g. what triangle signifies', Aristotle goes on: 'Grasping that this is, we enquire why it is; but it is difficult thus to get hold of things when we do not know that they are' (ὅπερ ἔχοντες ὅτι ἔστι, ζητοῦμεν διὰ τί ἔστιν· χαλεπὸν δ᾽ οὕτως ἐστὶ λαβεῖν ἃ μὴ ἴσμεν ὅτι ἔστιν; 93b32–3).

Here are two possible paraphrases[9] of this desperately obscure sentence and the one that follows it:

(i) A man who knows what 'X' signifies and *in addition* knows that there are such things can ask 'Why?' (i.e. 'What is X?'). But it is difficult for a man with *only* knowledge of what the name signifies (οὕτως, 'thus', means 'simply knowing what the name signifies') to come to grasp the nature of things which he does not even know to exist (for one who knows only what the name signifies does not know, save *per accidens*, that Xs exist);

(ii) A man who knows what the name 'X' signifies and that there are such things can ask what X is. But it is difficult for him to grasp X in its real nature, with its cause, (οὕτως, 'thus', means 'with knowledge of why it is', διὰ τί ἔστιν). For he knows only *per accidens*

---

[9] Another suggestion (which I find unconvincing though ingenious) will be found in Richard Sorabji's admirable paper 'Definitions: Why Necessary and in What Way?' in Berti (ed.), *Aristotle on Science*, 205–44.

I do not derive much light from Robert Bolton's discussion of this and other passages in his paper 'Essentialism and Semantic Theory in Aristotle,' *Philosophical Review*, 85 (1976), 514–44. He makes very large claims; but his understanding of individual passages is often seriously defective, and the way in which he puts them together to build up his 'theory' is not at all satisfactory.

that there are Xs, since one who knows of the existence of Xs only via the ordinary meaning of the name 'X' does not yet really know that there are Xs.

In (i) attention is drawn to the man who knows what a name 'X' signifies but has no idea whether there are any Xs. The essential contrast is between knowing what a name signifies and knowing that there are items to which it actually applies. In (ii) the essential contrast is between knowing both what a name signifies and that there are items to which it actually applies and knowing the real nature of those items.

This second interpretation can itself be understood in various ways. On one view—Zabarella's—what the name 'X' signifies is identical (in effect) with the conclusion of the relevant demonstrative syllogism. Thus, what 'thunder' signifies is a *noise in clouds*. A man who knows what 'thunder' signifies and that there is such a thing may be said to know that there is thunder. But since he does not know why the noise occurs in clouds, he does not know what thunder really is—nor, therefore, does he really know that there is thunder. Such a man is in no position to state what X is. It is only one who has demonstrative knowledge that there is thunder who can give the complete definition; and he can easily extract it from the demonstrative syllogism.

On another view, what the name 'X' signifies is taken *not* to be identical with part of the real definition. So one who knows only that there are items to which the name, in virtue of what it signifies, is applicable does not know (save *per accidens*) *that* there are Xs, and he will find it hard to discover *what* Xs are.

It will be seen that Zabarella finds exactly the same point in 93b32–5 as in 93a21 ff. It is a rather simple (and unexciting) point. If the complete definition of X is Y in Z because of M, it is demonstrable that Y is in Z, and only a person with the demonstration *knows* that Y is in Z. Any such person can readily produce the complete definition of X, extracting it from the relevant demonstration. Anyone who does not have the demonstration knows only *per accidens* that there are Xs.

According to the other main line of interpretation, both passages are speaking of the pre-conditions for successful investigation. They are both contrasting favourable and unfavourable starting-points. But whether the line between favourable and unfavourable is drawn in the same place in both passages is doubtful.

(3) What exactly *is* it that the scientific investigator has to know if he is to ask the question 'Why *p*?' (or 'What is *X*?'), and how does he come to know it? It might be supposed that it (the ὅτι) is a plain fact, and that knowledge of it is provided by sense perception—or rather, by sense perception and experience, since it will not be a singular proposition but a general one (not an individual item but a type or class of item) about which the investigator's question is asked. But the knowledge or supposition that *p* (where *p* is a generalization), or that there are *X*s, is not enough. The investigator must suppose also that *p* is a *scientifically explicable* truth, derivable from basic scientific laws or starting-points (ἀρχαί), or that *X*s constitute a *scientifically explicable* class of events or phenomena, a sort of 'natural kind', if he is to think appropriate the question 'What laws explain *p*?' or 'What is the causal explanation of *X*s?' No such explanation (διότι) can be found for accidental truths or casual concomitances; and it is only if one supposes that there is such an explanation that one will ask what it is. Thus the necessary presupposition of the scientist's enquiry 'Why *p*?' is that explicably-*p*. And if I ask the question 'What *is* thunder?' in a scientific sense ('the "is" of theoretical identification'), I am assuming not only that noises occur in clouds—that thunder as ordinarily tested for occurs—but further that there really is such a (single, scientific) thing as thunder, that the observed cases called thunder do constitute one real kind of event with a scientific explanation.

This is why Aristotle asserts that the question whether *p* is true or whether *X* exists is the question whether there is an explanation, a middle term (αἰτία, μέσον): the question whether *S* is *P* is the question whether there is a term *M* such that *S* is *P* because it is *M*, and the question whether there is such a thing as *Y* in *Z* is the question whether there is a term *M* such that *Y* is in *Z* because of *M*. On the face of it, these identifications are absurd. But when we remember that what is afoot is analysis of scientific enquiry, we can readily understand why Aristotle makes them. For within scientific discourse it is only non-accidental propositions or concomitances that are of interest. To ask a (scientific) 'Why *p*?' is to assume the (scientific) truth of *p*, and to ask the (scientific) 'What are *X*s?' is to assume the existence of *X*s as (scientific) entities. Thus, even if Aristotle is conflating two logically distinguishable steps—coming to believe that *p* and coming to believe that *p* is scientifically explicable—the pre-condition for the investigator's enquiry 'Why?' (διὰ τί) is indeed the supposition that there is a middle term for *p* that there is some term *M* such that it is because *S* is *M* and *M* is *P* that *S* is *P*.

(It might, alternatively, be argued that the supposition that there is a μέσον is not an *addition* to the belief that *p*, but already involved in it. For it might be said that, if *p* is a genuinely universal proposition, capable of generating unfulfilled hypotheticals, the jump to it from mere experience is already and precisely a jump from the belief that actual *S*s are *P*s to the belief that there is a lawlike connection in virtue of which every *S* is *P*.)

But how can anyone be justified in making the move from *p* to explicably-*p* *before* finding out the explanation? Aristotle speaks blithely of our recognizing or grasping that there is a middle term (γνόντες, 89b38, 90a8; λαβόντες, 90a22), and then going on to enquire what it is. He does not say what leads us to suppose or recognize that there is a middle term, why and with what justice we go from *p* to explicably-*p* or from the belief that *p* is true to the belief that it is necessarily true. Perhaps, however, this is not a damaging criticism. For he is analysing the structure of science, not giving practical advice. That an investigator must assume there to be an explanation in terms of scientific laws, or ἀρχαί, if he is to ask the scientific 'Why?', and that his assumption must be correct if the question is to permit of an answer, are statements about the logical relations of certain questions and answers; they do not purport to illuminate the general conditions for coming to correct assumptions, let alone to guide us to the acquisition of correct assumptions in individual cases.

Another criticism to which Aristotle's words expose him is this. In the actual progress of science, enquiry into the cause of something may very well be undertaken without there being knowledge or even a positive belief that it has a cause. One can look for an answer to 'Why *p*?' without taking for granted that there is an answer. The mere suspicion or hope that *p* is scientifically explicable is sufficient to set one out on a search for an explanation; what emerges in the search will confirm or squash the suspicion or hope. I do not think that this point constitutes a serious objection to what Aristotle is saying, although it suggests a way in which in a fuller account he could have added complications and refinements.

What does in fact give confidence that some proposition or con-
comitance is scientifically explicable? The most important general
point is surely this, that at any given stage in scientific progress the
laws and connections already reliably established provide the
framework and are used as guides to determine the likelihood that
some newly observed conjunction of features or events is law-
governed. (The same of course holds, *mutatis mutandis*, in the life
of an individual.) Aristotle does not, as far as I know, expressly
state this principle, but his practice (naturally enough) illustrates
it:[10] where a familiar kind of explanation can be envisaged, it is
εὔλογον to expect there to be one; an eccentric suggestion is ἄλογον
and ἄτοπον (or even πλασματῶδες).

Once he has come to think that *p* is explicable, or *X* definable,
how does the investigator proceed in order to discover the explanation or definition? Here again Aristotle's own practice (in various
fields of science and philosophy) will provide the main evidence for
his views. But a few general points about possible outcomes of the
investigation are made or suggested in the *Posterior Analytics* (especially II. 13–18), and these are possibilities which the investigator
will have to bear in mind from the start.

It may be found that the original question requires breaking
down into two or more questions; there is no *single* explanation of
the original proposition *p*. Two main types of case: (1) we asked
why *S*s are *P*s; but it may emerge that there are two kinds of *S*, and
that the reason why S_1s are P_1s is different from the reason why S_2s
are P_2s (cp. II. 13, 97b13–25 on μεγαλοψυχία, and Aristotle's fre-
quent discussion of πολλαχῶς λεγόμενα). (2) We asked why *S*s are
*P*s; but if *S*s are *A*s that are *B*s and *P*s are *C*s that are *D*s, the
explanation why *S*s are *P*s will break down into two explanations:
*A*s are *C*s because . . . , and *B*s are *D*s because . . . (Why do my
hybrid roses suffer from early blackspot? My roses suffer from
blackspot because . . . ; hybrids develop early because. . . .)

The original question may need revision for other reasons, for
example: (3) We asked why *S*s are *P*s; but it may be that *S* is a
species of a genus *G*, and that the only explanation why *S*s are *P*s
is the explanation why *G*s in general are *P*s. So there is no 'match-
ing' or 'commensurate' cause for the connection between *S* and *P*.
The specific character of *S*s is irrelevant to their being *P*s. (Why do

[10] For one nice application of the principle see *De divin.* I, 462b18–26.

hybrid roses get blackspot? There's no special reason why *hybrid*
roses get blackspot. Roses get blackspot because. . . .) Aristotle has
a good deal to say about cases of this general kind: explanation
should always be commensurate; science is concerned with what
pertains to a thing in itself, on account of itself, *qua* itself (καθ᾽ αὑτό,
δι᾽ αὑτό, ᾗ αὑτό).

He has much less to say about another range of cases where the
original formulation proves to require revision, where our initial
characterization of a kind of thing or event requires amendment if
the kind is to receive a full definition or explanation. (4) We asked
why *S*s are *P*s. But it is really *T*s that are *P*s (and we can discover
why). *S*s, or most *S*s, may happen to be *T*s, and if so, *S*s or most *S*s
are in fact *P*s; but this is not a truth derivable from the laws or ἀρχαί
of the science. Cases more or less like this are of the greatest
interest, and they are prominent in recent discussions of definition
and of theory change. It is perhaps in remarks on the philosopher's
use of widely held beliefs (ἔνδοξα) that Aristotle himself comes
closest to expounding relevant ideas about the clarification, reformulation, and revision of one's original beliefs and definitions.

III

Can we get a clear idea of the *ideal* of definition and explanation to
which Aristotle's theory points? As is his wont, Aristotle uses a
very few highly simplified examples to bring out certain points,
leaving us to make such additions and qualifications as are necessary to accommodate other essential features of his theory. Thus
the premisses of our thunder syllogism do not look much like basic
definitions or primitive existence propositions. One can, however,
see how the explanation of thunder would be carried forward in
accordance with Aristotle's general principles. Thunder is a noise
caused by quenching of fire in clouds. But what *is* noise? What *is*
quenching of fire? What *are* clouds? Noise is a certain movement of
the air (ἀέρος κίνησίς τις; *De Anima* II. 8, 420b11). The account of
quenching and of clouds will doubtless involve the basic qualities or
powers (δυνάμεις) associated with the four elements, together with
highly general laws of action and reaction. So a final explanation of
why thunder occurs and what it really is will show it to be a case of
very simple laws or connections that are widely exemplified and
easily intelligible. For a start, the same 'nature' (φύσις) will be

found in winds and earthquakes (*Meteor.* II. 9, 370a25–32; III. 1, 371b14–18).[11] In the end, a much wider range of natural phenomena should be susceptible of explanation within a unitary theory with relatively few and simple starting-points.[12]

If the quenching of fire is (say) the departure of a certain kind of hot and dry from a surrounding wet and cold mass, and the clouds in which thunder occurs are such a wet and cold mass surrounding that kind of hot and dry, the occurrence of thunder may be seen to be necessary. But it is doubtful whether this could be a final explanation: it seems unlikely that among the indemonstrable starting-points of a science there should be the assumptions that such departures occur and that such masses exist. Simple laws might be expected to explain—given that there are the four elements with their basic powers—why such masses should form and such departures occur. So the quest will go on for the fewest and simplest starting-points capable of explaining all the truths of the science. Aristotle's scientific ideal is often and rightly contrasted with the more mathematical ideal of Democritus or Plato. But the impetus to simplification and a sort of reductionism is no less strong in him, even if it is controlled by the recognition that there are radically different areas of enquiry, and that though for each a unified theory is to be sought, there will be none that explains them all.

If Aristotle's general scientific aim is reasonably clear and clearly good, there is no need to regard his theory of definition as dangerous or obscurantist. Provided that the encapsulation of scientific discovery and theory into new definitions is understood as a step in a process—a process capable of false steps—it need not be condemned as a fallacious attempt to prove the unprovable or a futile effort to turn contingent truths into conceptual necessities.

IV

I remarked at the beginning that the items we were to consider were those with a cause different from themselves (ὧν ἔστι τι ἕτερον αἴτιον τῆς οὐσίας; II. 9, 93b26). I should like to end by raising a puzzle

[11] For another example of the same 'nature' in various phenomena see *Meteor.* II. 3.

[12] Geoffrey Lloyd rightly complains that in this section I greatly exaggerate the extent to which Aristotle's science aims at simple starting-points of the kind I mention. He certainly does not think that the truths of biology are to be derived from basic laws about elementary materials.

about this. If the explanation of there being Y in Z is M, it can be said that the cause of the phenomenon Y in Z is something different from itself. But if this is made the ground for claiming that the phenomenon is really—is to be defined as—Y in Z because of M, is this not a case of cutting off the branch on which one sits? We think it possible to define those items which have some *other* cause (ἕτερόν τι αἴτιον). The result of our efforts is definition of items which, as defined, do *not* have some other cause. So how can the things we end up by defining be the ones we identified as capable of being defined?

A related point can be made by means of a question about our example. Is the full account of thunder:

(i) the noise in clouds, which is caused by quenching of fire;
or (ii) the noise in clouds that is caused by quenching of fire?

In (ii) 'that is caused by quenching' serves to specify what is being spoken of—the particular sort of noise in clouds which is so caused. In (i) 'which is caused by quenching' gives an additional piece of information (ἕτερόν τι) about an already independently specified phenomenon, the noise in clouds which we call thunder (the audibly familiar bangs). (i) incorporates the result of investigating what the familiar bangs are caused by; (ii) encapsulates the result in a redefinition (or real definition) of thunder. But how can the phenomenon referred to by 'the noise in clouds' in (i) be identical with that referred to by (ii) if the point of (ii), in contrast to (i), is to add a specificatory restriction to 'the noise in clouds'? Yet, if it is not identical, (ii) cannot after all count as a definition (or re-definition or real definition) of the thing we first picked out.

Such problems are, in more sophisticated forms, of some interest to contemporary philosophers; and that is why I thought it worth while to touch on them here, however briefly.

8

Change and Aristotle's Theological Argument

INTRODUCTION

Aristotle's general metaphysics starts from nature, seeking its causes and principles: matter, form, essence, and so on. His theology also starts from the world of change. The steps in his main argument for the existence of an unmoved mover are reasonably clear (although exactly where and how it fails can be disputed): there is change, and change (like time) is necessarily eternal; to guarantee that necessary eternality, there must be one eternal movement, and *its* cause (final cause) must itself be an eternal unchanging mover. This line of thought is expounded at length in *Physics* VIII (and resumed in *Metaphysics* Λ) as a deductive argument, and commentators are not wrong to refer to it as a 'proof' or 'demonstration' of the existence of an unmoved mover—which turns out to be Aristotle's god. In his theology, therefore, the existence of change provides not just the starting-point and subject-matter for investigation, but the first premiss of a proof—of *the* proof. There is, of course, much else in the discussion in *Metaphysics* Λ, especially on the nature and activity of god; but in what follows I shall be concerned only with the argument summarized above, and I shall feel free to refer to it as Aristotle's theological argument.

We might have expected that Aristotle would decline to say anything at all to justify accepting as a premiss the proposition that there is change. Even to say that the proposition is clear by 'induction' (*epagōgē*; *Physics* I. 2, 185a13–14) might suggest that its truth is less than primitive; and to take seriously anyone who denied it would surely be the mark of a fool (unless of course he were engaged—as in *Physics* I. 2–3—in exposing the fallacious

First published in 1991.

arguments of philosophical opponents). Aristotle does, nevertheless, make some points in defence of the proposition, in two passages of *Physics* VIII. 3. Much attention has been given to other
premisses of the theological argument, but these two passages have
been treated summarily by modern commentators. In the next
section I shall discuss these passages, which surely deserve close
examination, being concerned with the very first premiss of the
proof. In the third section I shall raise in a very general way one or
two questions connected with the fact that Aristotle's theology is
based on that first premiss: what can be the credentials or the value
of a conclusion derived from it? Accounts of Aristotle's methods in
philosophy and science (including Aristotle's accounts) do not
seem to deal adequately with *theologikē*, whose structure is different both from that of general metaphysics and from that of the
special sciences.

Although my aim in this essay is to draw attention to two insufficiently studied texts and to point to some insufficiently discussed
questions, my primary motive in writing it is to pay tribute to an old
friend and colleague and to his work in ancient philosophy.

THE TEXTS

First, *Physics* VIII. 3, 253a32–b6:

(a) To hold that everything is at rest, and to look for an argument for this—
dismissing sense-perception—is a sort of intellectual weakness, and it is to
question the whole of something [literally, 'a certain whole'] and not a
part. (b) Nor is it only against the physicist, but against practically all
sciences and all beliefs, because they all make use of change. (c) Further,
just as in mathematical arguments objections about the principles are
nothing to do with the mathematician (and similarly in other cases also), so
neither are questions about the present matter the concern of the physicist.
For it is a basic assumption [of his] that nature is a principle of change.

In (a) some scholars treat 'and it is to question . . .' as explaining
the intellectual weakness just referred to. It seems better to find
two distinct points in the section: it is silly to try to establish by
argument something that *sense perception* sufficiently refutes; and
the thesis that *everything* is at rest is not a (permissible) querying of
part of an area of study, but the (improper) querying of the whole
of it. What follows in (b) makes clear that the whole just mentioned

is physics, and takes the point further: it is not only physics that the thesis is upsetting, but 'practically all the sciences'. (c) is connected with the point about 'questioning the whole of something': the physicist can be expected to meet attacks on particular parts of his science, but not (*qua* physicist) to defend the very basis of his whole subject.

It is not clear exactly how the various points made in this passage are related, but there seem to be two main lines of thought. First, it is absurd to look for an argument where none could be as convincing as sense perception. The point is, of course, a familiar one in Aristotle. It is made again later in *Physics* VIII. 3 (254a30–3): 'to look for an argument for things where we are too well placed to need argument shows bad judgement of what is better and what is worse, of what does and what does not deserve credence'. In this passage Aristotle is dismissing attempts to argue for a thesis (that there is change) which we have superior non-argumentative grounds for believing; in the earlier passage (253a33) he was dismissing attempts to argue for a thesis (that there is no change) which we have superior non-argumentative grounds for rejecting. But both passages are insisting that in some matters sense perception provides a higher grade of trustworthiness and certainty than any argument could.

Secondly, our passage exploits the familiar methodological point that a given science cannot be called upon to establish its own foundations. That certainly relieves the *physikos* of the need to establish that there is *physis* (and change), but might leave open the question whose job it *is* to establish this. One suggestion is that it is the job of metaphysics, and that it is at this that Aristotle hints when he says '*practically* all the sciences' at 253b1. There is a relevant passage at *Physics* I. 2, 185a1–3: 'the geometer will no longer argue against one who denies his first principles—this is a task either for a different science or for a science common to all'. In his note on this passage[1] Ross suggests that the 'science common to all' is probably metaphysics. He refers to Aristotle's claim at *Metaphysics E.* 1, 1026a30, that first philosophy is 'universal in this way, because it is first', and takes 'universal' as equivalent to the 'common to all' of the *Physics* passage.

I shall return to the question whether Aristotle's metaphysics

---

[1] W. D. Ross, *Aristotle's Physics* (Oxford: Clarendon Press, 1936), 461.

can in fact be intended or expected to establish the first principles of physics. But as regards the interpretation of our passage, the exception implied by 'practically all the sciences', if indeed Aristotle has a definite exception in mind, may well be mathematics.

The second passage to be considered occurs later in the same chapter, at *Physics* VIII. 3, 254a23–30:

We have already said that it is impossible for everything to be at rest, but we may reiterate the point now. For even if *in reality* that is how it is, as some claim (saying that what is is infinite and changeless), nevertheless it certainly does not *appear* so according to sense-perception—it appears rather that many of the things there are do change. If therefore there is false belief (or, in general, belief), there is also change—and if there is imagination (*phantasia*), and if sometimes it seems [is thought to be] thus and sometimes otherwise. For imagination and belief seem [are thought] to be sorts of change.

The main argument here is a kind of *peritrope* argument. One who maintains that there is no change must hold to be false the general view that there is. But in holding this, he is admitting that there is false belief. But if there is false belief (or indeed any belief), then there is change—since belief is itself a sort of change. I say that this is a *kind* of *peritrope* argument; it is not of the form '*p* entails *q*, and *q* entails not-*p*', but rather (to put it roughly) of the form '*p* entails there being the belief that *q*, and there being the belief that *q* entails not-*p*'.

'The belief that *p*' is ambiguous. It may mean (in effect) 'the proposition *p*', or it may mean 'the psychological act or event or state of believing that *p*'. It is clear that Aristotle's argument requires the latter sense, since it is only in this sense that it could be plausibly claimed that a false belief (or any belief) is or necessarily involves a change. In principle, therefore, Aristotle's imaginary opponent could evade the argument by admitting that 'There is no change' entails 'It is false that there is change', but denying that there actually is any false believing that there is change.

More could be said about the overall structure of the argument, but I turn now to what is in any case an essential step, the claim that if there is belief, there is change. On Aristotle's own account in *De Anima*, perception and imagination and belief do indeed all involve physical change (though none *is* just a physical change). But it is not to be taken for granted that an opponent in argument will agree with Aristotle's own account. And even if it is a generally accepted view that they involve change (the *dokei* in 254a30 signalling an *endoxon*), the opponent will not be obliged for that reason to admit its truth. If he *were* so obliged, he would have been obliged *a fortiori* to admit the truth of the even more confidently held general view that there are changes, and he would have been out of business from the start.

It is just possible that an actual argument for the view that belief involves change can be found (hidden) in our passage, at 254a28, in the words 'if sometimes it seems thus and sometimes otherwise'. Ross paraphrases: 'if things seem sometimes so and sometimes otherwise' (*Physics*, 434). There is a certain ambiguity in the Greek and in the English, and it is necessary to draw a clear distinction between two interpretations. (Aristotle himself draws the distinction neatly in *De Anima* III. 2, 426b27: 'I now say that they are different, but not that they are different now.')

(1) I believe that sometimes the cat is awake and sometimes the cat is asleep [there is a belief in change];
(2) Sometimes I believe that the cat is awake and sometimes I believe that the cat is asleep [there is a change in belief].

In his introduction (*Physics*, 85) Ross writes: 'even the occurrence from time to time of these illusions itself implies change in our mental condition'. 'Occurrence from time to time' points to interpretation (2), and suggests that Ross is taking 'sometimes . . . sometimes . . .' to refer to different times in a person's history. But 'these illusions' suggests interpretation (1), which takes 'sometimes . . . sometimes . . .' to refer to the content of each belief ('illusion'). Without deciding between (1) and (2), we may ask what the implications for the argument are in either case.

On interpretation (1), Aristotle's words repeat the claim that in holding the belief that there is change to be false, our opponent is admitting that there is false belief—the belief that things are sometimes so and sometimes otherwise; he admits that there is *belief in change*. The words 'sometimes . . . sometimes . . .' merely constitute an explanation (surely unnecessary) of what the false belief that there is change (referred to at 254a27) amounts to. They add nothing of interest to the argument, and of course do nothing to justify the assumption that the existence of a belief in change implies the existence of any actual change.

On interpretation (2), the words in question refer to a *change in belief*—and such a ('mental') change is evidently an actual change. Nobody will seriously deny that there are in fact such changes—but this could not be thought to follow from the opponent's holding of his thesis in the obvious way in which the existence of belief in change can. Perhaps, however, it could be maintained that believing that there is change presupposes believing (having believed) one thing at one time and another thing at another? If so, we should have found in Aristotle an argument that does not rely on the assumption that holding *any* belief is (or involves) a change, but on the claim that holding the belief that there is change presupposes holding different beliefs at different times. This idea seems in itself to be worth considering; but whether we are justified in finding it here may depend on how the connected words 'if there is *phantasia*' in 254a28 are understood.

It is not at all clear why imagination should be brought in at this point. While it is true that it (like belief) does on Aristotle's view involve perception and therefore change, its mention here would seem only to complicate (and so weaken) the essential argument. I wonder whether one might not translate *phantasia* here by 'appearance' rather than 'imagination', and so take it to be picking up the *phainetai* of 254a26, which refers of course to perceptual appearance ('appear so according to sense perception'), not to imagination. The whole argument would then run: it appears to sense perception that there is change, so there is belief (people believe) that there is change, so there is change—whether it is a matter of 'appearing' or of 'believing': both appearing and believing are (thought to be) changes. This suggestion ties *phantasia* in a28 and a29 to the *phainetai* (*kata tēn aisthēsin*) of a26; and identifies the *hote men houtōs dokei, hote d' heteros* of a28–9 with the *doxa pseudēs* of a27 (this is to adopt interpretation (1) above). The proponent of the thesis will allow that there is the appearance of change (illusory according to him) and a belief in change (false according to him)—but both appearance and belief are themselves kinds of change. The whole passage then operates with just the two ideas of appearance and belief. If this is a possible way of understanding the pair of alternatives mentioned at a28, it seems attractive. If *not*, and if *phantasia* must be taken to introduce a new idea (imagination), it is tempting to take *hote men . . . hote de* as also introducing a new idea—change in belief (interpretation (2) above), and as insinuating the argument that believing that something changes (belief in change) presupposes believing at one time that it is F and believing at another that it is not F (change of belief).

QUESTIONS

In the two *Physics* passages we have considered, Aristotle defends the thesis that there is change by appealing to sense perception and belief; but he also claims that the physicist is not required to defend that thesis, his starting-point, any more than the mathematician is expected to defend *his* starting-point. A similar reference to the mathematician occurs at *Physics* I. 2, 184b25–185a3, where Aristotle says: 'the geometer will no longer argue against one who denies the principle of his science—this is a task either for a different science or for a science common to all'. By 'a different science' Aristotle no doubt has in mind (in the words of Hardie and Gaye[2]) 'another special science, if there is one, to which geometry is subordinate, as optics (e.g.) is to geometry'. If a science has no special science above it, it is only one 'common to all' that can give an account of its principles. So what of the 'hypothesis' of natural science, that there is change? Does theology confirm or justify that, whether as a special superordinate science or as a science 'common to all'? Unfortunately, that very thesis is the first premiss of the theologian's own demonstration that there is an unmoved mover. So in either case he would seem disqualified from the task of confirming or justifying it.

Aristotle's method in metaphysics is dialectical. In Ross's words,

the method adopted is, for the most part, not that of formal syllogistic argument from known premises to a conclusion which they establish. The truths which it is most important for metaphysics to establish are fundamental truths which cannot be inferred from anything more fundamental . . . Generally we may say that his method in the *Metaphysics* is not that of advance from premises to conclusion, but a working back from common-sense views and distinctions to some more precise truth of which they are an inaccurate expression, and the confirmation of such truth by pointing out the consequences of its denial.[3]

[2] R. P. Hardie and R. K. Gaye (trans.), *Physics*, in *The Works of Aristotle*, vol. II (Oxford: Clarendon Press, 1930).

[3] W. D. Ross, *Aristotle's* Metaphysics (Oxford: Clarendon Press, 1924), vol. I, p. lxxvii.

How, if not by inference, *can* the 'fundamental truths' be 'established'; and exactly what benefits in knowledge or understanding can the metaphysical project hope to bring? Working from *endoxa*, one may hope to clarify them and to work out their implications or presuppositions. But clarifying them will not prove them true; and identifying their implications or presuppositions cannot serve to verify of justify them, unless one has *independent* reason to accept (or to reject) those various implications or presuppositions. These questions have received magisterial treatment in Professor Irwin's recent work,[4] in connection with Aristotle's general metaphysics. It seems to me that a separate investigation is required into similar questions about Aristotle's special metaphysics or theology. Certainly the structure of theology—in which a deductive proof to establish the existence of the unmoved mover is central—is very different from that of general metaphysics; and the benefits that the conclusions of theology may be expected to provide are likely to be very different too.

The theological argument with which we are concerned purports to establish a fundamental truth, that there is an unmoved mover. How can it perform this important trick? The various steps in the argument rely on (what are taken to be) necessary truths—that time can have no beginning or end, that every change must be preceded by a change, and that there must be an explanation for every change. Are these principles themselves principles implicit in *endoxa*, or can they claim some independent validity? In any case, even if they bring extra—and indubitable—material into the argument, the first premiss—that there is change—remains indispensable, if the conclusion is to be other than hypothetical. Pure reason may perhaps see that if there is change, there must be an unmoved mover; but the conclusion that there *is* an unmoved mover cannot have a strength greater than that of the protasis 'there is change'— and this is not a truth of pure reason, but only an *endoxon*. So what are the credentials of the theological conclusion if it rests on such a basis? And what will be its power or usefulness?

Two lines of thought suggest themselves: (1) that there is change is not a mere *endoxon*; (2) although it is initially a mere *endoxon*, the conclusion of the theological argument turns it into something intelligible and confirms its truth.

---

[4] T. Irwin, *Aristotle's First Principles* (Oxford: Clarendon Press, 1988).

That there is change is certainly not one of a group of *endoxa* that can be set off against one another to generate *aporiai* in the way familiar to students of Aristotle's philosophical discussions. It is *the* basic hypothesis of *physikē*—more basic, one might even be tempted to say, than that there is *physis*, in so far as the recognition that there are changing things is logically prior to the recognition that (some) changing things have an internal principle of change. And Aristotle has good reason to claim (in *Physics* VIII. 3) that the occurrence of change is presupposed by (pretty well) all belief contents, and entailed by the occurrence of belief acts. But if, by a deductive argument, we can be *as* certain of God's existence as we are of the world around us and of our own existence as thinking beings, why should we ask more? We cannot really have any clear idea of what a conviction greater than this would be like. It would surely be a fine achievement to demonstrate that we have as much reason to believe in God as we have to believe in the existence of our world.

'A fine achievement'—but what good does it do us to be certain of the existence of Aristotle's god? We gain in understanding. The unmoved mover, as object of desire and imitation, explains the movements of the heavenly bodies and the persistence of natural kinds. So, just as in other branches of philosophy and science, we reach a point where we can *better understand* (but not prove to exist) the phenomena with which our enquiries started. The fact that there is change was a basic premiss for the proof of the existence of God; the existence of God makes that fact intelligible.

In this connection I should like to quote from Professor Jules Vuillemin's book *De la logique à la théologie*. He reports a remark made by Professor Victor Goldschmidt, commenting on Vuillemin's analysis of the argument for an unmoved mover. To paraphrase the remark:

While the existence of movement (and of *physis*) is a *principle* for the physicist, for the metaphysician it is merely a *hypothesis*, of which only he can give an account—as Aristotle in fact does in *Physics* VIII (a book that no longer belongs to the *physical* enquiries). Only the first mover, who does not belong to physics, can give an ontological basis to the physical hypothesis of the existence of movement.[5]

---

[5] Jules Vuillemin, *De la logique à la théologie* (Paris: Flammarion, 1967), 223.

In the light of that comment, Professor Vuillemin concedes that what he has himself earlier called the *first principle* of the proofs of an unmoved mover (viz. the premiss that movement exists) ought rather to be called a *hypothesis*. He continues:

Aristotle argues at first in the hypothetical mode: 'if there is movement, as sense-perception assures us, then . . .', to reach assertorically the conclusion: 'since there is a first mover, therefore movement exists'. The physical principle of the reality of movement is an absolute principle of metaphysical knowledge (*Idealgrund*) and, from this point of view, belief in the reality of the first mover depends on it. But this reality is in its turn an ontological principle grounding the reality of perceptual knowledge (*Realgrund*).[6]

The suggestion is, then, that while the existence of change explains our knowledge of the existence of an unmoved mover, the existence of an unmoved mover explains the existence of change. This suggestion seems to be open to two objections, or at least severe qualifications. In the first place, the 'downward path' of explanation does not get far without the aid of supplementary assumptions. Aristotle has an a priori argument for the circularity of the eternal movement of the outer sphere. But the behaviour of the sun that is required to produce seasons and the cycle of life is called in precisely in order to produce them. In short, not *much* of the change in the world is explained by the existence of an unmoved mover.

Secondly, the existence of an unmoved mover does not make it intelligible that there should *be* a changing world. It may be said that on Aristotelian principles an unmoved *mover* must actually cause movement; and so there must be at least the outer sphere. But this is an argument from a description; an eternal changeless being need not have been describable as 'an unmoved *mover*'. Moreover, in any case, there being an unmoved mover and an eternally moving sphere does not require there to be, or make it intelligible that there should be, planets and rocks and plants. The existence of an unmoved mover as an object of desire and emulation may explain why foxes behave as they do—by self-preservation and reproduction they maintain the species, thus partaking in the eternal and the divine as far as they can; but the existence of an unmoved mover does not explain why there are

---

[6] Jules Vuillemin, 224.

foxes. In short, even if God's existence makes intelligible (some of) the features of the world around us, it does not require or make intelligible the very existence of this world. The starting-point of the theological argument—that there is a world of change—is *precisely* what the conclusion—that there is an unmoved mover—does *not* explain. For Aristotle's theology, as much as for his physics, it remains an inexplicable 'hypothesis'. But Plotinus will recognize the existence of a problem, and will offer the doctrine of emanation as a solution to it.

9

Aristotle's Distinction between *Energeia* and *Kinēsis*

INTRODUCTION

In *Metaphysics* Θ. 6 Aristotle first gives a general explanation of the notion of *energeia* as opposed to *dunamis*—actuality as opposed to potentiality. He then draws a distinction between *energeia* and *kinēsis*. '*Kinēsis*' is Aristotle's regular word for change, including movement. *Kinēsis* is itself an *energeia* in the wide sense, an actuality as opposed to a potentiality. So in distinguishing it from *energeia*, Aristotle is evidently using '*energeia*' in a new and narrower sense. This distinction between *energeia* and *kinēsis* occurs in a number of places in Aristotle, and the commentators seem to be fairly happy about it. Yet it is not easy to understand precisely what distinction Aristotle has in mind.

There are several reasons why the distinction between *energeia* and *kinēsis* is worth studying. (a) It crops up, as will be seen, in a variety of important contexts in Aristotle. (b) It is closely related to the distinction between action (πρᾶξις) and production (ποίησις) which plays a leading part in Aristotle's ethical writings. (c) The difficulties we encounter in trying to give a clear and consistent interpretation of what Aristotle says about *energeia* and *kinēsis* are largely due to features of his thought and writing which cause equal trouble in other parts of his philosophy; so that to diagnose these features in this relatively limited area would be a help towards explaining his treatment of quite other topics. (d) The point or points that Aristotle is trying to bring out with this distinction are of continuing philosophical interest.

This essay is primarily aporetic and destructive. Some of the relevant passages are examined, and some difficulties are raised. The aim is to stimulate, not to close, discussion of the problems.

First published in 1965.

The words 'energeia' and 'kinēsis' will be left untranslated and, from now on, unitalicized. The word 'activities' will be used, where convenient, to cover both energeiai and kinēseis; this is not to imply that the performances, operations, etc., which are in question would all be naturally described in English as 'activities'.

METAPHYSICS Θ. 6

The passage on energeia and kinēsis, 1048b18–35, divides into two parts. Aristotle first speaks of actions (πράξεις), and distinguishes between those that are 'perfect' (τελείαι) and those that are not. Some actions have a limit (πέρας), others do not. An action that has a limit is not itself an end (τέλος) but is directed to an end or goal (οὗ ἕνεκα) which is not yet in existence during the course of the action. Such an action is not perfect. On the other hand, an action that has no limit is one which is an end, or one in which the end is present (ἐνυπάρχει τὸ τέλος); this is a perfect action. Aristotle now passes to remarks evidently intended to elucidate the foregoing distinction. In these remarks (1048b23–35) he distinguishes between energeiai and kinēseis by the repeated use of formulae which combine present tenses with perfect tenses. Thus he starts: 'at the same time one sees [or "is seeing"—there is no distinct continuous present in Greek] and has seen, understands and has understood, thinks and has thought; while it is not true that at the same time one learns and has learnt or is being cured and has been cured'. So seeing, understanding, and thinking are energeiai, learning and being cured are kinēseis. Among other examples he uses here are (for energeiai) living well and being happy, (for kinēseis) walking and house building.

What exactly is the force of Aristotle's point about present and perfect tenses? The earlier distinction between activities which have a limit and those which have not naturally suggests the distinction between activities which are indefinitely continuable and those which are not: I cannot go on building a house once I have built it, but I can go on thinking of something, though it is already true to say that I have thought of it. This is certainly one thing that Aristotle means to bring out by his present and perfect tense formulae. For after saying 'at the same time one is living well and has lived well, and is happy and has been happy', he goes on: 'otherwise it would have to stop at some time'. Thus he takes the propriety or impropriety of combining present and perfect tenses as tied to the possibility or impossibility of going on with the activity indefinitely. And when he continues: 'but in fact it is not [*sc.* necessary for it to stop at some time], but one lives and has lived', one naturally understands these last words to mean that a man can go on living though he has already lived. Perhaps this is the only point that Aristotle is making with his presents and perfects: the point, namely, that with some activities *X* the moment at which one can say 'he has *X*ed' necessarily terminates the period of *X*ing, while with other activities *Y* there is no absurdity in saying that a man is still going on *Y*ing even though it would already be true to say 'he has *Y*ed'.

Quite a different point has, however, often been read into Aristotle's 'at the same time one sees and has seen'. It has been taken as saying (not, or not only, that 'one sees' does not exclude 'one has seen', but) that whenever 'one sees' is true, so also is 'one has seen'—that is, that 'sees' *entails* 'has seen'; similarly, of course, for all the other energeia verbs. Thus Sir David Ross, in the introduction to his edition of the *Metaphysics*, says that an energeia 'is complete in each moment of itself; at the same moment you see and have seen, know and have known'.[1] Professor Ryle, in *Dilemmas*, says that in our passage Aristotle points out that you can say 'I have seen' as soon as you can say 'I see'.[2]

Now it seems highly doubtful whether this *is* pointed out in our passage. Anyone, I suppose, will understand 'it is not true that at the same time one learns and has learnt' as meaning—*not* that 'learns' does not *entail* 'has learnt' but—that 'learns' and 'has learnt' are *incompatible*. Surely, therefore, the contrasted formulae like 'sees and has seen' should mean simply that these pairs are compatible and *can* be true at the same time. This is the way the matter is explicitly put in *De Sophisticis Elenchis*, where Aristotle seeks to show that seeing belongs to a different category from making. He says (178a9): 'Is it possible at the same time to make and to have made the same thing? No. But it is possible to see something and at the same time to have seen the same thing.' This way of understanding the 'sees and has seen' formulae yields,

---

[1] W. D. Ross, *Aristotle's* Metaphysics (Oxford: Clarendon Press, 1924), vol. I, p. cxxviii.

[2] G. Ryle, *Dilemmas* (Cambridge: Cambridge University Press, 1954), 102.

as has been said, a perfectly clear and relevant point about continuability.

There is, however, other evidence to support the view that Aristotle holds that the present entails the perfect in the case of energeia verbs, even if this is not pointed out in the 'sees and has seen' passage of the *Metaphysics*. Firstly, the idea is naturally suggested by the distinction between activities which have and activities which lack a limit, the distinction drawn in the preceding section of the *Metaphysics* chapter. A limit points both ways. If you have already built a house, you cannot still be building it; but also, if you are still building it, you cannot yet have built it. There is a limit which both cannot be passed and must be reached. So, correspondingly, an action which altogether lacks a limit should be one not only continuable indefinitely but also fully performable in any period of time, however short. If it could be true to say that a man *X*es while denying that he has *X*ed, the activity *X*ing would not 'lack a limit'; the man would still be on his way to a limit—namely, the point at which it would be true to say that he has *X*ed. Thus the general characterization of perfect action in the earlier passage of the *Metaphysics* does suggest the idea that for such an action, an energeia, the present tense entails the perfect.

Secondly, a sentence in the *De Sensu* (446b2) has this implication. The relevant words are in an 'if' clause, but evidently express Aristotle's opinion. 'Everything at the same time hears and has heard, and in general perceives and has perceived, and there is no coming-into-being of them, but they *are* without *coming to be*.' I return later to these last phrases. The immediate point is that the word 'everything'—'everything at the same time hears and has heard'—seems to make this into a statement that 'hears' *entails* 'has heard'. Aristotle is not saying merely that 'hears and has heard' *can* hold, but that it does so in every case. Since be cannot mean that whenever anyone has heard something he must be going on doing so, he must mean that whenever anyone hears or is hearing, it must also be the case that he has heard.

Further evidence that Aristotle does think this can be derived from his discussion of pleasure at the beginning of *Nicomachean Ethics* x. 4. But I postpone consideration of this passage, and ask next what exactly we are to suppose Aristotle to mean if he holds that in the case of energeia verbs the present tense entails the perfect. Professor Ryle's suggestion on this deserves consideration.

It has already been criticized in print,[3] but I believe that it still has adherents. I quote:

Seeing and hearing are not processes. Aristotle points out, quite correctly, that I can say 'I have seen it' as soon as I can say 'I see it'. To generalise the point that I think he is making, there are many verbs part of the business of which is to declare a terminus. To find something puts 'Finis' to searching for it; to win a race brings the race to an end. Other verbs are verbs of starting. To launch a boat is to inaugurate its career on the water; to found a college is to get it to exist from then on. Now starting and stopping cannot themselves have starts or stops, or, *a fortiori*, middles either. Noon does not begin, go on and finish. . . . It cannot itself go on for a time, however short. It is not a process or a state.

It will, I think, be apparent why, with certain reservations, verbs which in this way declare termini cannot be used and are in fact not used in the continuous present or past tenses. . . . I can be looking for or looking at something, but I cannot be seeing it. At any given moment either I have not yet seen it or I have now seen it. The verb 'to see' does not signify an experience, i.e. something that I go through, am engaged in. It does not signify a sub-stretch of my life-story.[4]

Ryle thus construes Aristotle's thesis that 'sees' entails 'has seen' as making the point that 'see' is a got-it verb, and does not stand for anything that can go on for any time.

One fatal objection to this interpretation of Aristotle is to be found in the sentence already quoted, where Aristotle supports the statement that at the same time one lives well and has lived well by saying 'otherwise it would have to stop at some time'. This surely shows that he has in mind not a distinction between activities that go on through time and activities or acts that do not, but a contrast between activities whose character sets a limit to their continuance and activities whose character sets no limit. It is, of course, true that activities which do 'have to stop at some time' *cannot* be achievements of the got-it kind, since these, so far from having to stop at some time, cannot ever stop (or start). But no one wishing to distinguish activities that go on through time from those that do not would do it by saying that the former 'have to stop at some time', since this so evidently suggests a contrast with those

³ See R. J. Hirst, *The Problem of Perception* (London: Allen & Unwin, 1959), 132.
⁴ Ryle, *Dilemmas*, 102.

that *need* not stop, and not with those that cannot stop (or indeed start).

Secondly, whatever may be—or may have been thought by Aristotle to be—the case with 'see', some at least of the verbs that stand for energeiai as opposed to kinēseis in Aristotle are certainly not got-it verbs. Thinking (*νοεῖν*) or contemplating (*θεωρεῖν*; *Metaphysics* Θ. 8, 1050a36) is certainly an activity one can be engaged in for a time. Thus in *Metaphysics* Λ. 7, 1072b14–30 God is contrasted with men because he thinks continuously and eternally, while they can do so only for a short period of time (*μικρὸν χρόνον*). In *Nicomachean Ethics* x. 7, 1177a21 the activity of thought or contemplation is said to be the most continuous (and, in particular, more continuous than practical activity), 'since we can contemplate more continuously than we can *do* anything'. Again, the continuability through time of living or living well, and of being happy, other examples of energeiai, is obvious. Since Aristotle uses one and the same linguistic test to segregate seeing from kinēseis and to segregate thinking, living well, etc., from kinēseis, it cannot be right to construe his point about 'see' in a way that makes nonsense when applied to his other examples.

Thirdly, there is the general consideration that the Greek verbs translated 'see' and 'hear', correspond, in fact, not only to 'see' and 'hear', but also to 'look at' or 'keep in view' and 'listen to'; and further, that they have perfectly good continuous past tenses (they cannot be blamed for not having a present continuous form, since there is no such form in Greek). Clearly, then, the odds were very much against Aristotle's seeing, let alone clearly expressing, Ryle's point about perception verbs.

I conclude that it is no part of Aristotle's view of energeiai that they cannot go on through time, and that his energeiai verbs do not correspond to Ryle's got-it verbs. (They have a better chance of corresponding to Ryle's other class of achievement verbs, the 'keeping' ones.)

If 'everything at the same time hears and has heard' does not make Ryle's point, an obvious alternative is to hand. The 'has heard' can be taken to refer to a period of time preceding the moment to which the 'hears' refers.

First, let us say something that holds of both kinēseis and energeiai. If a man *starts* to X at time *t*, he cannot be said to *be X*ing at *t*; it is only at some moment later than *t*, say *w*, that he can be said to be *X*ing. Since no two moments are contiguous, there must be an interval between *t* and *w*; and however short this period (*t* to *w*), it is a period of *X*ing preceding the moment *w* at which the man is said to be *X*ing. Thus, as soon as it is true to say 'He is *X*ing', it is true to say 'He has been *X*ing'. Aristotle argues for all this at some length in *Physics* vi. 5 and 6, claiming that there is no absolutely first sub-period in a period of change or movement, but that 'everything that is in motion must have been in motion before' (236b33).

Let us now take an example—an example of a kinēsis as opposed to an energeia. If at *w* a man is building a house, he must have started to build at some time *t* prior to *w*, and he must have been at it for some period before *w*. However, it clearly does *not* follow from the fact that we can say at *w* 'He is building a house' that we cay say at *w*—with reference to the preceding period—'He has built a house'. Indeed, this we certainly *cannot* say. With energeiai, however, the case is different; with energeiai 'He is *X*ing' *entails* 'He has *X*ed'. The perfect can always be used of the period preceding a moment at which the present can be used.

If at *w* a man is playing a prelude, he must have been at it for some time; but what he has done in that time cannot be described by saying 'He has played a prelude'; nor, had he fallen dead at *w*, could we have included as the last item in his biography the statement 'He played a prelude'. But if at *w* he is gazing at a statue, not only must he have been doing so for some time, but what he has done in that time entitles us to say at *w*, 'He has gazed at the statue'; and had he fallen dead at *w*, his biography could have included at the end the statement 'He gazed at the statue'. So playing a prelude qualifies as a kinēsis, gazing at a statue as an energeia.

While Ryle's account of the present–perfect connection involves that an energeia cannot go on through time, this one implies that it must. There may be objections to thinking that seeing, for example, must occupy time, and even objections to thinking that Aristotle thought this. But the passages so far considered do not provide any evidence against the belief that Aristotle did think this. The *Metaphysics* passage, in particular, does not suggest the idea that an energeia cannot (or need not) occupy time; but rather, that there is no upper or lower limit to the time it may occupy, and that it is somehow equally and fully present throughout any such period.

NICOMACHEAN ETHICS x. 4

Aristotle does not say that he is here talking of the distinction between energeiai and kinēseis. But he likens pleasure or enjoyment (ἡδονή) to seeing, and contrasts both with kinēseis, using as examples of kinēseis house building and walking—which were also used as examples of kinēseis in the *Metaphysics* passage. Both the choice of examples and the general account of the contrast leave no doubt that it *is* the energeia–kinēsis distinction that he is using. Moreover, though he is going to say that enjoyment somehow *perfects* energeia (rather than that it *is* an energeia), it is fair to say, for the purposes of the present discussion and on the basis of x. 4, 1–4, that he classifies enjoying on the energeia side of the energeia–kinēsis distinction.

Seeing seems to be, with respect to any time whatever, perfect. For it does not lack anything whose coming into being later will perfect its form (τελειώσει αὐτῆς τὸ εἶδος); and pleasure also seems to be of this nature. For it is a whole, and at no time can one find a pleasure whose form will be completed if the pleasure lasts longer. For this reason too it is not a kinēsis. For every kinēsis (e.g. that of building) is in a time and for the sake of an end, and is perfect when it has made what it aims at. It is perfect therefore only in the whole time or at that final moment. In their parts and during the time they occupy, all kinēseis are imperfect, and are different in kind from the whole kinēsis and from each other. (1174a14–23)

Aristotle then proceeds to mention some of the different phases in the kinēsis of building a temple (1174a23–9).

The distinction between the form which is and the form which is not perfect with respect to any time whatever can most naturally be elucidated in terms of what can be said at various times. With a kinēsis the form is not perfect with respect to any time whatever: the perfect tense is applicable only at the end of a stretch of time, at the end of none of whose sub-stretches it was applicable. With an energeia the form is perfect with respect to any time whatever: the perfect tense is applicable at any moment in a stretch of time occupied by that energeia—that is, at the end of any sub-stretch, however short. 'Is gazing at the statue' entails 'has gazed at the statue'; 'is building the house' is inconsistent with 'has built the house'. If this is the correct interpretation of the *Ethics* distinction, it confirms that Aristotle does hold that with energeia verbs the present entails the perfect, and it confirms the way in which this was understood above (in opposition to Ryle's account).

It may be objected that Aristotle cannot mean to characterize energeiai in such a way that an energeia must go on through time, since he says: 'every kinesis is in a time and for the sake of an end' (1174a19). If in distinguishing energeiai from kinēseis he says that every kinēsis is 'in a time', is he not implying that an energeia need not occupy time? It is wrong, however, to regard the words 'in a time and for the sake of an end' as giving two independent criteria for being a kinēsis. There is no further suggestion in the context that occupying time (or necessarily occupying time) by itself distinguishes kinēseis from energeiai. The words 'in a time and for the sake of an end' go closely together to give a single criterion; a kinēsis occupies some *definite* time, limited by its arrival at its end—that is, its goal. The phrase makes the same point as is made in the *Metaphysics* by the equating of having a limit with having an end; there also the contrast was not with something occupying no time, but with something which did not occupy a fixed time determined by the goal to be reached. That Aristotle is in the *Ethics* making the *single* point when he says 'every kinesis is in a time and for the sake of an end' is confirmed by the way he goes on: 'and it is perfect when it has made what it aims at. It is perfect, therefore, only in the whole time or at that final moment.' Here, in what is evidently intended to explain the preceding short statement, the notions of end or goal and time are blended to provide a single criterion for being a kinēsis: namely, that only at the termination of a fixed period of time, or perhaps with reference to the whole of such a period, can a kinēsis be called perfect—the period, of course, being fixed by the necessity of reaching the appropriate goal. Thus the *Ethics* discussion, down to 1174b7, contains no suggestion that an energeia can occur without going on for any time.

After the discussion so far summarized has come (at 1174b7) to its conclusion that enjoyment is not a kinēsis but is something 'whole and perfect', Aristotle adds a further and different reason for the conclusion. He says: 'This would seem to be the case, too, from the fact that it is not possible to undergo kinēsis otherwise than in a time, but it is possible to have enjoyment [or perhaps, "be pleased"]; for what occurs in the "now" is something complete (τὸ γὰρ ἐν τῷ νῦν ὅλον τι).' That this is added as a *supplementary* argument confirms that in the preceding discussion Aristotle was not making the point that energeiai can occur in the 'now', while kinēseis cannot. However, it might be thought that this later statement that it is possible to have enjoyment in the 'now'—'otherwise than in a time'—is inconsistent with the distinction drawn in the preceding passage, if it was there assumed that energeiai go on through time. I am not quite clear what to say about this, for I am not sure what fact Aristotle is pointing to when he says that enjoyment or pleasure may occur 'not in a time'. But certainly the rule or criterion here suggested (rule 1), 'If *X*ing can occur not in a time, it is not a kinēsis' does not seem *inconsistent* with the rule implied in the previous discussion (rule 2), 'If at every moment in a period of *X*ing it is true to say "He has *X*ed", then *X*ing is not a kinēsis'. Now if, as I have argued, Aristotle believes that any energeia can go on through time, while it is evident that not every energeia can occur *not* in a time (e.g. living or living well), it is not surprising that Aristotle should have given his main accounts of the distinction between energeiai and kinēseis by reference to cases where energeiai do go on through time—that is, by using rule 2.

Indeed, granted that any energeia may continue through time, the first rule—'If *X*ing can occur not in a time, it is not a kinēsis'— does not provide an adequate way of distinguishing energeiai from kinēseis. That *X*ing can occur not in a time shows, by rule 1, that it is not a kinēsis (the point Aristotle is insisting on with regard to enjoyment), but it does not show that it is an energeia. For the starts and terminations of kinēseis are not in a time—do not last for any time—yet they are not themselves energeiai. So rule 1 can establish that *X*ing is not a kinēsis, but only rule 2 can establish that *X*ing is an energeia. In short, if Aristotle recognized the possibility of using some energeia verbs to stand for durationless acts, he threw this in as an additional contrast to kinēseis verbs, but he did not make this possibility either a necessary or a sufficient condition for being an energeia verb. The necessary and sufficient condition for being an energeia verb is that rule 2 be satisfied. Aristotle's main accounts of the distinction between energeiai and kinēseis do not presuppose that if *X*ing is an energeia, *X*ing must always occupy time. They do assume that if *X*ing is an energeia, *X*ing may go on through time, and they give a criterion for distinguishing energeiai from kinēseis by reference to the behaviour of energeia verbs in situations where they are used to describe what is going on through time.

A DIFFICULTY

I turn now to the main and obvious difficulty about Aristotle's account of energeia and kinēsis. In both the *Metaphysics* and the *Ethics* passages, he gives walking (βαδίζειν) as an example of a kinēsis. But how can this be so, if the criterion for X's being a kinēsis is that 'He has Xed' cannot be true of any part of a period of the whole of which it is true? For are not parts of walks walks? Now Aristotle perhaps realizes that what he has said about kinēseis as opposed to energeiai does not fit walking so easily as house building. At any rate, he follows his discussion of building in the *Ethics* with a separate section on walking (1174a29–b5). He argues that in walking (as in other forms of locomotion like flying) 'the whence and whither constitute the form' (τὸ πόθεν ποῖ εἰδοποιόν). In other words, he claims that no part of a walk does qualify for the same specific description as any other part of the walk or as the whole walk. If I walk from Oxford to Reading, the 'form' of the whole walk is its being a walk from Oxford to Reading, and this form is not achieved until I have reached Reading. Then, but at no earlier stage, can I say 'I have walked from Oxford to Reading'. I could earlier, on arrival at Wallingford, have said 'I have walked from Oxford to Wallingford'—but that again I could not have said at any time preceding the time of arrival at Wallingford.

Now certainly we can, as Aristotle tells us, provide different descriptions for the parts and the whole of any walk. Nor are the differences in question trivial or irrelevant: it is not as if Aristotle had distinguished portions of a walk by temporal references, which one could clearly do equally well for sub-stretches of a period of an energeia. Yet, granted that such different descriptions of parts of a walk and of the whole walk are always possible, and germane to what has been done *qua* walking, why cannot the same procedure be used to show that, say, enjoyment can be a kinēsis? Enjoyment, as Aristotle himself insists, is always the enjoyment of something; and that something may be a play, a symphony, or a battle. Suppose I have enjoyed hearing a symphony; this description—'I have enjoyed hearing the symphony'—is the full and proper description of what I have done; just as, if I have walked from A to Z, the proper description of what I have done is, according to Aristotle, 'I have walked from A to Z'. But 'I have enjoyed the symphony' is *not* something I can say 'with respect to any time whatever'—at the end of any sub-stretch of the total period—any more than 'I have

walked from A to Z' is. If called away in the middle of the symphony, I could no say that I had enjoyed hearing the symphony or
that I had heard the symphony (any more than the players, if
interrupted, could say that they had played the symphony). In
short, the procedure by which Aristotle makes walking count as a
kinēsis and not an energeia—the procedure of taking relatively
precise or specific descriptions of walks and showing that *they* do
not apply to parts of the walks—can be applied also to enjoying,
hearing, etc. If the rules for saying 'He has walked from A to Z'
prove that walking is a kinēsis, don't the rules for saying 'He has
heard the symphony' or 'He has enjoyed hearing the symphony'
prove that hearing and enjoying are kinēseis too?

It is not open to Aristotle to argue that hearing is, after all, an
energeia because in every part of the time during which the man
was listening to the symphony he could be said to have heard, or to
have heard something. For his proof that walking is a kinēsis depends upon asking not whether the man who walked from A to Z
could be said to have walked, or to have walked somewhere, in sub-
stretches of the time he took to go from A to Z, but whether he
could be said to have walked from A to Z in such sub-stretches.
Thus Aristotle could not claim that though hearing a symphony is
a kinēsis, hearing is an energeia, without having to admit that
though walking from A to Z is a kinēsis, walking is an energeia.

The difficulty would, of course, be removed if it could be shown
that Aristotle did not intend 'enjoy', 'hear', 'think', etc. to cover the
kind of case that the objection brings forward, but that he had in
mind only such cases as enjoying a scent, hearing a single sound,
dwelling on a single truth. But such a restriction on the meaning of
the terms would be utterly alien to ordinary Greek usage, and not
supported by Aristotle's usage elsewhere. Indeed, the point about
enjoyment in the *Ethics* is embedded in a discussion which assumes—of course—that one can enjoy all sorts of complex activities and experiences. Again, while the verbs translated 'think' and
'contemplate' are sometimes used by Aristotle of the grasp or
contemplation of single truths, they are equally used for trains of
thought or ratiocination. So, had Aristotle been clear that he
wanted to classify as energeiai only certain cases of hearing, enjoying, thinking, etc., he could not possibly have spoken as he does,
using the verbs without qualification.

It might be suggested that Aristotle is entitled to classify walking
as a kinēsis because variant descriptions can always be found for

the parts and the whole, and that he is entitled to classify hearing, etc. as energeiai because variant descriptions cannot always be found. Walking is always from some *A* to some *Z*, while hearing can be the hearing of a continuous unchanging note. But this defence of Aristotle fails. Firstly, he does not say or suggest that seeing and enjoying are energeiai because *some* instances of them satisfy the requirement 'perfect with respect to any time whatsoever'; he says without restriction that *they* satisfy this requirement. Secondly, if the key to the distinction between energeiai and kinēseis is the notion of 'perfection with respect to any time whatsoever', and if some cases of enjoyment, etc. satisfy this, and others do not, the only and obvious conclusion is that some enjoyment, etc. is energeia, and some is kinesis.

It is appropriate at this point to refer to a comment Ryle has made about Aristotle's treatment of pleasure. The view that he attributes to Aristotle (evidently on the basis of our passage) might make our difficulty about enjoying a symphony—and how you cannot be said to have done so until the end of it —irrelevant to Aristotle's thesis. I quote:

If enjoying something were a process from state to state, it would follow that a person could have begun to enjoy something but been prevented from finishing, as a person can begin his dinner but be prevented from completing it. But though a person may enjoy something for a short time or for a long time, he cannot have half an enjoyment. Enjoyments can be great or small, but not fractional.[5]

It is rather remarkable that Ryle can, as we saw, interpret Aristotle's remarks about seeing and other energeiai in the *Metaphysics* as meaning that they are not processes and cannot go on for a time, and can now interpret the *Ethics* passage, in which enjoyment is likened to seeing and contrasted with kinēsis, as meaning that enjoyment is not a process but can last for a time. It is hard to see how both these interpretations of the energeia–kinēsis distinction could be right. In fact, the second, as well as the first, seems to be wrong. It would, indeed, be odd to speak of having half an enjoyment, and fairly odd to speak of being prevented from finishing enjoying something. But these are not translations of any phrases Aristotle uses. *He* does not, to make *his* point, exploit any

5 G. Ryle, 'Proofs in Philosophy', *Revue internationale de philosophie*, 8 (1954), 150–7.

such words as 'interrupt', 'prevent from finishing', 'complete', or
'half'. His distinction depends on whether an activity is or is not
'perfect with respect to any time whatsoever'; and this, surely, is a
question whether one can or cannot apply the same description—
ascribe the same 'form'—to every sub-stretch of a given stretch. So
what Ryle says is clearly not a direct interpretation of Aristotle's
words. But it is not even a correct expansion of them. For Ryle's
class of expressions X such that one cannot speak of being prevented from finishing Xing is not the same as Aristotle's class of
expressions Y such that one can say 'He has Yed' at any moment in
a period of Ying. Consider 'enjoying the Choral Symphony'. This
will go into Ryle's class of X expressions, but not into Aristotle's
class of Y expressions. In general, that it is absurd to speak of being
'prevented from finishing' Xing does not entail that one can say 'He
has Xed' at any moment in a period of Xing.

Thus Ryle's interesting remarks about enjoying are not an acceptable exegesis of Aristotle, and do nothing to remove the major
difficulty that has been raised. This difficulty, to repeat, is that while
Aristotle's *descriptions* of his energeia–kinēsis distinction seem to
add up to a useful distinction, his treatment of examples is not in
accordance with that distinction. Nor can this be shrugged off by
saying that anyone is liable to throw in an infelicitous example. For
'enjoying' is no casual example, but the very topic of the *Ethics*
passage; while Aristotle goes out of his way to discuss walking at
some length, and to explain why it is to count as a kinēsis. Yet it was
precisely the cases of walking and enjoying that were used above to
show up the major difficulty. We seem, therefore, forced to conclude that there is a serious confusion in Aristotle's exposition of
the energeia–kinēsis distinction.

RECAPITULATION

I can perhaps pull together what has been said by quoting a passage
from an excellent paper by Professor Zeno Vendler. Vendler's
distinction between what he calls 'activities' and 'accomplishments'
seems to be the distinction Aristotle is telling us to make in his
accounts of the energeia–kinēsis distinction, while the examples
Vendler uses to illustrate the distinction bring out clearly how
unjustified Aristotle is in his blanket classification of hearing, etc. as

energeiai and walking, etc. as kinēseis. I have interposed a few references to Aristotle; Vendler himself does not refer to him.

First let us focus our attention on the group of verbs that admit continuous tenses. There is a marked cleavage within the group itself. If I say that someone is running or pushing a cart, my statement does not imply any assumption as to how long that running or pushing will go on; he might stop the next moment or he might keep running or pushing for half an hour ['lacks a limit']. On the other hand, if I say of a person that he is running a mile or of someone else that he is drawing a circle, then I do claim that the first one will keep running till he has covered the mile and that the second will keep drawing till he has drawn the circle. If they do not complete their activities, my statement will turn out to be false. Thus we see that while running or pushing a cart have no set terminal point ['lacks a limit'], running a mile and drawing a circle do have a 'climax', which has to be reached if the action is to be what it is claimed to be. In other words, if someone stops running a mile, he did not run a mile; if one stops drawing a circle, he did not draw a circle. But the man who stops running did run, and he who stops pushing the cart did push it. Running a mile and drawing a circle have to be finished, while it does not make sense to talk of finishing running or pushing a cart. . . . If it is true that someone has been running for half an hour, then it must be true that he has been running for every period within that half-hour ['perfect with respect to any time whatever', 'lacking nothing whose coming into being later will perfect its form']. But even if it is true that a runner has run a mile in four minutes, it cannot be true that he has run a mile in any period which is a real part of that time, although it remains true that he was running, or that he was engaged in running a mile during any substretch of those four minutes. Similarly, in case I wrote a letter in an hour, I did not write it in, say, the first quarter of the hour. It appears, then, that running and its kind go on in time in a homogeneous way ['form perfect with respect to any time whatever']; any part of the process is of the same nature as the whole. Not so with running a mile or writing a letter. . . . Let us call the first type, that of 'running', 'pushing a cart', and so forth *activity terms*, and the second type, that of 'running a mile', 'drawing a circle', and so forth *accomplishment terms*.[6]

OTHER TEXTS

The last section of this essay will contain a brief discussion of some further passages which might be expected to throw light on the energeia–kinēsis distinction.

---

[6] Zeno Vendler, 'Verbs and Times', *Philosophical Review*, 66 (1957), 143–60.

(a) In *Nicomachean Ethics* x. 3 Aristotle says that pleasure is not a kinēsis: 'for speed and slowness seem to be proper to every kinēsis . . . but neither of these holds of pleasure. For while we may *become* pleased quickly (as we may *become* angry quickly) we cannot *be* pleased quickly . . . while we *can* walk or grow or the like quickly.' Now one certainly might divide verbs into two classes according to whether they do or do not admit qualification by the adverbs 'quickly' and 'slowly'. But the suggestion that here we have the real ground for Aristotle's distinction between energeiai and kinēseis is not convincing. First, Aristotle does not exploit this elsewhere as a criterion for distinguishing energeiai from kinēseis. Next, he does not, even here, state in a general way that all energeiai verbs refuse, while all kinēsis verbs accept, such adverbial qualifications. Finally, though this adverbial criterion may indicate a philosophically important distinction between two types of verbs, one would expect it to be backed up and in a way explained by a fairly general characterization of the types of activity concerned. Since Aristotle attempts such a general account, particularly in the *Metaphysics* and *Ethics* passages examined earlier, it seems proper to examine *these* to see what the distinction amounts to, rather than to rely upon one brief and ungeneralized reference to the adverbial criterion.

(b) In the *De Sensu* passage already quoted (446b2), after saying that 'everything at the same time hears and has heard, and in general perceives and has perceived', Aristotle goes on: 'and there is no coming into being of them, but they *are* without *coming to be*'. Is this a new clue to the energeia–kinēsis distinction? In the *Ethics*, too (x. 4, 1174b12–13), after the proof that pleasure, like seeing, is not a coming into being or a kinēsis, Aristotle remarks that there is no coming into being *of* seeing or *of* pleasure. Unfortunately, it is hard to understand why Aristotle thinks it worth pointing this out in connection with the distinction between energeiai and kinēseis, for he holds that there is no coming into being of a kinēsis either. The point is stated and argued in *Physics* v. 2. 'There is not any kinēsis of a kinēsis, nor coming into being of a coming into being, nor in general change of change' (225b15). The obvious candidates for things *of* which there is a coming into being—things which *cannot* 'be without coming to be'—would be products of processes of making or terminal states following processes of change. But such products or states are relevant to the distinction between energeiai and kinēseis only in so far as kinēseis are processes *leading to* such products or states—that is, are (in a broad sense) comings-into-being—while energeiai are not. But this is simply to repeat the point Aristotle has already made, that energeiai are not themselves comings-into-being or kinēseis. It seems impossible to construe the statement that there is no coming into being *of* seeing in such a way as to make it relevant to the distinction between energeiai and kinēseis *without* construing it (or misconstruing it) as *equivalent* to the statement that seeing is not itself a coming-into-being. But then it does not offer any additional clue to the nature of the distinction under examination.

(c) It may be thought that I have wrongly neglected an important element in Aristotle's thinking about energeiai and kinēseis: the idea that energeiai are desired or desirable for their own sakes, while kinesēis are not. Two different suggestions are possible: (1) that Aristotle actually draws the distinction between energeiai and kinēseis with the aid of a psychological or evaluative criterion— that is, in terms of human desires as they are or as they ought to be; (2) that Aristotle does indeed draw the distinction in quite other terms (as has been supposed above), but that he is improperly influenced in his classifying of various candidates into the two classes by psychological or evaluative considerations. This latter would be a suggestion to explain discrepancies between Aristotle's account of his distinction and his treatment of particular examples; it would presuppose that there is some confusion in what he says. Since this essay is concerned only to show up the confusion, this suggested diagnosis of its cause can be left aside.

The first suggestion would presumably rely on the fact that in the *Metaphysics* and *Ethics* passages Aristotle uses such expressions as 'end' or 'goal', 'aims at', 'for the sake of' (τέλος, ἐφίεται, οὗ ἕνεκα). But Aristotle constantly uses such terms in contexts where no question of human or other conscious purpose or motive arises; and in the absence of any more definite indication that Aristotle is distinguishing energeiai from kinēseis by a test which has to do with desires and motives, it would be very rash to assume this. That house building is directed to the production of a house, has a house as its aim or goal, is, surely, put forward not as a fact about the motivation of builders, but as a fact about the concept of house building (a fact that can be expressed by the formula 'It is not true that at the same time one builds a house and has built it'). There may be logical, psychological, or ethical connections between the question whether *X*ing is an energeia or a kinēsis and the question whether people can, do, or ought to *X* for its own sake. But Aristotle does not seem to advocate answering the latter question as the way to discover the answer to the former question.

(d) In *Physics* III Aristotle asks what kinēsis is. He says that 'kinesis seems to be a kind of energeia, but imperfect' (201b30), and he goes on: 'the reason is that the potentiality whose energeia it is, is imperfect'. Now, since energeia in the narrow sense is itself in general the actualization of a potentiality, the suggestion here is that kinēsis is an imperfect actualization because it is the actualization of a certain type of potentiality, an imperfect one. One might, therefore, ask what makes a *potentiality* imperfect or not, in the hope of distinguishing kinēsis from energeia (in the narrow sense) indirectly, via the distinction between the types of potentiality of which each is the actualization. This is, of course, not the sort of procedure we expect to find Aristotle adopting or permitting, since he regularly insists that actuality is prior to potentiality in definition (λόγῳ) as well as in other ways, and we should therefore expect to find different types of potentiality defined in terms of differences between the respective actualizations, and not vice versa. If we hopefully neglect this point, and try to elucidate further the remarks in the *Physics*, we shall naturally turn to Aristotle's more or less formal definition of kinēsis in *Physics* III. 1, 201a11: 'the entelechy of that which is potentially, as such' (ἡ τοῦ δυνάμει ὄντος ἐντελέχεια, ᾗ τοιοῦτον); or 201b5: 'the entelechy of the potential, *qua* potential' (ἡ τοῦ δυνατοῦ, ᾗ δυνατόν, ἐντελέχεια). Though the word 'energeia' is not used in these phrases, it and its verb occur often throughout the discussion; and it will not be misleading for present purposes to equate 'entelechy' with 'energeia' (in the broad sense of 'actualization').

Now at first sight these definitions suggest that a kinēsis is not the actualization of a certain *kind* of potentiality (an imperfect one), but the actualization of potentiality in a certain aspect or way—'as such', '*qua* potential'. If, however, one asks what this kind of way is, one finds that only *some* potentialities are capable of being actualized in this way, and that *they* are not capable of being actualized in any other way. The potentiality capable of being actualized 'as such', '*qua* potentiality', is in fact just the *imperfect* potentiality. I quote Ross's note on *Physics* III. 1, 201a9–b15, where Aristotle explains his definition of kinēsis with the aid of the example of house building: the process of building is the actualization of the buildable *qua* buildable.

An aggregate of bricks, stones etc., may be regarded (1) as so many bricks, stones etc., (2) as potentially a house, (3) as potentially being in course of being fashioned into a house. The kinēsis of building is the actualisation not (1) of the materials *as* these materials (they are, previously to the kinēsis of building, already actually those materials), nor (2) of their potentiality of being a house (the *house* is the actualisation of this), but (3) of their potentiality of being fashioned into a house. Similarly every kinesis is an actualisation-of-a-potentiality which is a stage on the way to a further actualisation of potentiality, and only exists while the further potentiality is not yet actualised. Hence it is imperfect, and, though in a sense an energeia, is distinct from an energeia in the narrower sense in which 'energeia' implies that no element of potentiality is present at all.[7]

Thus the question whether a potentiality is imperfect *is* the question whether it is of the sort that is actualized '*qua* potential'—that is, over a period of time during no part of which it is fully actualized (for there remains an element of potentiality) and at the end of which it ceases to be being actualized (for there is no longer any potentiality). So the different-looking phrases in the *Physics* take us back in fact to the test indicated in the *Metaphysics* and *Ethics*: one can establish that *X*ing is an energeia and not a kinēsis if one can establish that it is not the actualization of an *imperfect* potentiality or of a potentiality '*qua* potential'; but one can establish this only by establishing that what is being done in any period of actual *X*ing is the same as what is being done in any other such period— that is, that the 'form' is perfect 'with respect to any time whatever'. The *Physics* account of kinēsis does not, therefore, provide any new independent criterion for the distinction between kinēsis and energeia.

(e) If the *Physics* account of kinēsis as the actualization of what is imperfect simply leads us back to the criterion of the *Metaphysics* and *Ethics*, the same phrase serves to make a rather different point in the *De Anima*. At III. 7, 431a4–7 Aristotle says that the transition from potential to actual perceiving is not a case of alteration, or indeed of kinēsis at all: 'for kinēsis, as we said, is an actualization of the *imperfect*; actualization in the unqualified sense—that is, of

---

[7] W. D. Ross, *Aristotle's* Physics (Oxford: Clarendon Press, 1936), 536. I have written 'kinēsis' where Ross writes 'movement', and 'actualisation' where he writes 'realisation'; I have transliterated one or two words he writes in Greek.

what is perfect—is different'. The word translated 'as we said' is omitted by most manuscripts. But in any case the reader will naturally refer back to II. 5, where again the distinction between potential and actual seeing and thinking is under discussion, and where kinēsis is said to be 'a kind of actualization, but imperfect'. In this chapter two types of potentiality are distinguished. Since an example of the actualization of one type is learning, and examples of actualizations of the other type are perceiving and thinking, we might hope to find in this distinction of types of potentiality an elucidation of the energeia–kinēsis distinction, for which perceiving and thinking, and on the other hand learning, are standard examples. In fact, however, Aristotle's explanation of the two types of potentiality in *De Anima* II. 5 reveals quite a different distinction. He contrasts, roughly, first-order abilities, abilities to do things, with second-order abilities, abilities to acquire first-order abilities. He says that in exercising a second-order ability, one is undergoing a change, developing one's nature (φύσις); while in exercising a first-order ability, one is not undergoing a change, one is simply exercising or expressing one's nature. A man capable of acquiring certain knowledge is in that respect imperfect—his nature remains not fully developed; the process of *acquiring* it is a journey towards an end or goal, arrival at which will make him (as far as this field of knowledge goes) perfect or perfected. He then *has* certain knowledge—that is, he has the ability to use it. When he does *this*, he is exploiting or expressing his perfected nature, not changing it or moving towards a further end or goal.

Aristotle, then, distinguishes between getting, having, and using a (first-order) ability; and he says that getting such an ability is undergoing a kinēsis, but using it is not a kinēsis, but an energeia. It is clear that this distinction, in spite of similarity of terminology and examples, is utterly different from that drawn elsewhere between energeia and kinēsis. For the distinction between acquiring and using an ability can itself be applied as well to (say) house building as to (say) knowledge of mathematics. When a *skilled* man builds a house, this will not, according to the *De Anima* distinction, be a kinēsis, but an energeia; for the man is not changing but expressing his nature, not acquiring, but exercising a perfection. Aristotle himself recognizes this; he says that 'it is not right to say that a wise man is altered whenever he displays wisdom, any more than that a house-builder is when he builds a house' (417b8–9).

Thus the *De Anima* distinction, though valuable in itself, is not the same as the usual energeia–kinēsis distinction. It tells us when to say that a man engaged in an activity is thereby *undergoing* a kinēsis, but it does not tell us which of the activities a man may be engaged in are themselves kinēseis. If Callias, a skilled man, is building a house, we are not to say that he is being changed (undergoing a kinēsis); yet what he is doing, house building, is, of course, a paradigm case of an activity that is a kinēsis and not an energeia. Some connection might be found between the distinction between acquiring and using abilities and the usual distinction between kinēsis and energeia; but the connection is not obvious, and is certainly not asserted or explained by Aristotle.

10

Aristotle's Definitions of *Psuchē*

In spite of the doubt he expresses as to the possibility or usefulness of giving a general definition of *psuchē*, Aristotle does offer such a definition in *De Anima* II. 1; indeed, he offers three. In this essay I wish to develop (in a simple, or even simpleminded, way) a main difficulty his formulae seem to involve, and to enquire into the root of the difficulty.

I

Aristotle's three formulae are:

(a) 'form of a natural body that has life potentially';
(b) 'the first actuality of a natural body that has life potentially';
(c) 'the first actuality of a natural body that has organs'.

What relation between *psuchē* and body is here intended? In his justly admired monograph *Identity and Spatio-Temporal Continuity* Professor David Wiggins suggests that 'the only logically hygienic way of sorting out Aristotle's analogy' is to take '[living] body: soul' as equivalent to 'flesh and bones: person'.[1] He offers Aristotle an interpretation of 'form' (or 'actuality') that makes form that which the matter constitutes: this wood, iron, etc. is an axe; this flesh and bones is a person. 'What we have done here is in effect to rediscover the "is" of constitution.'

I said that Wiggins *offers* Aristotle a certain interpretation. Indeed, he argues that Aristotle must, if pressed, accept it. He does

[1] David Wiggins, *Identity and Spatio-Temporal Continuity* (Oxford: Basil Blackwell, 1967), 48. I do not apologize for devoting some space to Wiggins's suggestion. I think that it is wrong, and that in general his paraphrases and interpretations of Aristotle are open to serious criticism. But his book is subtle and stimulating, and every part of it deserves careful consideration.

First published in 1973.

not, I think, claim that this is what Aristotle really meant; and he allows that 'Aristotle would insistently repudiate this whole line of argument'. Let us then consider what Aristotle does mean and whether he is open to the logical pressure Wiggins seeks to exert.

In the *Categories* Aristotle treats individual things as the basic entities—'primary substances'—and their *species* and *genera* as secondary substances. In later works he uses the distinction between matter and form in order to explain what an individual thing is. Here is a bronze sphere; we can distinguish what it is made of (bronze) from what makes that stuff a bronze sphere (sphericity). Aristotle regularly distinguishes form, matter, and 'the composite'. The last is the actual ('separable') thing, and to speak of form and matter is to speak of the form and the matter *of* such a thing. Whatever the obscurities or gaps in this Aristotelian account, it is surely clear that he has discovered 'the "is" of constitution'. Consider the following:

(1)	(2)	(3)
bronze	sphericity	a bronze sphere
wood and iron	ability to chop	an axe
bread and cheese	a certain arrangement	a sandwich
bricks and timber	ability to shelter	a house.

An item designated under (1) is (constitutes) an item under (3) if it has the form (shape, character, power) indicated under (2). Under (1) will normally be found material- or stuff-words; under (3), sortals; and under (2), names or descriptions of properties, structures, powers, and the like.[2]

We need not, then, doubt that the 'is' of constitution is a main weapon in Aristotle's armoury. But it is equally clear that he does not think or wish to suggest that a body—or flesh and bones—*constitutes* a *psuchē*. For he quite consistently applies the above triadic scheme in the following way:

(1)	(2)	(3)
body	*psuchē*	animal

An animal, he is always saying, is (or is made up of) *psuchē* and body. Strictly, the same is true of a plant, since a plant is *empsuchon*

---

[2] Notice that the form can equally well be called the form of the matter or the form of the composite: two aspects of the actual thing may be contrasted, or one aspect may be picked out.

('living'). If we confine ourselves to man, we have the triad 'body, *psuchē*, man'. What makes a body a man is its having *psuchē* (its being *empsuchon*). It would make no more sense to say that a man *is* a *psuchē* than to say that an axe *is* an ability to chop. An item under (1) constitutes an item under (3) in virtue of its possession of the item under (2); part of the point of the triadic scheme is to *contrast* the terms *psuchē* and *man* (or *animal* or *plant*).

How then does Wiggins come to think that Aristotle can be forced to a quite different account, one which actually identifies *psuchē* with *man* (or *person*)? Let us examine what he says in direct reply to an account like that just given.[3] The following sentences contain the gist of Wiggins's argument. 'Aristotle gives the form of axe as *chopping* and that of eye as *seeing*. . . . They [these concepts] come to much the same as being *an axe* or *being an eye*, but they are not strictly the same concepts as the concepts *axe* and *eye*.' 'There is an *f* such that in virtue of *psuchē* Kallias is a particular *f*. What value can *f* take? *Chopping* makes this an *axe*. *Psuchē* makes Kallias a *what*? . . . If the answer be *man* that is fine, but if the form *axe* makes this particular axe this *axe*, surely *psuchē* makes Kallias this particular *psuchē*. And for Kallias, then, *psuchē* and *man* must come to the same. The resolution which I shall offer Aristotle is precisely this—that the particular *f* is *this particular psuchē* or, equally good, *this particular man*.'

Now Aristotle certainly would give to Wiggins's question the answer 'a man'. Wiggins's claim that this commits him to equating *psuchē* and *man* depends upon the supposition that 'the form *axe* makes this particular axe this *axe*'. This presumably derives from the earlier passage where he says (a) that Aristotle gives the form of axe as *chopping*, and (b) that this concept comes to much the same as *being an axe*, although (c) it is not strictly the same concept as the concept *axe*. But (a) is incorrect, since it is not *chopping* but the *power* to chop (or, in the case of the eye, to see) that is the form, or 'first entelechy'. Chopping and seeing correspond to being awake; what corresponds to being alive (*empsuchon*) is being able to chop and having sight (*De Anima* II. 1, 412b27–413a1). (b) is also unacceptable. *Chopping* and *being an axe* are obviously quite disparate concepts. But even *the power to chop* (which is what Aristotle actually gives as the form of *axe*) and *being an axe* are, though

3 Wiggins, *Identity*, 76 n. 58.

intimately related, easily distinguishable. Aristotle himself noted in the *Categories* that 'being deprived and possessing are not privation and possession. . . . Having sight is not sight nor is being blind blindness.' 'The power to chop' and 'being able to chop' are not interchangeable expressions. Nor, moreover, are 'being able to chop' and 'being an axe': the former can, as the latter cannot, occur in a helpful answer to the question what makes this iron thing an *axe*. Finally, the admission in (c) is itself sufficient to destroy the argument Wiggins uses later to force on Aristotle the equation of *psuchē* and *man*. For if it is not, after all, the form *axe* (strictly speaking), but the form *being an axe* (or *being able to chop* or *the power to chop* or . . .), that makes this an *axe*, there is not the slightest presumption that the form *psuchē* makes Kallias a *psuchē*.

What Aristotle says about axes is that some wood and iron (matter) constitute an axe (composite) in virtue of its having the power to chop (form). Similarly, some part of the body is an eye because it has sight; and the body as a whole is a man because it has certain living powers, *psuchē*. *Psuchē* is the power a body must have if it is to be a man, as sight and the power to chop are what objects must have to be eyes or axes. There seems to be no justification for the suggestion that Aristotle either does or must identify *man* and *psuchē*.

It may be worth making two further remarks here to avert misunderstanding. First, it is of course true that Aristotle often speaks of man (horse, etc.) as an *eidos*, and that this is the very word translated 'form'. What is involved here, however, is not an implied identification of *man* with *psuchē* (his form), but a variation in the use of the term '*eidos*'. To speak of ambiguity might well be misleading, for the connection between the two uses is exceedingly close. Nevertheless, one can say that in some contexts '*eidos*' means 'form', and in others 'species'. The context usually makes perfectly clear which it means, but where necessary, Aristotle adds a phrase to put it beyond doubt. Thus '*eidos* of a genus' (e.g. *Metaphysics Z*. 4, 1030a12) plainly means 'species', whereas in '*eidos* and shape' (e.g. *De Anima* II. 1, 412a8) and 'actuality and *eidos*' (e.g. *Metaphysics H*. 3, 1043a32) 'form' is clearly intended. So the double use of the word '*eidos*' is no reason for confusing—or supposing that Aristotle confuses—form with species or, more generally, form with composite substance.

Secondly, Aristotle says, especially in *Metaphysics Z*, some difficult things about 'what-it-is-to-be-X'. The following will serve as a rough but sufficient reminder. To ask why an X is an X is, according to Aristotle, to ask why certain specified matter is (constitutes) an X; and to answer such a question, one must give the form of X. The form is thus the 'what-it-is-to-be-X.' Not, of course, that an X is *identical* with its form—an X is a composite of form and matter.[4] But the form is what the matter has to get or have if it is to become or be an X; for the matter, to become or to be an X is precisely to get or to have the form. Now if an expression 'E' designates a form and not a composite, there is, of course, no question corresponding to the question why an X is an X as construed above, and hence no clear meaning for the expression 'what-it-is-to-be-E'. Aristotle puts this contrast rather misleadingly when he says (in effect) that X is not identical with what-it-is-to-be-X, whereas E is identical with what-it-is-to-be-E. This last is misleading because it suggests what it is designed to deny, that E is the sort of term to which an analysis into matter and form can be applied. X must be distinguished from its formal defining character E; but E is neither the same as nor different from *its* formal defining character, since it *is* (and does not *have*) a form.

Aristotle thinks that it is not always obvious whether a word 'W' signifies, or on some occasion is used to signify, a composite or a form. He points out that in such a case one cannot give an unqualified answer to the question 'Is W identical with what-it-is-to-be-W?' For if 'W' signifies a composite, the answer is 'No'; if a form, the answer is 'Yes'. The examples Aristotle usually has in mind seem to be geometrical ('circle'); but he also makes his point by reference to 'man'. He says: 'For "soul" and "to be soul" are the same, but "to be man" and "man" are not the same, unless indeed the soul is to be called man; and thus on one interpretation the thing is the same as its essence, and on another it is not' (*Metaphysics H.* 3, 1043b2–4). What Aristotle alludes to here, and in one or two other places, is the possibility that 'man' may sometimes be used to designate not, as usual, the composite of matter and form, but the form alone,

---

[4] One can, of course, ask 'What is it for something to be an X?' and expect the answer to mention matter as well as form. Aristotle is well aware of this, and indeed often asks and answers such questions. But his use of phrases like 'what-it-is-to-be-X' derives not from *this* question, but from that indicated in the text. To put it otherwise, it depends upon the constitutive use of 'to be'—'These bricks, etc. are a house'—and not upon the classificatory use—'The thing in the drawer is a typewriter'.

psuchē. It is far from clear what he has in mind. What is clear and immediately relevant is that the passages in question are few, whereas he constantly and systematically *contrasts* man as composite with *psuchē* as form. Moreover, it is in the context of the distinction between *psuchē* and body that reference is made to a possible use of 'man' as equivalent to '*psuchē*': the use envisaged is not a use of '*psuchē*' to stand for the composite, but a use of 'man' to stand for the form. In other works, if one did use 'man' to stand for the form, to say of a body that it was a man would precisely not be to say what it *constituted.* This option therefore would not serve Wiggins's purpose.

II

Can we then say that Aristotle's account of *psuchē* stands in no need of any 'sorting out', that it is already 'logically hygienic'? Hardly. For it is not clear how the notions of form and matter or of actuality and potentiality are in this case to be understood. They normally find application where the relevant matter (or what is potentially an X) can be picked out and (re-) identified in both an unformed and an in-formed state (or both as potentially and as actually an X). Take first the concepts of form and matter. They are introduced by Aristotle to explain change. Certain matter or material can be shaped or otherwise worked on (given a form) and made into a so-and-so (the composite). In the simplest type of example, the material of which the composite is made is the very same material from which it was made; and the same material will survive the destruction of the composite. We can of course distinguish form from matter in regard to things we have not made and things which may escape dissolution as long as we like to think; but in making the distinction, we are implying the possibility of this material's not always having been (and not always going to be) informed in this way. In order that the matter–form distinction should be clearly applicable to anything, that a thing should be capable of being seen as a composite of matter and form, it is necessary that the material constituent should be capable of being picked out. 'Constituent' is no doubt an unhappy word: it is because matter and form are not, in the ordinary sense, constituents that no question arises as to how they combine into a unity. We might speak of the material 'aspect'. To speak of a composite *qua* material or in its material aspect is to refer to some material whose identity as that material does not depend on its being *so* shaped or in-formed.

It is less easy to regard actuality and potentiality as two 'aspects' of an actual thing. For to say that something is potentially an *X* seems to exclude its now being actually an *X*. Aristotle distinguishes two very different types of case in *Metaphysics* Θ. 6. (a) Unwrought material is potentially a statue; after the sculptor's work, it is actually a statue. Now in the statue matter and form can be distinguished, and it seems to Aristotle not unnatural to speak of the matter as potentiality (it is, after all, what was capable of receiving the form) and the form as actuality (it is what had to be imposed on the matter if there was to be an actual statue). Thus 'potentiality' and 'actuality' can come to be used not only for successive phases, but also for aspects of the composite which are present simultaneously; but this is only because of reliance on the idea of the matter as it was before being in-formed. This notion of compresent potentiality and actuality involves the assumption that the material of the actual thing was not always, or at least need not have been, in-formed in *this* way. (b) The other type of case is that in which a power or disposition is contrasted with its actualization. What is implied in talk of powers or dispositions is closely analogous to what was implied in talk of matter. A particular performance displays or manifests a power or disposition that could have been present before this performance (and usually was) and can survive it (and usually will). Where '*dunamis*' means 'power', *dunamis* at *t* is not incompatible with actual exercise of *dunamis* at *t*. Power is displayed in the exercise of it (whereas mere potentiality gives way to its actualization).

It seems, then, that both the matter–form distinction and the potentiality–actuality distinction (in the two types of case just mentioned) depend upon the idea that something that is actually the case might not have been: this stuff might not have been so arranged, the capacity being now displayed might have remained undisplayed. 'It is the nature of matter to be capable both of being and of not being ⟨such and such⟩' (*Metaphysics* Z. 15, 1039b29).

The problem with Aristotle's application of the matter–form distinction to living things is that the body that is here the matter is itself 'already' necessarily living. For the body is this head, these arms, etc. (or this flesh, these bones, etc.), but there was no such thing as this head before birth, and there will not be a head, properly speaking, after death. In short—and I am of course only summarizing Aristotle—the material in this case is *not* capable of existing *except* as the material of an animal, as matter *so in-formed*. The body we are told to pick out as the material 'constituent' of the animal depends for its very identity on its being alive, in-formed by *psuchē*.

There is a parallel difficulty with the notions of actuality and potentiality. Aristotle characterizes the animal's body as 'potentially alive' and as 'having organs'—such organs, clearly, as eyes, hands, heart, etc. But to be such an organ is to have a certain power (as the eye has sight; *De Anima* II. 1, 412b18–22), and to be a body with a set of organs is to have certain powers—nutritive, perceptual, locomotive, etc. There is, of course, such a thing as the actualization of any of these powers—their exercise on particular occasions; but it is not that to which Aristotle is referring when he calls *psuchē* 'the first actuality of a natural body that has organs'. He calls it the *first* actuality precisely to make clear (as he explains) that what he is trying to define is the life that a living creature has even when completely dormant, not active waking life—that would be the *second* actuality. If being alive, whether for an organ or for a whole body, is having certain powers (not necessarily exercising them) and to be an organ or a human body is to possess such powers, no distinction can be drawn for organs and bodies between their being potentially alive and their being actually alive. They are necessarily actually alive. If they lack the relevant powers, they are just not organs or human bodies; if they have them, they are *eo ipso* alive.

To sum up, Aristotle's definitions of *psuchē* resist interpretation because (i) the contrast of form and matter in a composite makes ready sense only where the matter can be picked out in such a way that it could be conceived as existing without that form, but (ii) his account of the body and bodily organs makes unintelligible, given the homonymy principle, the suggestion that this body or these organs might lack or have lacked *psuchē*. The complaint is not that Aristotle's concept of matter and form commits him to the impossible notion that what has form must lack it—that the same matter both has and has not the form—but that it commits him to something that he cannot allow to be possible in the case of living beings: namely, that what has form might have lacked it—that the same matter both has and might not have had the form.

III

What is the root of the difficulty? Is there something special about the concept of 'living thing' that makes it recalcitrant to Aristotle's treatment? Or ought he just to give a different account of the matter of which *psuchē* is to be the form?

(a) It might be suggested that Aristotle could evade the difficulty simply be dropping the homonymy principle, at least as regards living versus dead (or severed) organs or bodies. He could then allow an animal's 'organic body' after death to count still as a body (and the same body), and a dead or severed hand to count still as a hand (and the same hand). He would thus be able to give good sense—as we have demanded that he should—to the idea that this body, which is in fact living, *might not* be living; one day, indeed, it will certainly not be.

There are various ways in which this suggestion could be understood, but I shall mention only one. It involves raising a question about the interpretation of the homonymy principle. Let it be granted that if an organ *O* or a tool *T* is, by definition, something capable of performing a certain function, then it would in losing this capability cease to be an *O* or a *T*, strictly speaking. (It might be a broken or a ruined *T*, but not therefore a *T simpliciter*.) But what counts as 'losing' the capability? Aristotle's position is not entirely clear. Consider first a blunt axe that can perfectly well be re-sharpened. Has this 'lost' its capacity in the required sense? It would seem more natural to hold that it is a permanent loss of power, not a temporary disorder or malaise, that causes an axe to be no longer an axe, strictly speaking. Aristotle does not tell us what his principle requires us to say about a blunt axe, only what to say about an axe that has 'lost' its capacity. (Have I lost my pen if I've only mislaid it?) Consider next a faultless carburettor that has been taken from the car and lies on the bench. Is it disqualified from counting as a carburettor (strictly) because it cannot in this condition[5] inject fuel? Is a newly made rudder not yet a rudder (strictly) because not yet installed in a boat? Aristotle argues warmly (in *Metaphysics* Θ. 3) against those who refuse to ascribe a power to anything unless it is actually being exercised. But his own account signally fails to make plain which of the circumstances and conditions that are necessary conditions of a thing's exercising a power are also necessary conditions of its simply having the power. A carburettor cannot inject fuel when dismantled; but are we therefore to say of a dismantled carburettor that it cannot inject fuel?

Because Aristotle does not discuss whether or how the homonymy principle applies to the blunt axe and the dismantled carburettor, it is impossible to decide what he would say if confronted, as he might be today or tomorrow, with severed but reusable limbs and organs or dead but revivable bodies. By the same token, we cannot be sure whether to take him to be making a conceptual claim or asserting a depressing empirical proposition when he says (at *Cat.* 13a34–6) that 'one who has gone blind does not recover sight nor does a bald man regain his hair nor does a toothless man grow new ones'.

Here, then, is one suggestion we can offer Aristotle: that he should maintain the homonymy principle in a form that would not prevent a blunt axe and a dismantled carburettor from counting as an axe and a carburettor (strictly speaking), and that he should recognize as a possibility the reuse of severed organs and the reactivation of dead bodies. I am sure that this suggestion does not go to the root of the problem. But it would be a mistake to dismiss it offhand on the ground that talk of reviving a dead body is simply contradictory, or on the ground that what Aristotle was seeking to elucidate was the old-fashioned concept of life and not the rather different one that after future medical advances our grandchildren may have.

(b) Could not Aristotle take as matter not the body as a set of organs but the body as made up of certain stuffs? The dead or severed hand is still, is it not, the same *flesh and bones*? Professor Wiggins is happy about this, treating flesh and bones as parallel to

---

[5] Perhaps 'in this condition' is a bad phrase. What we are considering now is not a faulty state of the object but its separation from the environment that provides it with the opportunity to function.

the iron of which an axe is made. *His* only difficulty is over the competition that, as he thinks, arises for possession of the matter: this flesh and bones constitutes a human body, but also a person; and these (he argues) have different principles of individuation. There certainly are places where Aristotle treats flesh and bone as matter, in contrast to anhomoeomerous parts. 'The matter for animals is their parts—the anhomoeomerous parts for every whole animal, the homoeomerous parts for the anhomoeomerous, and those bodies we call elements for the homoeomerous' (*G.A.* I. 1, 715a9–11). 'The homoeomerous bodies are composed of the elements, and serve in turn as material for all the works of nature' (*Meteor.* IV. 12, 389b26–8). Where Aristotle discusses problems about form and matter in connection with man he commonly mentions flesh and bone as matter, rather than limbs and organs. See, for example, *Metaphysics Z*. 8, 1034a6, *I*. 9, 1058b7, and *Z*. 10–11, where it is instructive to notice that Aristotle mentions organs when arguing that form cannot be defined without reference to material parts, but 'homoeomerous' parts when advancing the opposite point of view.

Nevertheless, Aristotle regularly maintains that flesh and bone are defined by the work they do, and that therefore in a dead body they are only homonymously called flesh and bone. Thus in *Meteor.* IV. 12, after he has spoken of organs and tools—'all are defined by their function'—and has explained that the sightless eye or the wooden saw is an eye or a saw only homonymously, he goes on: 'So also with flesh; but its function is less obvious than that of the tongue' (390a14–15). Again, in *De Gen. et Corr.* I. 5: 'That growth has taken place proportionally is more obvious as regards anhomoeomerous parts like the hand. For there the fact that the matter is distinct from the form is more obvious than in the case of flesh and the homoeomerous parts. That is why one would be more inclined to think that in a dead body there was still flesh and bone than that there was still a hand or an arm' (321b28–32). In *G.A.* II. 1 a contrast between homoeomerous and organic ('instrumental') parts is combined with an insistence that the former too have a function, and that the homonymy principle applies to both equally: 'For it is not face nor flesh unless it has soul: after their death it will be equivocal to say that the one is a face and the other flesh, as it would be if they were made of stone or wood. The homoeomerous parts and the instrumental parts are produced simultaneously. We would not say that an axe or other instrument was made by fire alone; no more would we say it of hand or foot. The same applies to flesh, for it too has a certain function' (734b24–31, trans. Balme[6]).

If, then, flesh and bone, properly so called, are necessarily living—or parts of what is living—to take them rather than eyes, hands, etc. as the 'matter' of an animal does not avoid the basic difficulty. The parallel with the iron of an axe is inexact. For though an axe must be made with iron (material with certain powers), iron can exist otherwise than in axes, whereas flesh is by definition in a living thing. We cannot, therefore, take much comfort from Wiggins's assurance: 'Of course we can specify the matter as "this flesh and bones".' Nor, by way of compensation, need we worry about his problem—how flesh and bones can be (constitute) a living body *and* a person. For this is not a problem for Aristotle, who holds that to be a person (a man) *is* to be a living body (of a certain sort). Wiggins's problem arises from his ill-advised suggestion that '*psuchē*' means 'person' ('For our purposes it will not do very much harm to think of *psuchē* as much the same notion as *person*'.[7]). The real difficulty for Aristotle is not how it can be true both that this flesh and bones constitutes a living body and that this flesh and bones constitutes a man (or a person); it is how it can be illuminating to say *either* of these—essentially equivalent—things if flesh and bones can occur only as constituents of living bodies.

III

If neither the anhomoeomerous parts nor the homoeomerous parts of bodies seem able to play successfully the role of matter, because they are inseparable from *psuchē*, might inanimate materials like the four elements do better? Aristotle does of course think that the bodies of animals and plants are, like every other material thing, made up ultimately from the elements. In some places he actually refers to them as the 'matter' correlative to the form of man (e.g. *Metaphysics* Λ. 5, 1071a14); and he often mentions them by way of

---

[6] D. M. Balme (trans.), *Aristotle De Partibus Animalium I and De Generatione Animalium I* (Oxford: Clarendon Press, 1972), 61.

[7] Wiggins, *Identity*, 46.

material cause when contrasting this with the formal or final cause. Nevertheless, it is really quite clear that he would not be willing to say that a human body is (is made of) earth and water, or that the elements are potentially men. They are altogether too remote. In *Metaphysics* Θ. 7 Aristotle raises the question *when* something is potentially so-and-so:

E.g., is earth potentially a man? No—but rather when it has already become seed, and perhaps not even then. . . . A thing is potentially all those things which it will be of itself if nothing external hinders it. E.g., the seed is not yet potentially man; for it must be deposited in something other than itself and undergo a change. But once it has through its own motive principle got such and such attributes, then it is potentially a man. (1049a1–16)

If earth, etc. are too remote to count as the matter of a human body, could they count as the matter of the *lowest* kind of living thing, plants? Does Aristotle's difficulty arise from the attempt, whose feasibility he himself casts doubt on, to give a *general* account of *psuchē*? Certainly he holds both that the different 'souls' or living powers form a logically developing series, and that in the development of a man one power precedes another. For example, *G.A.* I. 3, 736a32–b8:

One could not class the foetus as soulless, in every way devoid of life; for the seeds and foetuses of animals are no less alive than plants, and are fertile up to a point. It is plain enough that they have nutritive soul . . . , but as they progress they have also the perceptive soul in virtue of which they are animal. . . . For they do not become simultaneously animal and man, or animal and horse, and so on; for the end is the last to be produced, and the end of each animal's generation is that which is peculiar to it. (trans. Balme; cp. 736b13, 778b32–779a2)

So it would make sense to say of a human body that it might have failed to grow to maturity, that it might have remained at the merely vegetable or merely animal stage. That a given body has *this psuchē* (the human) is contingent if it might have failed to develop beyond the animal stage.

It is quite likely that careful study of Aristotle's views on the actual processes of generation and growth would throw new light on some of his general doctrines. But talk of the lower forms of life or of early phases in a man's life cannot diminish our main difficulty. For even if plants and human embryos are 'nearer' to earth and water than men are, they are nevertheless alive; and for them too, therefore, the 'body potentially alive' of Aristotle's definition must be not earth and water but plant fibre, etc. and flesh, etc. Aristotle himself insists in an important passage of *De Anima* II. I that 'it is not the body that has lost the *psuchē* that is "potentially such as to be alive", but *the body that has it*; a seed and a fruit is potentially such a body' (412b25-7, cp. *G.A.* II. 3). Seeds, etc. are not yet 'potentially alive' in the sense this expression has in Aristotle's definition of *psuchē*, though they are potentially—they will with luck grow into—bodies that are potentially alive—bodies, in fact, of plants or animals. Until there is a living thing, then, there is no 'body potentially alive'; and once there is, its body is necessarily actually alive.

IV

It would clearly be wrong to say that the concepts of matter and form, or of potentiality and actuality, are improperly transferred by Aristotle from the account of process and change to the analysis of substance concepts. For they are perfectly clear and helpful analytic tools in many cases, even if their understanding and application does depend on presuppositions about change. The question is why they cause trouble elsewhere. I will end by mentioning two directions in which it may be useful to look.

We may be struck by the fact that artefacts provide the easiest and most straightforward examples of things whose ingredients or components evidently retain their character or identity from before (and also after) the 'lifetime' of the things. But not everything we can make is like this. The timber, hinges, and screws can still be seen when the cupboard is built, but the eggs and sugar are lost in the cake. If, as a result of cooking, *a* and *b* combine to form the homogeneous stuff *c*, *a* and *b* are no longer there to be picked out. We can refer to the *a* and *b* we started with, and perhaps we can recover the *a* and *b* again by some process. But *a* and *b* are present now, if at all, only potentially. Actual bricks constitute an actual wall, though those very same bricks might not have done so. But here is quite a different story: potential *a* and *b* are 'in' actual *c*, though they might have been actual *a* and *b*. Chemical change, in short, which yields a new sort of stuff, cannot easily accommodate an account tailor-made for other operations. (Compare the constant but often misleading use of mechanical terms and analogies for biological processes and events.) This is the difficulty for Aristotle with the basic living materials such as flesh and bone. They are produced, as he explains in detail in the biological works, by processes like cooking; and they have powers and characteristics that, though explicable by reference to the powers of their ingredients, are new, emergent powers and characteristics.

This, then, may be one fairly deep source of trouble. Where things or materials are produced, whether in nature or by technology, by chemical action, the matter–form analysis is in difficulty. One can refer to the material that by such-and-such a process *became* this (and perhaps may be recovered *from* this); but this will not explain what it is that *is* this.

A second point, related but distinct, is this. Once Aristotle moves from examples like 'bronze sphere', he gets to things that have functions, that can do specific jobs. As is well known, he likes to identify the 'end' or 'final cause' of an object with its essence or 'formal cause' (e.g. *Physics* II. 7, 198a25). But this creates a problem. For the job to be done determines the shape or structure or proportions, as well as the material ingredients, of the thing; and the thing's ability to do its job depends not only on what it is made of, but also on shape, structure, etc. The thing's ability to do a certain job is not *identical with* its shape, structure, etc. So if this ability (*A*) is treated as the form of a functional object, what are we to count as its matter? If the ingredients alone, what has become of the shape, structure, etc. (the original paradigm of form)? But if the ingredients plus shape etc.—that is, the materials *thus organized*— then the matter (so understood) *necessarily* has *A*. Powers are surely consequential attributes in the sense that if one object has a power that another lacks, this must be due to some other difference, an 'internal' difference of composition or structure. Aristotle would not, I think, wish to entertain the idea that two things might have different powers without there being any basis for this difference in their material constitution.

Here, therefore, is another source of trouble. A thing's power is not related to its material constitution (ingredients plus structure) in the same way in which a thing's structure is related to its ingredients; and the distinction between matter and form that works for ingredients and structure cannot be expected to do so for constitution and power. Somewhat the same may be said of potentiality and actuality: it is easy to distinguish the possession of a power from its exercise, but not easy to construe the possession of a power as itself the exercise of one.

II

Aristotle on *Eudaimonia*

I

Like most great philosophical works, Aristotle's *Nicomachean Ethics* raises more questions than it answers. Two central issues as to which it is not even quite clear what Aristotle's view really is are, first, what is the criterion of right action and of moral virtue? and, second, what is the best life for a man to lead? The first question is raised very explicitly by Aristotle himself at the beginning of book VI, where he recalls that moral virtue (or excellence of character) was defined as a mean determined by the rule or standard that the wise man would employ, and now says that this statement, though true, was not clear: we need also to discover what *is* the right rule and what *is* the standard that fixes it. Unfortunately, he does not subsequently take up this question in any direct way. The difficulty about the second question is not that he fails to discuss it—it is, after all, the centre of his target—or that he fails to answer it, but that he seems to give two answers. Most of the *Ethics* implies that good action is—or is a major element in—man's best life, but eventually, in book X, purely contemplative activity is said to be perfect *eudaimonia*; and Aristotle does not tell us how to combine or relate these two ideas.

One way of answering the two questions brings them into close connection. For if Aristotle really holds, in the end, that it is contemplation (*theōria*) that is *eudaimonia*, a possible—or even inevitable—answer to the first question is that right actions are right precisely in virtue of their making possible or in some way promoting *theōria*, and that the states of character commendable as virtues or excellences are so commendable because they are states that favour the one ultimately worthwhile state and activity, the state of theoretical wisdom (*sophia*) and the activity of *theōria*. Professors

First published in 1974.

Gauthier and Jolif, in their commentary,[1] take some such view; and since they recognize that Aristotle sometimes stresses the 'immanent character' of moral action, they find here a major incoherence in his thought. They themselves seek to explain why he falls into this incoherence (recognizing the moral value of virtuous actions and yet treating them as 'means to arrive at happiness') by suggesting that in his account of action he brings into play ideas that properly apply not to actions but to productive activities—he fails to free himself from an inappropriate way of speaking and from the associated way of thinking.

Professor Hintikka too has argued recently[2] that Aristotle remained enslaved to a certain traditional Greek way of thought ('conceptual teleology'), and that this is why his analysis of human action uses the ends-and-means schema, though this 'does not sit very happily with some of the kinds of human action which he considered most important'. According to Hintikka, since Aristotle could not 'accommodate within his conceptual system' an activity that did not have an end (*telos*), he had to provide a *telos* even for activities he wanted precisely to distinguish from productive activities, and so he fell into the absurdity of speaking of an activity of the former kind as *its own end*.

Mr Hardie, also believing that Aristotle fails in book I of the *Nicomachean Ethics* to think clearly about means and ends, claims that this fact helps to explain why he confuses the idea of an 'inclusive' end and the idea of a 'dominant' end.[3] Hardie attributes to Aristotle as an 'occasional insight' the thought that the best life will involve a variety of aims and interests, but finds that the other doctrine—that *eudaimonia* must be identified with one supremely desired activity—is Aristotle's standard view, and not merely something to which he moves in book X. Dr Kenny agrees in interpreting book I as treating the pursuit of *eudaimonia* as the

[1] R. A. Gauthier and J. Y. Jolif, *L'Éthique à Nicomaque* (Paris and Louvain: Publications Universitaires de Louvain, 1958). Quotations are from ii. 5–7, 199, 574, 886.

[2] J. Hintikka, 'Remarks on Praxis, Poiesis, and Ergon in Plato and in Aristotle', *Annales Universitatis Turkuensis* Sarja—Series B Osa-Tom. 126 (1973) (*Studia philosophica in honorem Sven Krohn*), Turku. Quotations are from pp. 54, 55, 58.

[3] W. F. R. Hardie, 'The Final Good in Aristotle's Ethics', *Philosophy*, 40 (1965), 277–95. Quotations are from pp. 277 and 279. (See also Hardie's *Aristotle's Ethical Theory* (Oxford: Clarendon Press, 1968), esp. ch. 2.)

pursuit of a single dominant aim: 'Aristotle considers happiness only in the dominant sense.'[4]

In this essay I shall question some of the views about the *Nicomachean Ethics* that I have been outlining. In particular I shall contend that in book I (and generally until book X) Aristotle is expounding an 'inclusive' doctrine of *eudaimonia*, and that there is no need to suppose that he was led into confusion on this matter by some inadequacy in his understanding of means and ends.

II

It may be useful before turning to the text, to make two preliminary points. First, the terms 'inclusive' and 'dominant', which have been prominent in recent discussion, need to be used with some care. The term 'inclusive' suggests the contrast between a single aim or 'good' and a plurality, while the term 'dominant' suggests the contrast between a group whose members are roughly equal and a group one of whose members is much superior to the rest. When used as a contrasting pair of terms, how are they to be understood? By 'an inclusive end' might be meant any end combining or including two or more values or activities or goods; or there might be meant an end in which different components have roughly equal value (or at least are such that no one component is incommensurably more valuable than another). By 'a dominant end' might be meant a *monolithic* end, an end consisting of just one valued activity or good; or there might be meant that element in an end combining two or more independently valued goods that has a dominant or preponderating or paramount importance. The former (strong) sense of 'dominant end' is being used when Hardie claims that in book I (apart from his occasional insight) Aristotle 'makes the supreme end not inclusive but dominant, the object of one prime desire, philosophy'; the latter (weak) sense when he says that 'some inclusive ends will include a dominant end'. It is clearly in the strong sense of 'dominant' (and the contrasting weak sense of 'inclusive') that Hardie and Kenny claim that book I expounds *eudaimonia* as a dominant and not an inclusive end.

[4] A. Kenny, 'Happiness', *Proceedings of the Aristotelian Society*, 66 (1965–6), 93–102. Quotations are from pp. 99 and 101.

The second point concerns the nature of Aristotle's enquiries about *eudaimonia* in book I. It is not always easy to decide what kind of question he is answering—for example, a linguistic, a conceptual, or an evaluative question. At one end of the scale, there is the observation that all agree in using the *word eudaimonia* to stand for that which is 'the highest of all practicable goods', and that all take the expressions 'living well' and 'doing well' to be equivalent to it. At the other end, there is the substantial question 'What *is eudaimonia*?', a question that invites alternative candidates, and to which Aristotle offers, with his own arguments, his own answer (or two answers). In between there are remarks about *eudaimonia*, and about what we all think about it, which could be construed as helping to elucidate the very concept of *eudaimonia* or as moves towards answering the questions 'What is *eudaimonia*'? 'What form of life satisfies the concept?' It will not be necessary to attempt exact demarcations. But it is important to bear in mind that two things might be meant by the assertion that Aristotle makes *eudaimonia* a dominant end: first, that, according to him, consideration of the logical force of the term *eudaimonia*, and of its place in a network of concepts ('good', 'end', etc.), shows that *eudaimonia* is necessarily a dominant end; or, secondly, that, according to him, although it is not part of the very *concept* of *eudaimonia* that it should be a single activity, yet it is in fact so—the life that fills the bill proves on enquiry to be 'monolithic', although this is not directly deducible from the terms of the bill itself. In claiming that Aristotle expounds in book I an 'inclusive' and not a monolithic doctrine of *eudaimonia*, I was referring both to his account of the concept itself—or what one might call in a broad sense the meaning of the word—and to his view about the life that satisfies the concept and deserves the name.

III

At the very start of the *Nicomachean Ethics* (I. I) we find Aristotle expounding and using the notion of an end, and connecting it with terms like 'good' and 'for the sake of'. He distinguishes between activities that have ends apart from themselves (e.g. products like bridles or outcomes like victory) and others that are their own ends. After remarking that where an activity has a separate end that end is better than the activity, he says that one activity or skill, *A*, may be subordinate to another, *B*, and he gives some examples—cases in fact where what *A* produces is used or exploited by *B*. He then makes a statement that is often neglected and never (I think) given its full weight: 'it makes no difference whether the activities themselves are the ends of the actions or something else apart from these, as in the case of the above-mentioned crafts' (1094a16–18). He is clearly saying here that his point about the subordination of one activity to another has application not only where (as in his examples) the subordinate activity produces a product or outcome which the superior activity uses, but also where the subordinate activity has no such end apart from itself, but is its own end. Commentators have not been sufficiently puzzled as to what Aristotle has in mind. It is, after all, not obvious what is meant by saying that one action or activity is for the sake of another, in cases where the first does not terminate in a product or outcome which the second can then use or exploit. It is no doubt true, as Stewart remarks, that a builder may walk to his work.[5] But it is not clear that walking to get to the building site is properly to be regarded as an activity that is its own end. Walking to get somewhere is more like fighting for victory: its success or failure depends on the outcome, and that is its point.

It would be natural to expect that, corresponding to the initial distinction between activities, there would be a fundamental distinction between the ways in which activities of the two different types could be subordinate to another activity. The idea of the use or exploitation of a product or outcome being inappropriate where the subordinate activity is not directed to a product or outcome, what immediately suggests itself instead is a relation like that of part to whole, the relation an activity or end may have to an activity or end that includes or embraces it. Many different types of case could be distinguished. But, to seek no more precision than immediate needs require, one may think of the relation of putting to playing golf or of playing golf to having a good holiday. One does not putt *in order to* play golf as one buys a club in order to play golf; and this distinction matches that between activities that do not and those that do produce a product. It will be 'because' you wanted to play golf that you are putting, and 'for the sake' of a good holiday

5 J. A. Stewart, *Notes on the* Nicomachean Ethics (Oxford: Clarendon Press, 1892), i. 12.

that you are playing golf; but this is because putting and golfing are *constituents of* or *ingredients in* golfing and having a good holiday respectively, not because they are necessary preliminaries. Putting *is* playing golf (though not all that playing golf is), and golfing (in a somewhat different way) *is* having a good holiday (though not all that having a good holiday is).

Now the idea that some things are done for their own sake and may yet be done for the sake of something else is precisely the idea Aristotle will need and use in talking of good actions and *eudaimonia*. For *eudaimonia*—what all men want—is not, he insists, the result or outcome of a lifetime's effort; it is not something to look forward to (like a contented retirement), it is a life, enjoyable and worth while all through. Various bits of it must themselves be enjoyable and worthwhile, not just means for bringing about subsequent bits. That the primary ingredients of *eudaimonia* are for the sake of *eudaimonia* is not incompatible with their being ends in themselves; for *eudaimonia* is constituted by activities that are ends in themselves. More of this in a moment. The main point I want to make about *Nicomachean Ethics* I. I is that it is unreasonable to suggest that Aristotle is slipping into an inherited usage when in fact he is very obviously introducing and expounding distinctions vital for what follows. Hintikka, in the paper from which I have quoted, seems to assume that the word '*telos*' ('end') must mean an end produced by (instrumental) means, and that 'for the sake of' necessarily brings in the idea of an end separate from the action. But the word '*telos*' is by no means so narrowly confined, and it is absurd to rely on the implications (or supposed implications) of a translation, rather than on the substance of what the philosopher is evidently saying. Why should Hintikka, in any case, identify having a 'well-defined end or aim' with doing something as a means to producing an outcome? If I play chess because I want to enjoy myself, is not that a well-defined aim? And can we ourselves not speak of 'doing something for its own sake'? Of course, an action cannot be 'a means to performing itself'—but Aristotle's words are not, like these, nonsensical; and his meaning seems clear enough.

Unlike Hintikka, Gauthier and Jolif have no trouble over action being its own end. They recognize the importance of 'l'affirmation par Aristôte, dès les premières lignes de l'*Éthique*, du caractère immanent de l'action morale', though they add regretfully that its force is 'limitée par les lignes 1094a16–18 [quoted above] et par la contradiction qu'elles incluent'. In their note on this last sentence they say: 'on ne voit pas . . . comment les actions morales, dont c'est la nature d'être à elles-mêmes leur propre fin, pourront ultérieurement être ordonnées à autre chose pour former une série hiérarchisée'. They call this one of Aristotle's 'incohérences foncières'. 'Au lieu d'être sa fin à elle-même, l'action morale devient un moyen de *faire* autre chose qu'elle-même, le bonheur.' I have tried to suggest that this offending sentence may in fact invite us to think of a kind of subordination which makes it perfectly possible to say that moral action is for the sake of *eudaimonia* without implying that it is a means to producing ('faire') something other than itself.

IV

Aristotle's thought on this matter is more fully developed in the first part of chapter 7 (1097a15–b21), where he starts from points about 'good' and 'end' and 'for the sake of' which come from chapter 1, and concludes with the statement that *eudaimonia* is something final and self-sufficient, and the end of action. In asking what we aim at in action, what its 'good' is, Aristotle says that if there is just one end (*telos*) of all action, this will be its good; if more, they will be its good. Now, he goes on, there evidently *are* more ends than one, but some are chosen for something else, and so they are not all *teleia* (final). But the best, the highest good, will be something *teleion*. So if only one end is *teleion*, that will be what we are looking for; if more than one are *teleia*, it will be the one that is most *teleion* (τελειότατον).

No reader or listener could be at all clear at this point as to what is meant by 'most *teleion*'. The word '*teleion*' has been introduced to separate off ends desired in themselves from ends desired as means to other ends. What is meant by the suggestion that there may be degrees of finality among ends all of which are desired for themselves? Aristotle goes on at once to explain how, among ends all of which are final, one end can be more final than another: *A* is more final than *B* if, though *B* is sought for its own sake (and hence is indeed a final and not merely intermediate goal), it is also sought for the sake of *A*. And that end is more final than any other, final without qualification (τέλειον ἁπλῶς), which is always sought for its own sake and never for the sake of anything else. Such, he continues, is *eudaimonia*: there may be plenty of things (such as pleasure and virtue) that we value for themselves, but yet we say too that we value them for the sake of *eudaimonia*, whereas nobody ever aims at *eudaimonia* for the sake of one of them (or, in general, for anything other than itself).

Surely Aristotle is here making a clear conceptual point, not a rash and probably false empirical claim. To put it at its crudest; one can answer such a question as 'Why do you seek pleasure?' by saying that you see it and seek it as an element in the most desirable sort of life; but one cannot answer or be expected to answer the question 'Why do you seek the most desirable sort of life?' The answer to the question about pleasure does not imply that pleasure is not intrinsically worth while but only a means to an end. It implies, rather, that pleasure *is* intrinsically worth while, being an element in *eudaimonia*. *Eudaimonia* is the most desirable sort of life, the life that contains all intrinsically worthwhile activities.

This idea, that takes up the thought suggested in the last sentence of chapter 1, is expressed again in the following lines, where the term 'self-sufficient' is introduced. That is self-sufficient (αὔταρκες) in the relevant sense which, taken alone (μονούμενον), makes life desirable and lacking in nothing (μηδενὸς ἐνδεᾶ). *Eudaimonia* does just that. For, Aristotle says, we regard it as the most worth while of all things, *not* being counted as one good thing among others (πάντων αἱρετωτάτην μὴ συναριθμουμένην)—for *then* (if it *were* simply the most worth while of a *number* of candidates) the addition of any of the other things would make it better, more worth while, and it would *not* have been lacking in nothing. He is saying, then, that *eudaimonia*, being absolutely final and genuinely self-sufficient, is more desirable than anything else, in that it *includes* everything desirable in itself. It is best, and better than everything else, not in the way that bacon is better than eggs and than tomatoes (and therefore the best *of the three* to choose), but in the way that bacon, eggs, and tomatoes is a better breakfast than either bacon or eggs or tomatoes—and is indeed the best breakfast without qualification.

It is impossible to exaggerate the importance of this emphatic part of chapter 7 in connection with Aristotle's elucidation of the concept of *eudaimonia*. He is not here running over rival popular views about what is desirable; nor is he yet working out his own account of the best life. He is explaining the logical force of the word *eudaimonia* and its relation to terms like 'end' and 'good'. This is all a matter of report and analysis, containing nothing capable of provoking moral or practical dispute. Aristotle's two points are: (i) you cannot say of *eudaimonia* that you seek it for the sake of anything else, whereas you can say of anything else that you seek it for the sake of *eudaimonia*; (ii) you cannot say you would prefer *eudaimonia* plus something extra to *eudaimonia*. These points are of course connected. For if you could say that you would prefer *eudaimonia* plus something extra to *eudaimonia*, you could say that you sought *eudaimonia* for the sake of something else: namely, the greater end consisting of *eudaimonia* plus something extra. The first point is that *eudaimonia* is inclusive of all intrinsic goods; and if that is so by definition, it is unintelligible to suggest that *eudaimonia* might be improved by addition. This ends and clinches one part of Aristotle's discussion, and he marks quite clearly the transition to the different and more contentious question to be dealt with in what follows: '*eudaimonia*, then, is something final and self-sufficient, and is the end of action. However, while the statement that *eudaimonia* is the chief good probably seems indisputable (ὁμολογούμενόν τι), what is still wanted is a clearer account of *what it is*'.

It is not necessary to claim that Aristotle has made quite clear how there may be 'components' in the best life or how they may be interrelated. The very idea of constructing a compound end out of two or more independent ends may rouse suspicion. Is the compound to be thought of as a mere aggregate or as an organized system? If the former, the move to *eudaimonia* seems trivial—nor is it obvious that goods can be just added together. If the latter, if there is supposed to be a unifying plan, what is it? For present purposes it is enough to claim that Aristotle understands the concept of *eudaimonia* in such a way the *eudaimonia* necessarily includes all activities that are valuable, that he applies the notion of *A*'s being for the sake of *B* to the relation between any such activity and *eudaimonia*, and that it is in this sense that he holds that good actions are for the sake of *eudaimonia*.

Commentators have not, I think, given due weight to these inter-

locking passages about the finality and self-sufficiency of
eudaimonia. Gauthier and Jolif follow Burnet[6] in giving a correct
account of the latter passage, and they say: '[Le] bonheur ne saurait
s'additioner à quoi que ce soit pour faire une *somme* qui vaudrait
mieux que lui; il est en effet lui-même la somme qui inclut tous les
biens.' Unfortunately, they fail to connect this with the earlier
passage in which Aristotle speaks of ends that are indeed final yet
subordinate to one supreme end, *eudaimonia.* Nor do they refer
to this text when considering (and rejecting) the suggestion that
Aristotle's general idea of *eudaimonia* is of a whole composed of
parts.

Mr Hardie also recognizes that the self-sufficiency passage suggests an inclusive end; yet he offers the previous sections as part of
the evidence that Aristotle's main view is different. Aristotle's
explicit view, he says, 'as opposed to his occasional insight, makes
the supreme end not inclusive but dominant, the object of one
prime desire, philosophy. This is so even when, as in E.N. 1. 7, he
has in mind that, *prima facie*, there is not only one final end'; and
Hardie then quotes: '[I]f there are more than one, the most final of
these will be what we are seeking.' I do not think that '*prima facie*'
does justice to 'if more than one, then the most final'. It seems to
imply that Aristotle is saying that, though there may seem at first
sight to be several final ends, there can really be only one final end,
and the others must really be only means to it. But there is, of
course, no 'seems'. The hypothesis is that there *are* several final
ends. When Aristotle says that, if so, we are seeking the most final,
he is surely not laying down that only one of them (*theōria*) is *really*
a final end. What he has in mind with this use of 'most final' must
be discovered by considering the explanation he immediately gives
(an explanation which Hardie, very remarkably, does not quote).
For certainly the idea of degrees of finality calls for elucidation.
The explanation he gives introduces the idea of an objective that is
indeed a final end, sought for its own sake, but that is nevertheless
also sought for the sake of something else. So the *most* final end is
that never sought for the sake of anything else because it includes
all final ends. That there *is* such an end whenever there are several
final ends is not then a piece of unargued dogma; it follows naturally from the very idea of an 'inclusive' end. Such, Aristotle imme-

    [6] J. Burnet, *The Ethics of Aristotle* (London: Methuen, 1900), 33.

diately continues, is *eudaimonia* (not, we note, *theōria* or *nous*)—
and he then passes to the self-sufficiency point which, as Hardie
himself recognizes, implies the inclusive approach.

Dr Kenny, on the other hand, in his paper 'Happiness', actually
reverses the sense of the passage about self-sufficiency. He attributes to Aristotle the remark that 'other goods added to happiness will add up to something more choiceworthy', and he says that
this 'makes it clear that Aristotle did not consider happiness an
inclusive state made up of independent goods'. This interpretation
will not, I am convinced, survive a careful consideration of the
immediate context (especially Aristotle's description of the 'self-
sufficient' as 'lacking nothing' and his statement that *eudaimonia* is
best 'not being counted as one good thing among others'). Nor are
other passages in which the quite special character of the concept
eudaimonia is dwelt upon compatible with this interpretation of
eudaimonia as happiness. It is indeed only if one is willing, with
Kenny, to treat 'happiness' as a fair translation of the word
eudaimonia that one can feel the slightest temptation to take the
self-sufficiency passage as he does. This willingness is the fatal flaw
in his paper considered as a contribution to the understanding
of Aristotle. The point is important enough to deserve a brief
digression.

It may be true, as Kenny says, that happiness is not everything,
that not everyone seeks it, and that it can be renounced in favour of
other goals. What Aristotle says, however, is that *eudaimonia* is the
one final good that all men seek; and he would not find intelligible
the suggestion that a man might renounce it in favour of some other
goal. Nor is Aristotle here expressing a personal view about what is
worth while or about human nature. It is in elucidation of the very
concept that he asserts and emphasizes the unique and supreme
value of *eudaimonia* (especially in I. 4, I. 7, I. 12). The word
eudaimonia has a force not at all like 'happiness', 'comfort', or
'pleasure', but more like 'the best possible life' (where 'best' has
not a narrowly moral sense). This is why there can be plenty of
disagreement as to what form of life *is eudaimonia*, but no disagreement that *eudaimonia* is what we all want.

Kenny points out that someone might renounce happiness because the only possible way to achieve his own happiness would
involve doing wrong. He writes: 'In such a case, we might say, the
agent must have the long-term goal of acting virtuously: but this

would be a goal in a different way from happiness, a goal identified with a certain kind of action, and not a goal to be secured by action.' How would the situation envisaged be described by Aristotle? If I find it necessary to undergo privation or suffering in order to do my duty, I shall have to recognize that my life will fall short of *eudaimonia*. But what I *renounce* is comfort in favour of right action, not *eudaimonia* in favour of right action. Nor could Aristotle possibly contrast *eudaimonia* with acting virtuously, on the ground that *eudaimonia* is 'a goal to be secured by action', while acting virtuously is 'a goal identified with a certain kind of action'. Comfort and prosperity may be goals to be secured by action, but *eudaimonia* is precisely *not* such a goal. It is doing well (εὐπραξία), not the result of doing well; a life, not the reward of a life. Nearly everything Kenny says about happiness goes to show that the word 'happiness' is not a proper translation of the word *eudaimonia*.

V

On what other grounds, then, may it be contended that Aristotle's idea of *eudaimonia* in book I is the idea of a 'dominant' end, a 'single object of desire'? Hardie takes the notorious first sentence of chapter 2 as expressing this idea—not indeed as asserting it, but as introducing it hypothetically. The sentence and following section run as follows in Ross's translation:

> If, then, there is some end of the things we do, which we desire for its own sake (everything else being desired for the sake of this), and if we do not choose everything for the sake of something else (for at that rate the process would go on to infinity, so that our desire would be empty and vain), clearly this must be the good and the chief good. Will not the knowledge of it, then, have a great influence on life? Shall we not, like archers who have a mark to aim at, be more likely to hit upon what is right?[7]

It is commonly supposed that Aristotle is guilty of a fallacy in the first sentence, the fallacy of arguing that since every purposive activity aims at some end desired for itself, there must be some end

[7] W. D. Ross, *Aristotle: The Nicomachean Ethics* (Oxford: Clarendon Press, 1925), 1–2.

desired for itself at which every purposive activity aims. Hardie acquits Aristotle. He writes:

Aristotle does not here prove, nor need we understand him as claiming to prove, that there is only *one* end which is desired for itself. He points out correctly that, if there are objects which are desired but not desired for themselves, there must be *some* object which is desired for itself. The passage further suggests that, if there were *one* such object and one only, this fact would be important and helpful for the conduct of life.

It is, however, not so easy to acquit Aristotle. For what would be the point of the second part of the protasis—the clause 'if we do not choose everything for the sake of something else' together with the proof that we do not—unless it were intended to establish as true the first part of the protasis—'there is some end of the things we do, which we desire for its own sake (everything else being desired for the sake of this)'? If the second part were simply a correct remark—irrelevant to, or a mere consequence of, the first part—it would be absurdly placed and serve no purpose.

The outline structure of the sentence is 'if *p* and not-*q*, then *r*'. Nobody will suggest that the not-*q* is here a condition additional to *p*. The one natural way to read the sentence as a coherent whole is to suppose that *q* is mentioned as the only alternative to *p*. In that case a proof of not-*q* would be a proof of *p*. So when Aristotle gives his admirable proof of not-*q*, he is purporting to prove *p*; and the sentence as a whole therefore amounts to the assertion that *r*.

This interpretation is confirmed by the fact that in what follows Aristotle does assume that *r* is true. Hardie attributes to him the suggestion that if there *were* only one object desired for itself, this fact *would* be important. But what Aristotle says is that knowledge of it '*has* (ἔχει) a great influence'; and he says we must try 'to determine what it *is* (τί ποτ' ἐστί), and of which of the sciences or capacities it *is* the object'; and he proceeds to try to do so.

There is, then, a fallacious argument embedded in the first sentence of chapter 2. But further consideration of the context and Aristotle's general approach may help to explain and excuse. What, after all, is the conclusion to which Aristotle's argument is directed? That there is some end desired for itself, everything else being desired for it. This need not be taken to mean that there is a 'single object of desire', in the sense of a monolithic as opposed to 'inclusive' end. Indeed, the immediately following references to the political art as *architectonic* and as having an end that *embraces* the ends of other arts are themselves (as Hardie allows) indicative of an inclusive conception. If, however, the idea is admitted of an end that includes every independently desired end, the possibility presents itself of constructing one (inclusive) end from any plurality of separate ends and of speaking of the one compound or inclusive end as the highest good for the sake of which we seek each of the ingredient ends.

Enough has been said about other passages to suggest that this notion is indeed central to Aristotle's account of *eudaimonia* in book I. The sentence at the beginning of chapter 2 precedes a passage that points to the inclusive conception. It immediately follows (and is connected by an inferential particle with) the remark I discussed earlier to the effect that activities that have no separate product can nevertheless be subordinate to, and for the sake of, higher activities—a remark which itself invites interpretation in terms of 'inclusive' or 'embracing' ends. This being the context and the drift of Aristotle's thought, it is perhaps not so surprising that he should commit the fallacy we have found it impossible to acquit him of. For the fallacy would disappear if an extra premiss were introduced—namely, that where there are two or more separate ends each desired for itself, we can say that there is just one (compound) end such that each of those separate ends is desired not only for itself but also for *it*.

VI

Up to the middle of I. 7, then, Aristotle has explained that the concept of *eudaimonia* is that of the complete and perfectly satisfying life. He has also mentioned various popular ideas as to what sort of life would fulfil that requirement, and he has accepted without discussion some fairly obvious views about certain goods that presumably deserve a place in the best life. Next, in the second part of chapter 7, he develops the *ergon* argument, thus beginning to work out his own account. Something must now be said about the way in which this argument terminates.

Consideration of man's *ergon* (specific function or characteristic work) leads Aristotle to the thesis that *eudaimonia*, man's highest good, is an active life of 'the element that has a rational principle'.

This would of course cover practical as well as theoretical rational activity. However, Aristotle's final conclusion adds what is usually taken to be a restriction to theoretical or contemplative thought, *theōria*, and to express therefore a narrow, as opposed to an inclusive, view of *eudaimonia*. For he says: 'The good for man turns out to be the activity of soul in accordance with virtue, and if there are more than one virtue, in accordance with the best and most complete' (or 'most final', *teleiotaton*); and it is supposed that this last must refer to *sophia*, the virtue of *theōria*. However, there is absolutely nothing in what precedes that would justify any such restriction. Aristotle has clearly stated that the principle of the *ergon* argument is that one must ask what powers and activities are peculiar to and distinctive of man. He has answered by referring to man's power of thought; and that this is what distinguishes man from lower animals is standard doctrine. But no argument has been adduced to suggest that one type of thought is any more distinctive of man than another. In fact, practical reason, so far from being in any way less distinctive of man than theoretical, is really more so; for man shares with Aristotle's god the activity of *theōria*.

Aristotle does have his arguments, of course, for regarding *theoria* as a higher form of activity than practical thought and action guided by reason. He will even come to say that though it is not *qua* man (but *qua* possessing something divine) that a man can engage in *theōria*, yet a man (like any other system) is most properly to be identified with what is best and noblest in him. But it is clear that these arguments and ideas are not stated in the *ergon* argument, and involve quite different considerations. The only proper conclusion of the *ergon* argument would be: 'if there are more than one virtue, then in accordance with all of them'. This is precisely how the conclusion is drawn in the *Eudemian Ethics* (1219a35–9): 'Since we saw that *eudaimonia* is something complete (*teleion*), and life is either complete or incomplete, and so also virtue—one being whole virtue, another a part—and the activity of what is incomplete is itself incomplete, *eudaimonia* must be the activity of a complete life in accordance with complete virtue (κατ' ἀρετὴν τελείαν). The reference to whole and part makes clear that by 'complete virtue' here is meant all virtues.

If, then, the *Nicomachean Ethics* addition—'if there are more than one virtue, in accordance with the best and most complete'— is a reference by Aristotle to a 'monolithic' doctrine, the doctrine that *eudaimonia* is really to be found in just one activity, *theōria*, it is entirely unsupported by the previous argument, part of whose conclusion it purports to be. Moreover, it is not called for—and has not been prepared for—by the conceptual clarification of the notion of *eudaimonia* earlier in the book and chapter; for it has not there been said that the end for man must be 'monolithic' (or even contain a dominant component). Thus such a restriction will be an ill-fitting and at first unintelligible intrusion of a view only to be explained and expounded much later. Now this is certainly a possibility, but not, in the circumstances, a very strong one. For we are not dealing with a work that in general shows obvious signs that marginal notes and later additions or revisions have got incorporated but not properly integrated into the text. Nor is the case like that of the *De Anima*, in which there are several anticipatory references to 'separable reason' before that difficult doctrine is explicitly stated. For there the remarks do not appear as part of conclusions of arguments; they are the lecturer's reminders of a possibility later to be explored, they keep the door open for a new character's later arrival. Here, however, in the *Nicomachean Ethics*, something is being affirmed categorically, and at a critical stage of the work, and as a crucial part of the conclusion of a carefully constructed argument.

Is there not any alternative to construing 'the best and most complete virtue' as an allusion to *sophia*? After all, it must be allowed that the meaning of the expression 'most complete virtue' or 'most final virtue' (τελειοτάτη ἀρετή) is not perfectly obvious. An alternative may suggest itself if we recall that earlier passage in the same chapter, concerning ends and final ends. For there too there was a sudden baffling use of the term 'most final'—and there it was explained. 'Most final' meant 'final without qualification', and referred to the comprehensive end that includes all partial ends. One who has just been told how to understand 'if there are more than one end, we seek the most final' will surely interpret in a similar or parallel way the words 'if there are more than one virtue, then the best and most final'. So he will interpret it as referring to total virtue, the combination of all virtues. And he will find that this interpretation gives a sense to the conclusion of the *ergon* argument that is exactly what the argument itself requires.

This suggestion is confirmed by two later passages in book I, where Aristotle uses the term 'teleia arete' and clearly is not referring to *sophia* (or any one particular virtue), but rather to comprehensive or complete virtue. The first of these passages (I. 9, 10) is explicitly taking up the conclusion of the *ergon* argument—'there is required, *as we said*, both complete virtue (*aretēs teleias*) and a complete life'. The second (I. 13, 1) equally obviously relies upon it: 'since *eudaimonia* is an activity of soul in accordance with complete virtue (*aretēn teleian*), we must investigate virtue'. And the whole further development of the work, with its detailed discussion of moral virtues and its stress upon the intrinsic value of good action, follows naturally if (but only if) the conclusion of the *ergon* argument is understood to refer to *complete* and not to some one *particular* virtue.

VII

It is obviously not possible here to survey all the evidence and arguments for and against the thesis that Aristotle's account of *eudaimonia* in book I is decidedly 'inclusive'; but one question should be touched on briefly. If such is indeed Aristotle's account, it may well be asked why he does not state it more plainly and unambiguously, using the terminology of parts and whole as in the *Eudemian Ethics*. One possibility worth considering is that he realizes in the *Nicomachean Ethics* that the notion of *parts* is really much too crude. To say that *eudaimonia* is a whole made up of parts does indeed make it quite clear that you are expounding an 'inclusive' and not a 'dominant' or 'monolithic' end. But it leaves quite unclear what kind of partition can be meant and how such 'parts' are put together. Plato already brings out in the *Protagoras* the difficulty of understanding the suggestion that there are different virtues which are 'parts' of complete virtue. Aristotle is particularly conscious of the variety of ways in which different factors contribute to a good life, and also of the fact that the distinguishable is not necessarily separable. So it may be that the reason why he does not speak of parts of a whole in *Nicomachean Ethics* I is not that he now sees *eudaimonia* as other than inclusive, but that he now has a greater awareness of how difficult it is to say exactly how the notion of 'inclusion' is to be understood. It may have seemed less misleading to speak (rather vaguely) of 'contributing to a final end' than to use an expression like 'parts of a whole', which sounds entirely straightforward but is not really so.

VIII

I have argued with respect to *Nicomachean Ethics* I that when Aristotle says that *A* is for the sake of *B*, he need not mean that *A* is a means to subsequent *B*, but may mean that *A* contributes as a constituent to *B*; that this is what he does mean when he says that good actions are for the sake of *eudaimonia*; and that he does not argue or imply that *eudaimonia* consists in a single type of activity, *theōria*. This is a defence of Aristotle against the charge that in book I a confusion about means and ends leads him to hold that action has value only as a means to *theōria*. But the original questions are now, of course, reopened: what, according to Aristotle, does make virtuous actions virtuous? and how are action and *theōria* related in his final account of the best life for man? I shall conclude with some exceedingly brief remarks on these questions.

It might be suggested that Aristotle's answer to the first question is that actions are virtuous in so far as they promote *theōria*, even if that answer is not argued for or implied in the first book. But although book X, using new arguments, certainly ranks *theōria* above the life of action as a higher *eudaimonia*, it does not assert roundly—let alone seek to show in any detail—that what makes any good and admirable action good and admirable is its tendency to promote *theōria*. Nor can this thesis be properly read into Aristotle's statement in book VI (1145a6–9) that practical wisdom does not use or issue orders to *sophia* but sees that it comes into being and issues orders for its sake. He is here concerned to deal with a problem someone might raise (1143b33–5): is it not paradoxical if practical wisdom, though inferior to *sophia*, 'is to be put in authority over it, as seems to be implied by the fact that the art which produces anything rules and issues commands about that thing'? Aristotle's reply does not amount to the unnecessarily strong claim that *every* decision of practical wisdom, *every* correct judgement what to do, is determined by the single objective of promoting *theōria*. It is sufficient, to meet the difficulty proposed, for him to insist that since *theōria* is an activity valuable in itself, the man of practical wisdom will seek to promote it and its virtue *sophia*, and that *that* is the relation between practical wisdom and *sophia*. To say this, that practical wisdom does not control *sophia* but makes it possible, is not to say that making it possible is the only thing that practical wisdom has to do.

It has sometimes been thought that the last chapter of the *Eudemian Ethics* offers an explicit answer to our question. Aristotle says here that whatever choice or acquisition of natural goods most produces 'the contemplation of god' is best, and any that prevents 'the service and contemplation of god' is bad. However, Aristotle is not addressing himself at this point to the question what makes good and virtuous actions good and virtuous. Such actions he has described earlier in the chapter as praiseworthy and as done for their own sake by truly good men. It is when he passes from good actions to things like money, honour, and friends—things which are indeed naturally good, but which are nevertheless capable of being misused and harmful, and which are not objects of praise—that he raises the question of a criterion or test (ὅϱος). The test is only to determine when and within what limits natural goods should be chosen or acquired, and it is to provide this test that the promotion of contemplation is mentioned. So while here, as in *Nicomachean Ethics* x, the value of contemplation is emphasized, it is clearly not put forward as the foundation of morality or as providing the ultimate criterion for the rightness of right actions.

Aristotle does not then commit himself to the thesis that actions are valuable only in so far as they promote *theōria*. But no alternative answer to our first question seems to present itself. He holds, no doubt, that good actions spring from and appeal to good states of character, and that good states of character are good because they are the healthy and balanced condition of a man. But it will be obvious sooner or later that this is a circle or a blind alley. Again, it is no doubt true and important that the good man does what he does 'because it is noble' (ὅτι ϰαλόν), and that the right thing to do is what the good man would do. But such remarks do not begin to reveal any principle or test whereby the man of practical wisdom can decide what *is* the noble or the right thing to do. Perhaps, indeed, he can 'see', without having to work out, what to do; and that will make him an admirable adviser if we want to know what to do. But if we are enquiring about the 'why?' rather than the 'what?', references to the good man's settled character and reliable judgement are not helpful.

The other question—what is the best life for a man to lead—also remains without a satisfactory answer. A life of *theōria* would certainly be the best of all lives—and such indeed is the life Aristotle attributes to his god. But, as he himself allows, *theōria* by itself does not constitute a possible life for a man. A man is a sort of compound (*syntheton*), an animal who lives and moves in time, but has the ability occasionally to engage in an activity that somehow escapes time and touches the eternal. So you do not give a man a complete rule or recipe for life by telling him to engage in *theōria*. Any human life must include action, and in the best life practical wisdom and moral virtue will therefore be displayed as well as *sophia*. But then the question is unavoidable: if *theōria* and virtuous action are both valuable forms of activity—independently though not equally valuable—how should they be combined in the best possible human life? What really is, in full, the recipe?

Aristotle's failure to tackle this question may be due in part to the fact that he often considers a philosopher's life and a statesman's life as alternatives, following here a traditional pattern of thought, the 'comparison of lives'. They are indeed alternatives, if (as is presumably the case) concentration on *theōria* is incompatible with concentration on great public issues. But the philosopher's life here in question as one alternative is not a life simply of *theōria*, any more than the statesman's is a life of continuous public action. To contrast the philosopher with the statesman is to leave out of account the innumerable activities common to both. But it is precisely the relation, in the best life, between *theōria* and such activities—the ordinary actions of daily life—that requires elucidation. In so far, then, as he is concerned to pick out the philosopher's life and the statesman's life as the two worthiest ideals and to rank the former higher than the latter, Aristotle is not obliged to ask how in the philosopher's life the distinctive activity of *theōria* is to be combined with humbler practical activities—any more than to ask how in the statesman's life domestic claims are to weigh against public ones.

However, there must surely be some deeper explanation why Aristotle so signally fails to attempt an answer to the question how *theōria* and virtuous action would combine in the best human life. The question is theoretically crucial for his project in the *Ethics*, and must also have been of practical importance for him. The truth is, I suggest, that the question is incapable of even an outline answer that Aristotle could accept. For he does not wish to claim that actions have value only in so far as they (directly or indirectly) promote *theōria*; and it would have been desperately difficult for him to maintain such a claim while adhering reasonably closely to ordinary moral views. But if actions can be virtuous and valuable not only in so far as they are promoting *theōria*, the need for Aristotle to give a rule for combining *theōria* with virtuous action in the best life is matched by the impossibility of his doing so, given that *theōria* is the incommensurably more valuable activity.

It may seem that one could say: maximize *theōria*, and for the rest act well; and Aristotle's own famous injunction 'to make ourselves immortal as far as we can' (ἔφ' ὅσον ἐνδέχεται ἀθανατίζειν) might be understood in this way. Such a rule, giving absolute priority to *theōria*, would certainly avoid conflicting claims: it will only be if and when *theōria* cannot be engaged in and nothing can be done to promote *theōria* in any way that the other value will enter into consideration. However, the consequences of such a rule would be no less paradoxical than the consequences of the outright denial of any independent value to action. For the implication of the denial is that one should do anything, however seemingly monstrous, if doing it has the slightest tendency to promote *theōria*—and such an act would on this view actually be good and virtuous. The implication of the absolute priority rule is also that one should do anything, however monstrous, if doing it has the slightest tendency to promote *theōria*—though such an act would on this view actually still be monstrous.

The only way to avoid such paradoxical and inhuman consequences would be to allow a certain amount of compromise and trading between *theōria* and virtuous action, treating the one as more important, but not incomparably more important, than the other. But how can there be a trading relation between the divine and the merely human? Aristotle's theology and anthropology make it inevitable that his answer to the question about *eudaimonia* should be broken-backed. Just as he cannot in the *De Anima* fit his account of separable reason—which is not the form of a body—into his general theory that the soul is the form of the body, so he cannot make intelligible in the *Ethics* the nature of man as a compound of 'something divine' and much that is not divine.

How can there be a coalition between such parties? But if the nature of man is thus unintelligible, the best life for man must remain incapable of clear specification even in principle. Nor can it now seem surprising that Aristotle fails also to answer the other question, the question about morality. For the *kind* of answer we should expect of him would be one based on a thesis about the *nature* of man, and no satisfactory account of that kind *can* be given while the nature of man remains obscure and mysterious.

Aristotle is, of course, in good company—in the company of all philosophers who hold that one element in man is supremely valuable, but are unwilling to embrace the paradoxical and extremist conclusions about life that that view implies. And a parallel difficulty is felt in many religions by the enthusiastic. How can the true believer justify taking any thought for the future or devoting any attention to the problems and pleasures of this mortal life? *Sub specie aeternitatis* are not such daily concerns of infinitely little importance? In fact, compromises are made, and theologians explain that nobody need feel guilty at making them. But the suspicion remains that a man who really believed in the supreme importance of some absolute could not continue to live in much the same way as others.

12

Aristotle on 'Good' and the Categories

In the *Nicomachean Ethics* I. 6, 1096a23–9 Aristotle argues that goodness is not a single common universal: if it were, it would be 'said' in only one category, whereas in fact it is, like *being*, 'said' in all the categories. Aristotle discusses in many places the transcategorial character of ὄν and of ἕν, but most of his accounts of types of goodness or senses of 'good' do not rest upon the point about categories—a point which is, however, taken up in the traditional treatment of *bonum* along with *ens* and *unum* as categorially unclassifiable. The *Ethics* passage is therefore of considerable interest, and it has not, I think, received sufficient attention or final elucidation from the commentators. The present discussion will be far from exhaustive, but it may raise some questions worth further examination. It is perhaps a matter for apology that in a paper written in honour or Dr Walzer I have neglected to consider the relevant passage of the *Eudemian Ethics* (A. 8, 1217b25–34); but since the argument there may be different from that in the Nicomachean version, it seems safer to start by looking at the latter on its own.

Aristotle explains the statement that *good* is spoken of in as many ways as *being* (i.e. in all the categories) in a parenthesis which translates as follows: 'for it is said both in the category of substance, as god and reason, and in quality—the virtues, and in quantity—the moderate, and in relation—the useful, and in time—the opportune, and in place—the locality, and so on'. The central question is how to fill out the examples Aristotle here gives so crisply.

I

The most obvious way is to suppose that the terms listed are offered as subjects of sentences in which the predicate is 'good', thus:

First published in 1972.

God is good.

The virtues are good.

The moderate is good.

The useful is good.

I shall refer to this as interpretation *A*. Most commentators seem to adopt *A*. It is not always clear how they think that Aristotle's argument goes. The argument might be that simply because the subject terms in these sentences stand for items in different categories, the common predicate 'good' must be being used in diverse senses or ways. The sweeping principle here invoked would clearly be a very powerful generator of multivocity, and perhaps too powerful. There seems no obvious reason why one should accept it, or—what is more to the point—why Aristotle should suppose or imply that the principle is an obvious part or corollary of the doctrine of categories.

In *Aristotle's Ethical Theory*, Mr W. F. R. Hardie has provided Aristotle with a more persuasive argument.[1] According to this, the desired conclusion depends not simply on the fact that 'good' is predicated of items in different categories, but on the fact that it is *essentially* predicated of such items. The examples Aristotle lists— virtues, the useful, and so on—are essentially good; and the principle on which the argument relies is that items in different categories cannot have some common element in their essences. By 'essentially' Hardie means more than 'necessarily'; the essence is what is expressed in the definition of the item. There can, of course, be necessary properties of a subject which are no part of its essence, and whose names do not therefore occur in its definition. The strict interpretation of 'essentially' is certainly called for if this account of the argument is to have a decisive advantage over the first. For the principle that any feature that attaches necessarily to an item in one category cannot attach necessarily to an item in another would seem hardly less arbitrary than the principle that any feature that attaches (whether necessarily or accidentally) to an item in one category cannot attach to an item in another. The argument looks very much better when it is supposed that the relevant predicate is part of the definition of the subject, gives (part of) its essence. We have now something approaching an identity statement; and in such a statement the predicate item cannot fail to be in the same

[1] W. F. R. Hardie, *Aristotle's Ethical Theory* (Oxford: Clarendon Press, 1968), 56–8.

category as the subject item. It will follow that 'good' is being used in different ways, standing for items in different categories, when it is predicated essentially of the virtues on the one hand and of the useful on the other, since the virtues and the useful are themselves in different categories.

There seem to be two difficulties in this construal of Aristotle's argument. Firstly, it seems to require and rely upon the principle that the differentia of an item in a given category is itself in that category.[2] This principle goes far beyond the obvious fact that the two sides of an identity statement (including one which gives a definition) cannot stand for items in different categories. Since Aristotle nowhere discusses adequately the status of differentiae in relation to the categorial scheme, it is difficult to be sure whether he held this principle or, if so, why. His uncertain touch in the matter is exemplified in the passage of the *Categories* (3a21–8) where he distinguishes the differentia of substance from substance, but says of it things which could not be said of qualities, quantities, etc. It would be unfortunate if the *Ethics* argument relied on a strict doctrine about differentiae which is not a clear and settled part of Aristotle's thought elsewhere.

It might be suggested that a rather different principle about the differentiae would suffice to justify Aristotle's argument: the principle, namely, that the differentia of an item in one category cannot be the differentia of an item in another. This rule guarantees that 'good' has different senses in our examples, if in them 'good' gives the differentia of the subject term in each case. It is a rule that Aristotle formulates in various versions, and he relies on one of them in dealing with an important problem in *Metaphysics* Z. 12. Yet he allows that it is not easy always to set up definitions that accord with the rule that the differentia ἐπιφέρει τὸ γένος; and his own practice often seems to break it. It would thus be somewhat arbitrary if he assumed its universal validity in order to establish the multivocity of 'good'.[3]

A more fundamental difficulty concerns the propriety of applying doctrines about differentiae to the terms in question in the *Ethics* passage. Whether we think of the relatively simple scheme

---

[2] I assume that, on Hardie's view, 'good' gives the differentia and not the genus of the subject; virtue, e.g., is a ἕξις of a certain kind: namely, a good ἕξις.

[3] A fuller study of the point here touched on would of course have to distinguish between: (a) if *f* is the differentia of an item in one category, it cannot be the *differentia* of an item in another; and (b) if *f* is the differentia of an item in one category, it cannot belong to an item in another.

of the *Categories* or of the complex discussions in the *Metaphysics*, it is clear that there are severe restrictions on the terms which get places in the categorial scheme or which permit of strict definition—have a τί ἦν εἶναι. Neither 'hero' nor 'doctor' stands for an item with a unique place in the categorial scheme: each is an abbreviation, and the items in question are man (a substance), valour (a quality), and healing (an action) or the science of healing (a quality). Heroes and doctors are not species of man or of anything else (cp. *Metaphysics Z*. 4 and *I*. 2). Now is it to be supposed that terms like τὸ μέτριον and τὸ χρήσιμον figure as species in the genus–species pyramids falling under quantity and relation? The classification into moderate and immoderate, useful and useless, would seem to cut across any natural genus–species articulation of these categories. Yet unless τὸ μέτριον and τὸ χρήσιμον sit squarely in such a classification, principles about differentiae cannot get to work. If we are reduced to saying that the *word* 'moderate' means 'good quantity', and the *word* 'useful' means 'good relation', the argument for the multivocity of 'good' will have to rest not on a principle about the differentiae of proper species, but on the blanket thesis that no predicate attaching to items in one category can attach in the same sense to items in another. Suppose that some predicate '*f*' could attach in the same sense to *A* (a substance) and to *B* (a quality). We could then *invent* words '*a*' and '*b*' meaning '*A* that is *f*' and '*B* that is *f*' respectively. But we clearly could not now argue that '*f*' has two senses on the ground that '*a* is *f*' and '*b* is *f*' predicate '*f*' essentially of items in different categories. By inventing the words '*a*' and '*b*', we have not created two proper species; but unless *a* and *b* are proper species, nothing can, strictly speaking, be predicated essentially of either—neither of them has an essence, any more than does *hero* or *doctor*. Thus the force of Hardie's appeal to a principle about differentiae is lost unless it can be shown that the terms in Aristotle's examples stand for genuine species and are not merely portmanteau words.

II

I turn now to a quite different way of filling out Aristotle's examples (interpretation *B*). Perhaps the terms he lists are to be thought of not as subjects but as predicates of sentences:

... is god.

... are the virtues.

... is the moderate.

... is the useful.

Gauthier and Jolif seem to adopt this view in one note, where they write: 'Si nous disons que le bien de Coriscos, c'est le dieu qui est en lui, c'est à dire l'intellect . . . , nous désignons son essence . . . ; si nous disons que ce sont les vertus, nous désignons ses qualités; si nous disons que c'est la mesure, nous désignons la quantité de nourriture ou la quantité d'effort . . . qui lui convient.'[4] In their next note, however, they say: 'De même, lorsqu'on dit que l'intellect est le bien de l'homme et lorsqu'on dit que les vertus sont le bien de l'homme, le mot bien n'a pas le même sens, puisqu'il désigne ici l'essence et là la qualité.'[5] It is not easy to see the precise form of the argument being attributed to Aristotle.

Interpretation *B* has been explicitly adopted and argued for in an interesting paper by L. A. Kosman.[6] According to him, the sentences Aristotle has in mind are not sentences which contain the word 'good' at all, but are sentences used to make disguised ascriptions of goodness. When we say that Socrates is courageous, we predicate in the category of quality—courage being a quality—but we also thereby predicate good of him. Similarly, to say that something is in the right amount is to predicate quantity, but also implicitly to say that it is good.

The instances that Aristotle gives, then, are not the subjects of exemplary predicative statements, but rather the predicates of such statements. They make clear that the multivocity of 'good' is exhibited not only in the fact that many sorts of things may be said to be good, but more in the fact that predicates of radically different types are in fact disguised means of predicating the good in radically different senses. (p. 174)

The point that we praise or commend things by the use of diverse predicates is an important one, and very relevant to the question whether 'good' has a single meaning or stands for a single quality. But it does not seem easy to derive this point from Aristotle's text

---

[4] R. A. Gauthiel and J. Y. Jolif, *L'Éthique à Nicomaque* (Paris and Louvain: Publications Universitaires de Louvain, 1958), II. i. 40.

[5] Ibid.

[6] L. A. Kosman, 'Predicating the Good', *Phronesis*, 13 (1968), 171–4; subsequent page references are given in parentheses in the text.

in the way Kosman suggests. It would be surprising if Aristotle were illustrating the diversity of senses of 'good' by allusion to examples that do not contain the word; this is not how he or anyone else normally proceeds when exhibiting any kind of ambiguity in a term. The context does not warn us that the rather sophisticated notion of a *disguised* predication of good is in play. Kosman suggests as a parallel a remark Aristotle makes in the course of his discussion of ὄν in *Metaphysics Δ*. 7, where he points out that 'A man walks' is equivalent to 'A man is walking'. 'What this shows is that it is possible in Greek as in English to predicate being without explicitly using the verb "εἶναι" or "to be"' (p. 173). So, Kosman argues, if categorially different forms of being can be ascribed without explicit use of the verb 'to be', categorially different forms of goodness can be ascribed without explicit use of the word 'good'. However, the straightforward grammatical fact that 'walks' and 'is walking' are equivalent is not quite on all fours with the rather more subtle point that to say '*X* is brave' is a disguised way of predicating good of *X*; and even if the *Metaphysics* point about being can lead our minds to Kosman's point about good, it will be an ingenious reader of the *Ethics* who makes the connection.

Moreover, and more important, the argument for multivocity will not work in the same way for goodness as for being. If 'is' in 'is walking' has a different sense from 'is' in 'is white', the reason is that walking and white are items (ὄντα) in different categories. The basic argument for the multivocity of ὄν is that it means 'substance' in 'Man is ὄν', 'quality' in 'White is ὄν', and so on (*Metaphysics Γ*. 2, Z. 1); and there are familiar reasons why substance, quality, etc. cannot be treated as species of a single supreme genus *being*. If, however, we expand 'is brave' and 'is of the right amount' into 'is good (in the brave way)' and 'is good (in the right amount way)', what is the basic argument for the multivocity of 'good'? No doubt bravery is necessarily good, and the right amount is necessarily good; but the doctrine of categories that tells us that items in different categories are ὄντα in different senses does not tell us that items in different categories cannot exemplify (even necessarily) one and the same property—that a predicate attaching (even necessarily) to items in different categories cannot be univocal. Thus, even if we allow the idea of a disguised predication of good, the actual argument for the multivocity of good is in effect an argument like that required by interpretation *A*; no term that applies (necessarily) to items in different categories is being used univocally. This argument, I have suggested, falls short of being evidently acceptable.

III

Perhaps it is possible to reach a point similar to that which Kosman attributes to Aristotle, but by a rather different route (interpretation *C*). Suppose we take Aristotle's examples as follows:

... is good because (in that it is) god.
... is good because (in that it is) virtuous.
... is good because (in that it is) moderate.
... is good because (in that it is) useful.

There is to be no implication that the subject terms are in different categories. The point is that the ground for predicating 'good' in the different cases is radically different. If I say that Callias is good and am asked 'How do you mean, "good"?', or 'Why do you call him good?', I answer 'He is brave and honest'. But other things may be commended as good for other reasons, and indeed other sorts of reason—because they are of the right size or useful for some purpose. The criteria for commending different things as good are diverse, and fall into different categories; and this is enough to show that 'good' does not stand for some single common quality.

This expansion of Aristotle's argument brings it into line with the way in which he typically shows a predicate not to be univocal. Thus in *Metaphysics Γ*. 2, he explains the multiple role of ὄν by comparison with 'healthy' and 'medical'. One thing is healthy because it is productive of health (τῷ ποιεῖν), another thing because it is receptive of it (ὅτι δεκτική). Similarly, some items are ὄντα because—or in that—they are substances (ὅτι οὐσίαι), others in that they are attributes (ὅτι πάθη οὐσίας). Aristotle takes it that the phrases introduced by τῷ or ὅτι (or sometimes ὥς) give the sense of the predicate in the relevant example; they tell what it amounts to in each case to apply the predicate.

In chapter 15 of *Topics A* Aristotle examines various ways of establishing homonymy. One passage deals with 'good' precisely in the way interpretation *C* suggests:

One should examine also the genera of the predications corresponding to the word (τὰ γένη τῶν κατὰ τοὔνομα κατηγοριῶν) to see whether they are the same in all cases. For if they are not the same, what is said is clearly homonymous. Thus, for example, the good in food is the *productive* of pleasure but in medicine is the productive of health; while for a soul it is its being *qualified* (e.g. temperate or brave or just), and similarly for a man. But in some cases it is the *when*, i.e. the opportune; for the opportune is called good. And often the quantity, as with the moderate; for the moderate too is called good. It follows that the good is homonymous. (107a3–12)

It is clear in the earlier examples that Aristotle is contemplating sentences like 'This man is good', 'This food is good', and drawing attention to the categorially diverse grounds on which the predicate is assigned. The later examples are less fully given, but he doubtless means that sometimes something is called good because opportune, sometimes because moderate—and these grounds again differ radically from the relational and qualitative grounds appropriate to the previous cases.

This passage exhibits the diversity of meaning of 'good' by drawing attention to the categorial diversity of the features one would mention in explaining one's predicating 'good' of various items. This is precisely the line of thought which interpretation *C* finds in the *Ethics* passage. Though the two texts have not been brought together by modern commentators, the possible connection between them has not escaped notice. Pacius remarks in his note on the *Topics* section: 'Ostendit boni homonymiam: quia refertur ad quatuor categorias; actionem, qualitatem, quando, et quantitatem. potest etiam ad alias categorias referri, ut ipse Aristeles docet lib. I *Ethicorum* cap. 4. *ubi hoc loco utitur contra ideas Platonicas.*'[7] Alexander in his commentary on the *Topics* follows up his (correct) elucidation of the passage quoted above by indicating examples taken from the other categories (including god and reason for substance);[8] and it is fairly clear that he has the *Ethics* passage in mind.

The advantages of interpretation *C* are, then, that it gives Aristotle an excellent point, one that he certainly makes about 'good' elsewhere, and one that does not depend upon any arbitrary

[7] J. Pacius, *In Porphyrii Isagogen et Aristotelis organum Commentarius Analyticus* (Aureliae Allobrogum, Ex Typis Vignonian is, 1605), 363.

[8] Alexander of Aphrodisias, *In Aristotelis Topicorum Libros Octo Commentaria*, ed. Max Wallies, Commentaria in Aristotelem Graeca II. 2 (Berlin: G. Reimer, 1891).

or esoteric doctrine (other than the general doctrine of categories); and that it assumes that the examples Aristotle has in mind in the *Ethics* are just the sort of examples he normally uses to exhibit multivocity, examples which all use the predicate in question but where the account (λόγος) of the predicate—the explanation of what in the different cases it conveys or what justifies its application—varies from example to example.

Can this interpretation be reconciled with the actual run of the words in the *Ethics*? Consider the sentence: 'For "good" is said . . . in the category of quality: the virtues.' Interpretation *A* fills out with 'the virtues are good'; interpretation *B* with '. . . are virtues (or: is virtuous)'. Interpretation *C* does not take 'the virtues' as a part of the example Aristotle has in mind, but as a reference to what features are being assigned to, e.g., Callias when he is called good: that 'good' is here predicated 'in the category of quality' is shown by the fact that 'good' here refers to excellence in quality, virtues. The exceedingly compressed form of words is, I think, compatible with the expansions of both *A* and *B*, but is no less consistent with interpretation *C*. 'Good' is said in the category of quality when it is virtues that are being attributed, as when 'good' is said of Callias. It is true, of course, that to say 'Callias is good' is not to *say* 'Callias is brave and honest'; but it is such features of Callias that the speaker will have in mind, and the hearer will have to realize or discover this if he is fully to understand the speaker's remark.

The purpose of this brief discussion has been fulfilled if I have made interpretation *C* seem at least worth considering. Of the many difficulties that need fuller examination, I pick only two for comment. First, it may be said that the point being attributed to Aristotle has in fact no necessary connection with the categories. If the fact that the criteria for calling different things good differ shows something important about 'good' (say, that it does not stand for a single simple characteristic), it shows this whether or not the various criteria are features in different categories. In other words, an argument from variety of criteria to multiplicity of sense will generate not ten but an indefinitely large number of senses of 'good'. There is, of course, no doubt that Aristotle recognizes that 'good' is predicated of a man, a woman, and a slave on the basis of *different* qualities—though in each case on the basis of *qualities*. Why, then, should he speak as though the senses of 'good' like 'being' are ten and not very much more numerous? Perhaps the difficulty may be mitigated by noting a parallel in the case of 'being'. The doctrine is that there are ten senses of ὄν. Yet in detailed consideration of what it is to be this, that, or the other thing in *Metaphysics* H. 2 Aristotle implies a much greater variety of senses of 'is': 'Some things are characterized by the mode of composition, e.g. the things formed by blending, such as honey-water; and others by being bound together, e.g. a bundle; and others by being glued together, e.g. a book; and others by being nailed together, e.g. a casket . . . Clearly then the word "is" has just as many meanings' (1042b15–26). So Aristotle's usual willingness to operate with just a few senses of 'is' (corresponding to the categories) does not preclude him from recognizing finer distinctions when this serves his purpose. Similarly, an insistence that features of things in virtue of which they are called good can be radically different, in different categories, is not incompatible with the recognition that in cases where the features in question are in the same category they may nevertheless be different. This would no doubt be a highly unsatisfactory position if the main objective were to settle precisely the rules for counting the number of senses of 'good'. It is less regrettable when the main point is to show against Plato that there are a number of different senses, or, better, that 'good' is not always applied for the same reason—goodness is not a single uniform property.

Secondly, it may be asked how interpretation *C* can accommodate an example in the category of substance. For the criteria for calling various things good are features of the things, features that fall under non-substance categories; and being a so-and-so, a substance of a certain kind, is not a feature of a thing. To meet this difficulty, one must suppose that when Aristotle speaks of god and reason—or divine reason—he is not giving one among many possible examples for the predication of 'good' in the category of substance. God is just the one case of such predication, because the answer to the question 'Why do you call god good?' is precisely 'Because he is god': he provides in some way the ultimate standard by which other things are judged, the standard of perfection which other things can variously aspire to approach or imitate. Aristotle makes this sort of point with respect to *eudaimonia* in *Nicomachean Ethics* I. 12. *Eudaimonia* is above being praised as good, for it is that by reference to which other things are called good. Being the source and ground of goods (τὴν ἀρχὴν καὶ τὸ αἴτιον τῶν ἀγαθῶν), we call it 'honoured and divine' (τίμιόν τι καὶ θεῖον τίθεμεν). It is of course good, supremely so, but not through coming up to some standard (satisfying certain criteria), but by setting the standard. In '*Eudaimonia* is good', 'is good' functions quite differently from the way it functions in, say, 'Health is good'. The point Aristotle makes here about *eudaimonia* in connection with human actions and virtues can be made at a different level about god or divine reason: it is towards this that the whole Aristotelian cosmos strives, each part in its own way. This account of the reference to god in the *Ethics* passage may seem rather forced, but the ideas on which it depends are not remote. *Nicomachean Ethics* I. 12 gives the notion of a standard by which other things are called good, and the idea that god is the ultimate standard is central to Aristotle's whole account of the cosmos and its teleology. It is not only interpretation *C* that finds some difficulty in handling this example: it is, after all, not easy to understand the suggestion that in 'God is good' one is giving the *differentia* of the subject.

13

Aristotle on Action

Aristotle's statements about action and choice seem to involve serious inconsistencies—and on topics central to ethics and to his *Ethics*. Here are some samples.[1]

(a) Aristotle holds that when we choose to do something, we always choose with a view to some end, for the sake of something; but he also insists that a man who does a virtuous act is not doing it virtuously—is not displaying virtue—unless he has chosen it 'for itself'.

(b) Actions are done for the sake of other things, and things we can do are not themselves the ends with a view to which we do them; yet action (*prāxis*) differs from production (*poiēsis*), according to Aristotle, precisely because it is its own end.

(c) In recommending the theoretical life, Aristotle says that whereas contemplation 'aims at no end beyond itself', fine actions do 'aim at some end and are not desirable for their own sake'; but in recommending the life of action, he says that doing noble and good deeds is a thing desirable for its own sake, and that 'those activities are desirable in themselves from which nothing is sought beyond the activity'.

Passages like these suggest two problems. First, how can action be good in itself if it is valued as a means to *eudaimonia*? Secondly, how can an action be something done to bring about an outcome, and yet be distinguished from a production because done for its own sake? The first problem invites discussion of Aristotle's view of morality and its foundation: is it valuable in itself or only because it promotes something else? The second—with which the present note is concerned—calls for an examination of Aristotle's

---

[1] *Nicomachean Ethics* I. 1; II. 4; III. 3; VI. 2, 4, 5, 12; X. 6, 7.

First published in 1978.

concept of an action, and of his distinction between *prāxis* and *poiēsis*.[2]

Commentators discussing this distinction often fail to face the real difficulty, that actions often or always *are* productions, and productions often or always *are* actions. (The idea that some periods of the day are occupied by action episodes and others by production episodes would obviously be absurd even if 'production' referred only to the exercise of special techniques or skills, since a period of such exercise could certainly be a period during which an action, of promise keeping for example, was being performed. In fact, however, Aristotle's notion of production is not limited either to technical performances or to the making of material objects.) The brave man's action *is* fighting uphill to relieve the garrison, and the just man is paying off his debt *by* mending his neighbour's fence. How, then, is one to understand the thesis that paying off a debt is an action, but mending a fence is a production? I propose to examine one or two passages in which Aristotle speaks of choosing to do something 'for itself' or of doing something *hekousiōs* (intentionally), in order to see if they throw any light on the problem. For Aristotle closely connects the concept of *prāxis* with choice; and a man's actions, properly speaking, for which he can be praised or blamed, are confined to what he does if not from choice at least *hekousiōs*.

In *Nicomachean Ethics* II. 4 Aristotle confronts a puzzle: how can he say—as he has said—that men become just by doing just things, when surely men who do just things are already, *eo ipso*, just? He first remarks that even in the case of skills correct performance does not suffice to prove the performer's possession of the relevant skill. He goes on to make further points specially relevant to virtues as opposed to skills. It is not enough that the thing done should itself have a certain character, say justice, in order to justify the inference that it is done justly and that the agent is a just man; it is necessary that he should do it knowingly, choosing to do it for itself, and from a settled disposition. Actual things done (*prāgmata*) are

---

[2] In October 1974 I delivered at the Chapel Hill Colloquium in Philosophy a paper entitled 'Aristotle on Action'. The first part discussed the place of action in *eudaimonia*, and it expressed views similar to those in 'Aristotle on *Eudaimonia*', *Proceedings of the British Academy*, 60 (1974), 335–55; repr. here as Ch. 11. It is the second part of that paper that is here published, more or less as it was given. A number of workers in the Aristotelian vineyard have suggested that it would be useful to have it in print, in spite of its evident limitations.

called just if they are such as a just man would do. But it is not he who does them that is just, but he who does them in the way in which just men do.

Aristotle thus draws a strong contrast between *what* is done— which might have been done from various motives or inadvertently—and *why* it is done. If inferences to the character of the agent are to be made from the character of the thing done, it must have been done 'for itself'. This last, however, seems to be an unhappy formulation. For the 'actual thing done' must be some performance—such as mending a neighbour's fence—which is in fact (in the circumstances) just, though it might be done by someone ignorant of or indifferent to its justice. But when it is asked whether the doer chose to do it for *itself*, the question is of course whether he chose to do it because it was just, not whether he chose to do it because it was mending a neighbour's fence. How can doing something because it is ϕ be doing it for itself or for its own sake unless the thing done is specified precisely as ϕ? Only if the action is designated not as mending a fence but as *the ϕ act* does the expression 'for itself' get the necessary grip. Yet the ϕ act *is* some such performance as mending a fence, and it does not seem natural to say in such a case that the agent has done two things at the same time. It is easy to understand how Aristotle, not having addressed himself to this theoretical difficulty, should have said of an action both that it is done for itself and that it is done for the sake of something else: the ϕ act *is* done for itself, the mending of a fence is *not* done for its own sake but for its ϕ-ness.

It may be thought that to take mending a fence as one's example of an 'actual thing done' is to make it unnecessarily difficult to interpret the requirement that the just agent should choose to do what he does 'for itself'. Mending a fence is all too obviously something in itself unattractive; nor is it by any means always the just thing to do. However, Aristotle's position would hardly be easier if an example like repaying a debt were used. It is not always just to repay a debt either. In any case, even if what is done could be given a description such that *any* such act would be just, yet such an act would inevitably have other characteristics too. What 'for itself' points to will be clear only if the act is brought before us precisely *as* having the relevant characteristic, e.g. *as* the just act: it is not enough that it should actually or even necessarily have it.

One way of bringing out the point at issue is to distinguish two ways of understanding the expression 'do something that is ϕ'. It may mean 'do something (that is ϕ)', where there is no implication that the doer necessarily knows or supposes that what he does is ϕ. Or it may mean 'do something-that-is-ϕ', where it is implied that the doer knows or supposes it to be ϕ (whether or not he does it *because* it is ϕ, 'for itself'). Aristotle comes close to this kind of formulation in *Nicomachean Ethics* v. 8. Here, before contrasting the character of what is done with the character of the agent (along the same lines as ii. 4), he raises a preliminary question: before asking whether someone did a just act 'for itself' (or for ulterior motives), we must ask whether he *did a just act* at all, properly speaking.

Aristotle first distinguishes between 'doing a thing that is in fact wrong' and 'doing wrong' (*adikein*, a single word). To do-wrong is to do something wrong knowingly and intentionally. If one does what is as a matter of fact wrong but does not know that what one is doing is wrong, one cannot be said to do wrong (save *per accidens*) (v. 8. 1). Later in the chapter (v. 8. 4) Aristotle applies the same principle to expressions like 'doing what is right' and 'doing things that are wrong'. A man who has been *compelled* to return a deposit cannot be said to have done right or even to have *done what is right*, save *per accidens*. So it seems that what a man can be said to have done strictly, without qualification, not *per accidens*, is what he has done unforced and knowingly.

The contrast between doing something, properly speaking, and only doing something *per accidens*, differs from the earlier contrast between doing something for itself and doing it for an ulterior motive. But here again what is involved is a context that does not permit free substitution of alternative descriptions of the agent's performance. In the strict use a man 'does——' only if he 'does——knowingly'. An action of his, then, is not something some of whose features or circumstances he may be ignorant of. Rather it must be *defined* by features he is aware of, since it is only *as* so defined that he can be said to have done it *knowingly*, and hence to have *done* it at all (strictly speaking).

Aristotle implies, then, that nothing a man does unknowingly can count as an action of his. Does he recognize that, since there are on any occasion a great number of facts an agent knows about what he is doing, there will be a great number of different ways of characterizing what he is doing knowingly? Does he see that what is done may be subject to praise under one description and blame under another, or may constitute one offence under one description and a different one under another, or may invite moral appraisal under one description and technical appraisal under another?

In *Nicomachean Ethics* v. 8, between the sections already summarized, Aristotle explains what counts as *hekousion*: 'whatever of the things in his power a man does in knowledge and not ignorance of either the person, the instrument, or the result—e.g. whom he strikes, what he strikes with, and with what result—and ⟨knowing⟩ each of them not *per accidens*'.[3] This last requirement is explained by an example: you may know that you are striking a man, but not know that the man is your father; so, Aristotle implies, you do not know *whom* you are striking (your father) save *per accidens*. Similarly, he adds, as regards the result and the whole action.

Here, then, Aristotle touches on some of the various factors or circumstances of any practical situation—whose number and diversity he often, of course, stresses; and he uses the notion of knowing *per accidens*, a notion that is essentially connected with the idea that free substitution of extensionally equivalent expressions is not always permissible. Yet he conspicuously fails to remark that though on his account you do not strike your father *hekousiōs*, you do strike a man *hekousiōs*; or that, in virtue of different known factors in a given situation, a man may be accused of—and offer diverse excuses for—different offences. Aristotle's mind is clearly on giving conditions for ascribing responsibility for an act as already specified in the accusation 'He struck his father a fatal blow with a sword'.

We must, however, examine Aristotle's fuller account of actions and excuses in *Nicomachean Ethics* III. I. He starts with the privative term, *akousion*: a man can deny responsibility for something done—claim that it was *akousion*—if he can plead force or ignorance. By 'force' is meant real physical force, where it would in fact be misleading to say that the man had *done* anything—'the *archē* [originating principle] is outside and nothing is contributed by the person who acts or rather is acted on'. By 'ignorance' is meant

---

[3] The flow of the sentence is in favour of understanding 'knowing' rather than 'doing' before 'each of them'. (For 'knowing *per accidens*' see e.g. *Posterior Analytics* 76a1, 93a25, 93b25.)

ignorance of facts, circumstances, and consequences, not ignorance of 'the universal', of what is good or lawful. Corresponding to these negative tests for *akousion*—not due to an *archē* in the person, not known—is the positive formula: the *hekousion* is 'that whose originating principle is in the agent himself, he being aware of the particular circumstances of the action'.

Various questions arise as to the interpretation of the ignorance test, and Aristotle discusses some of them. But the point of concern to us he does not bring out, and indeed his way of speaking serves to conceal it. I give someone a drink not knowing it to be poison—I think it will refresh, but in fact it will kill. Ignorance makes my act *akousion*. *What* act? Clearly what I did through ignorance was to poison my friend, not to give him a drink. The ignorance that makes my act *akousion* is ignorance of a feature that goes to define that act, and not ignorance of a feature that simply characterizes it.

Now some of Aristotle's formulations could perhaps be construed in such a way as to accommodate this point. When, after referring to the various circumstances of action, he says that 'the man ignorant of any of these acts *akousiōs*' (III. 1, 15), we might take him to mean that corresponding to ignorance of any factor there will be some act the man can be said to have done *akousiōs*. And when he says that that is *hekousion* which a man does in knowledge of person, instrument, and result (v. 8, 3), we might take him to be using only by way of example a case where the performance in question is specified as the bringing about of a certain result by using a certain instrument on a certain person. This would then be consistent with his allowing that that is also *hekousion* which a man does in knowledge of person and instrument (but in ignorance of result): he struck his father *hekousiōs* (though he struck his father a fatal blow *akousiōs*).

These would, however, be very forced ways of interpreting Aristotle's words. His own approach is indicated by the fact that, after going through a number of things of which one might be ignorant, he says that one who was ignorant of any of these is thought to have acted *akousiōs*—and especially if he was ignorant on the most important points (III. 1. 18). It is clear that Aristotle is not associating knowledge or ignorance of this, that, or the other with various act descriptions involving this, that, or the other, with respect to each of which the question 'Did he do it *hekousiōs*?' could be asked. Rather, he is asking simply whether a man 'acted *hekousiōs*' on some occasion, and saying that he did so only if he knew all the important circumstances. It is easy to understand why Aristotle should have spoken as he does. In a simple exposition he considers simple and striking cases. We all know what Oedipus did, and we are quite willing to say simply that he 'acted *akousiōs*'. The enormity of the charge of striking his father a fatal blow pushes aside any minor infelicities of which he may simultaneously have been guilty, and even submerges the quite serious charge (which he might well find it harder to evade) of having struck a man. In such a dramatic case one can ask simply whether a man 'acted *hekousiōs*', or whether he 'did it *hekousiōs*', without entering into or even noticing theoretical questions about the identification of actions.

It is difficult, however, to see how closer consideration could have left Aristotle satisfied with his way of speaking. For whether he identified the thing done ('it') with the person's bodily movement M or with the total package $M(a, b, c \ldots)$—where the letters in brackets stand for various circumstances, etc.—he would find it impossible to raise the questions that we (and the courts) want to raise. But if he treated $M(a)$, $M(b)$, etc. as different things done (perhaps different offences), about each of which separately the question whether it was done *hekousiōs* could be asked, he could not say that the knowledge required for an affirmative answer was knowledge of all or of the most important factors in the situation. The knowledge required for an affirmative answer to the question about $M(a)$ would be simply the knowledge that M would be $M(a)$.

It might be said that though what a man does on a particular occasion must be (as it were) taken apart in this way—the question about intention or 'voluntariness' being directed not at the whole package but at the elements in it, $M(a)$, $M(b)$, etc.—yet what a man does *hekousiōs* on a particular occasion can be treated as a single action (*the* action he performed)—say, $M(a, g, m \ldots)$, where the letters in brackets stand for the circumstances etc. known to the agent. Certainly, however much he disliked some of the circumstances, however much he regretted that doing $M(a)$ would be doing $M(g)$, he did know that it was precisely this package—$M(a, g, m \ldots)$ that he was taking, and he took it because on the whole he wanted to do so rather than not.

There are, nevertheless, still reasons for picking $M(a, g, m \ldots)$ apart. Firstly, he may well have to go to different courts to meet different charges in respect of $M(a)$, $M(g)$ etc. In one court $M(a)$ will be the action complained of, and that it was also $M(g)$ will be, perhaps, a mitigating circumstance. Secondly, even if our knowledge that he took the package because on the whole he wanted to make it superfluous to ask separately whether $M(a)$ was *hekousion*, whether $M(g)$ was *hekousion*, etc., we may well want to ask with respect to each whether he was glad or sorry (or indifferent) that he was doing *that*. Was *that* what made him take the whole package, or was it perhaps an element he regretted but had to accept in order to get some other? He wanted $M(a, g, m \ldots)$ on the whole. Was it perhaps only (or precisely) $M(a)$ that he *really* wanted?

This takes us back to the first part of Aristotle's account of the *hekousion*—'that whose *archē* [originating principle] is in the agent himself, he being aware of the particular circumstances'. The *archē* relevant for action is no doubt desire, *orexis*. (For, as Aristotle recognizes, not every internal *archē* leads to performances classifiable—even given knowledge—as *hekousia*. Many processes of a biological kind are not influenced by our wishes and desires; they are not *hekousia*, and they are not *akousia* either; v. 8.3, 1135a33–b2.) But of what exactly is desire the originating principle? Is it, to use the above crude symbolism, M or $M(a)$ or $M(a, g, m \ldots)$ or $M(a, b, c \ldots)$? Does Aristotle's general account of human and animal movement throw any light on this?

The central features of this account are familiar. If an object of thought or imagination becomes an object of desire, a man's faculty of desire is stimulated and moves him towards realizing or achieving it. Three 'causes'—or explanatory factors—are mentioned here: the final cause, the object of desire; the efficient cause, the man's actual desire; and the formal cause, the essence or definition of the movement produced. In a certain way these three 'causes' coincide, as Aristotle says, for example in *Physics* B. II. 3, where he takes his illustrations from productive crafts.

It would appear, then, that *what* action precisely has been performed—what action is genuinely explained by the *archē* in the agent—depends on what the object of thought and desire was. Unfortunately, difficulties at once arise. Aristotle often gives as the object of desire (or of its species, appetite and wish) a *characteristic* (like the pleasant, the noble), and not something that could strictly be *done*. When he does speak of what we may want to *do*, he is naturally often concerned with cases in which deliberation is involved, where one thing is done as a means to another, or where the pros and cons of a course of action have to be weighed up. So an immediate distinction presents itself between what one primarily wants to do and what one wants to do derivatively, in so far as one thinks it necessary to achieve one's real aim. Should we then say that what we *really* want to do, or want to do without qualification, is only what we want non-derivatively to do? Aristotle comes close to this in *Nicomachean Ethics* VII. 9.1: 'if a person chooses or pursues this for the sake of that, *per se* it is that that he pursues and chooses, but *per accidens* it is this. But when we speak without qualification we mean what is *per se*'. This suggests a series or hierarchy of descriptions of what a man does because he desires to, each successive description coming nearer to revealing exactly what he aims at. In our simple case, $M(a, g, m \ldots)$ comes first, and is followed by $M(a)$: his wanting the package was derivative from his wanting $M(a)$. But if it is always for some desirable characteristic that a possible line of action appeals, there will be $M(\phi)$ after $M(a)$ in the series. Desire is then the *archē* of $M(a, g, m \ldots)$, $M(a)$, and $M(\phi)$—but primarily of the last and only derivatively of the others.

It is clear, I think, that what Aristotle says about desire as the originating principle of action does not provide an answer to the sorts of question about actions and action descriptions that were left unanswered by his discussions of responsibility. Moreover, his account of the *physiology* of animal movement, which shows how desire operates as a physical (non-intentional) process leading to muscular and limb movements (how desire is in a way the *archē* of M), gives no clue as to how the physiological story is connected to the psychological one, or how questions about the individuation of movements are related to questions about the individuation of actions.

I conclude that while Aristotle has much to tell us about the responsibility for actions, the motives of actions, and the physiology of actions, he does not direct his gaze steadily upon the questions 'What *is* an action?' and 'What is *an* action?'. It is not that such questions would be beyond him. He revels in questions of this kind, and he has the conceptual and linguistic equipment needed to tackle them. Whatever the reasons why he did not tackle these questions head-on, it seems likely that this failure is itself the reason for many of the 'incoherences' and 'contradictions' to be found in passages such as those I quoted at the beginning.

14

An Aristotelian Argument about Virtue

1. In *Nicomachean Ethics* III. 5 Aristotle argues that virtues and vices—good and bad states of character—are 'in our power' or 'up to us' (*eph hēmin*) and 'voluntary' (*hekousia*). He needs to establish this thesis, a thesis which I shall label '*T*', in order to justify the practice of praising people for their virtues and blaming them for their vices. He will at the same time be removing a dangerous objection that might be raised to the practice of praising and blaming people for *actions* they do voluntarily, the objection that if a man* cannot help the state of character which determines his choices and decisions, he can hardly be blamed for them or (consequently) for the actions he does voluntarily.

In the last two main sections of the chapter Aristotle wrestles (without decisive success) against the contentions (i) that one cannot help being the sort of person one is, and (ii) that it is by nature that a man values what he values, and against the conclusion that our virtues and vices are therefore *not* in our power or voluntary. The main ideas he deploys against these contentions are (i) that one could have helped *becoming* the sort of person one is, and (ii) that whatever the importance of a man's nature in setting his aims, it is he, after all, who carries them out. These sections of *Nicomachean Ethics* III. 5 have been much discussed, and rightly. Here however, I wish to examine more closely than is usually done the argument contained in the first few lines of the chapter (III. 5. 1–3, 1113b3–14), a self-contained argument sharply distinct from the later ones and much more direct than they are.

---

* I apologize for Aristotle's use of the masculine gender in discussions about virtue and vice; but the author, to be historically accurate, could not have used the impersonal pronoun 'one' and the possessive 'one's' in order to avoid criticisms which are bound to arise [Note by editor of *Paideia*].

First published in 1978.

2. Before turning to this argument for the thesis *T*, we should remark that it is far from obvious how the terms 'in our power' and 'voluntary' are to be understood in the case of states of character (*hexeis*). For *acts* all is reasonably clear: if an act is in my power, I can do it if I choose; and if I do so choose, the act done is a voluntary act. The acts which are in my power—acts which, if done, are voluntary acts—are those whose 'starting-point' or 'origin' (*archē*) is 'in' me. 'Now the man acts voluntarily. For the *archē* that moves his limbs in such actions is in him, and things whose *archē* is in a man himself are in his power to do or not to do. Such actions therefore are voluntary' (III. 1. 6, 1110a15–18; cp. III. 1. 20, 1111a22–4). 'Things whose *archai* are in us are themselves up to us and voluntary' (III. 5. 6, 1113b21–2). The *archē* to which Aristotle refers in these passages is evidently desire in some form. In central cases it is that form of desire called choice (*prohairesis*), or—going deeper—the state of character (*hexis*) revealed in choice.

Let us now consider not actions but *hexeis* themselves. If a *hexis* is said to be in my power, does this mean that I can have it, or be in it, if I choose? (Does it even make *sense* to suggest that I can now if I wish choose, or decide, to *be* (say) fond of children or kind and gentle?) Or does it mean only that I can, if I choose, *become*—or, weaker still, try to become—fond of children, or kind and gentle? Again, how does the test 'Is the *archē* in him?' work in the case of states of character? We can treat a man's *hexis* as an internal *archē* of voluntary acts; can it itself be voluntary because it derives from a (further) internal *archē*? To put the point in a less Aristotelian way: I am held responsible for *x* if it results from my desire or choice or state of character; can I in the same way and by the same test be held responsible for my desire or choice or state of character?

3. The passage we are to examine begins as follows:

(1) While it is the end that is wished for, it is steps directed to the end that are deliberated about and chosen; and so actions to do with these are in accordance with choice and are voluntary. But the exercise of the virtues are to do with these. (2) Therefore [*T*] virtue too [*sc.* as well as *acts* we deliberate about and choose to do, III. 3. 7, 19] is in our power, and vice equally. (III. 5. 1–2, 1113b3–7)[1]

[1] I read, with nearly all modern editors, δή at 1113b6 and ἄρα at 113b13.

As it stands, this is too compressed to be clear or convincing. The argument suggested is perhaps this (call it argument *A*):

(i) acts deliberately done to promote an end are voluntary, and (ii) exercises of virtue and vice are acts deliberately done to promote an end; therefore (iii) virtue and vice are voluntary.

From (i) and (ii) it no doubt follows that the exercises of virtues are voluntary acts. Why should it be thought to follow that virtues themselves are voluntary? Exercises of my skill at golf or of my innate ability to waggle my ears are up to me, in my power, and voluntary; does it follow that the skill itself and the ability itself are in my power and voluntary—whatever that would mean?

Aristotle proceeds to fill out his argument, and also to justify that final addition, 'and vice equally'. He first establishes very neatly a symmetry between acts and omissions (doings and refrainings) and a further symmetry between good and bad performances (whether acts or omissions). He then links good (bad) performances with being a good (bad) person—that is, with virtue (vice).

(2) ... For where acting is in our power, so is not acting; and where not acting is, so is acting. Thus, if acting, where that is fine, is in our power, not acting, which will be base, will also be in our power; and if not acting, where that is fine, is in our power, acting, which will be base, will also be in our power. (3) But if it is in our power to do fine acts and base acts—and equally in our power not to do these—and this is what our being good and bad was, it follows that [*T*] being virtuous and vicious is in our power. (III. 5. 2–3, 1113b7–14)

Although this last sentence is conditional in form, it is clear that Aristotle is asserting, and takes himself to have established, that virtue and vice are indeed in our power. The thesis *T*, first asserted as following from argument *A* above, is now supported by the following argument (argument *B*).

(i) it is in our power to do good (bad) acts, and (ii) doing good (bad) acts is what being good (bad) is; therefore (iii) it is in our power to be good (bad).

This argument is clearer, fuller, and more plausible than argument *A* as an argument for the thesis that virtue and vice are in our power. Whereas argument *A* slips invalidly from premises about performances to a conclusion about *hexeis*, argument *B* contains a premiss that explicitly identifies doing certain acts with having a certain *hexis*. It is the use of this contention, that the possession of a virtue or vice *consists in* the doing of certain acts, which distinguishes our argument from subsequent arguments in the chapter. For they appeal to a quite different point: that the possession of a virtue or vice *results from* the doing of certain acts.

The commentators fail to stress—or, in most cases, even to notice—this clear distinction. In their summaries they tend to carry the notion of the genesis of virtues back into this first argument—which really says nothing at all about how people *become* virtuous. Consequently, no serious critical attention is given to the argument which Aristotle actually propounds here.[2] Even commentators who remark that the opening argument of the chapter is inadequate fail to analyse or discuss it at any length.[3]

4. Aristotle formulates the crucial second premiss of argument *B* with a 'was'—'This is what our being good or bad was'—and it is natural to ask whether he is alluding to something previously said or whether this is the vaguer imperfect used in mentioning a common or familiar doctrine. Some commentators refer to II. I. 4, 1103a34–b2, where Aristotle says that it is by doing just acts that we become just, by doing brave acts that we become brave. But it is clear that this remark—and the whole chapter—is about the *acquisition* of virtue: it is from performances of the appropriate kind that a *hexis* comes into being (II. I. 7, 1103b12–22). At II. 2.8 and II. 3.11 Aristotle remarks that a *hexis* is exercised in performances of the same kind as the performances that produce, promote, or destroy the *hexis*; but this is far from asserting the identity which our second premiss asserts. Consequently, most commentators refer to III. 2. 11, 1112a1–3, where Aristotle says: 'it is by choosing what is good or bad that we are men of a certain character'. He says this to contrast choice with belief, since a man is clearly *not* good or bad in virtue of having certain beliefs.

There are several reasons why this passage will not serve as backing for the second premiss of argument *B*. First, a contrast may be drawn between choice of the good and good action. As Aristotle points out at x. 8. 5, choices and intentions are sometimes

---

[2] See e.g. Heliodorus, Aquinas, Grant, Burnet, Joachim, Dirlmeier, Gauthier and Jolif, in their commentaries.

[3] Ramsauer, *ad loc.* and Loening, in *Die Zurechnungslehre des Aristoteles* (Jena: Gustav Fischer, 1903), 257.

frustrated; and it is perhaps by choices and intentions rather than by actual performances that moral character is revealed (III. 2. 1). So there is a distinction between the thesis that character is a matter of what we choose to do and the thesis that it is a matter of what we do. Secondly, chosen actions are—and are according to Aristotle—only a subclass of voluntary actions. So there is a distinction between the thesis that character is a matter of what we choose to do and the wider thesis of argument *B* that it is a matter of what we do voluntarily.

A final objection to finding in III. 2. 11 the backing for the second premiss of argument *B* is that *if* the premiss is interpreted as being about what we choose to do, the validity of the argument is threatened. It will be valid only if the first premiss is reformulated thus: 'It is in our power *to choose to do* good (bad) acts.' But, apart from the fact that that is not what the text says, it is not obvious how it is to be understood. For if we consider what 'in our power' means, and how Aristotle explains it, we find it difficult to apply the phrase to *choosing*. Roughly, the *archē* in me whose consequences are actions which are in my power and voluntary is desire or desire guided by thought—choice. (When a man is *himself* described as *archē* and 'father' of his actions—III. 5. 5—it is because he is a choosing animal: 'Choice is desiring reason or reasoning desire, and such an *archē* is a man'; VI. 2. 5.) So to apply to desire or choice itself the terms 'in our power' and 'voluntary' that are applicable to actions is to generate an unintelligible regress, unless the terms are construed differently. But how?

5. I conclude that none of the references which are commonly suggested[4] provide a satisfactory explanation of the 'was' in Aristotle's formulation of the second premiss of argument *B*, and that it is better to take it simply as indicating that the proposition being expressed is a familiar one. In any event, I wish now to turn to the argument itself. The key difficulty has already been brought into view; but the clearest way to present it will be to recall what Aristotle says in II. 4, an important discussion of the relation of virtue, the *hexis*, to actions. It starts from a puzzle that someone might propound: Aristotle has insisted that one becomes (e.g.) just

---

[4] Gauthier and Jolif hold that the 'was' at 1113b13 refers to the hypothesis of 1113b8–10 (and they propose emendations designed to reinforce their suggestion). I do not think that this is at all convincing.

by doing just acts; but surely one who does just acts is *already* just. No, answers Aristotle. To be a just person requires not only that one do just acts but that one do them in or from a certain state of character (*hexis*). The doing of just acts brings a person into possession of that *hexis*; it is only the just acts he subsequently does which are exercises of the virtue, which he now has. A 'just act' is the act a just man would do, but to be a just man requires that one should do such acts knowingly, choosing them for their own sakes, and from a settled disposition. Aristotle expresses the same point very forcibly in VI. II. 7, 1144a13–20.

Suppose that *a, b, c, . . .* are just acts which a man could do—*a* might be, for example, paying a debt to Callias. The contrast which Aristotle is drawing may be put roughly but sharply in this way:

(1) If a non-just man does *a, b, c . . .*, he *becomes* just;
(2) if a man does *a qua* just, *b qua* just, *c qua* just, . . . he *is* just.

(I take it that to do *a qua* just is to do it knowing it to be just and because it is just, and that Aristotle holds that a person who regularly does just acts *qua* just is indeed a just person.) There are two crucial differences between (1) and (2). First, *a, b, c . . .* are certainly 'in a man's power'—he can do them if (for whatever reason and from whatever motive) he wants to; but it is not clear that it is in his power to do *a qua* just, *b qua* just, . . . Can a man decide or choose *to act from a certain motive*, to *act for a certain reason*? He can, from kindness, choose to help the child; but can he choose to help the child from kindness—and not from some other motive? No doubt there are ways in which we can try to develop and strengthen certain motives in ourselves, and in which we can try to concentrate on certain features of situations. In general, however, one may say that to decide is to be influenced in some direction by one's desires, etc., and that one cannot decide to be so influenced (decide to decide). So the performances mentioned in (1) are 'in a man's power', those in (2) are not.

The second difference between (1) and (2) is that the former asserts a causal connection, while the second puts forward something like an analysis. Now Aristotle has a reasonably clear view as to whether the consequences of voluntary acts count as voluntary: it depends on whether the agent could foresee the consequences. And it fits in with that general view that he should be willing to say that a man became (e.g.) unjust *voluntarily* if he did voluntarily things which, as he knew, would have this result. In the case of a thesis like (2), however, it is not safe to assume that what can be said of each performance mentioned in the protasis can be said of the state of affairs mentioned in the apodosis. Being an expert may well be a matter of doing this, that, and the other skilfully, and if a man is an expert, such skilful performances are in his power; but it is not therefore natural to say that it is in his power *to be an expert*. Thus, even if the performances specified in the protasis of (2) were in a man's power, the thesis would by no means suffice to establish that being just is in a man's power.

6. The verdict on argument *B* must be that the second premiss as it stands is false, and that, if it is filled out—as in thesis (2)—in order that it may be true, the argument collapses, because the first premiss cannot plausibly be amended in the way that would be necessary to make the argument valid. Aristotle is himself well aware of the essential point. Not only does he stress it in the passages referred to above (II. 4 and VI. 11. 7); he actually brings it to bear upon the very problem of what is in our power. In v. 9. 14, 1137a4–9 he says: 'Men think that to do unjust acts is in their power, and that for that reason being just is also easy. But this is not the case. For to sleep with one's neighbour's wife, or to hit a bystander, or to hand over a gift of money, is easy and in our power; but to do these things *in a certain state of character* is neither easy nor in our power.'

It is odd, then, that Aristotle puts forward without adverse comment the argument at the beginning of III. 5. It is of course clear from the remainder of the chapter that he does not suppose that argument to have been a clincher. He in fact turns to quite different arguments, which rest on a thesis as to how virtues/vices are brought into being, not on a thesis as to what virtues/vices are. Perhaps it would have required disproportionate time to explain exactly why the first argument was unsatisfactory. For although it is easy enough to indicate roughly—as I have indicated—what is amiss, a proper discussion would involve difficult and complex questions. For example, is there not a distinction between doing an act that is fine and doing a fine act? In III. 5. 2–3 Aristotle moves without remark from the former to the latter way of speaking. But in v. 8–9 he argues *inter alia* that the expression 'did' a 'just act' properly applies only to one who knew what he did was just and did it because it was just. In short, the innocent-looking argument at the beginning of III. 5 raises so many tricky issues when examined closely that Aristotle was perhaps wise to drop it like a hot potato and to move on. (The main ideas needed to clarify the issues are, however, to be found in the *Ethics*, notably in II. 4 and v. 8–9). Here I have simply tried to show that the argument does deserve close examination, and I have tried to indicate some of the issues that are involved.[5]

---

[5] One or two related points are made in my 'Aristotle on Action', *Mind*, 87 (Oct. 1978); repr. above as Ch. 13. A full discussion would need to compare *Nicomachean Ethics* III. 1–5 with the interestingly different treatment of much the same questions in *Eudemian Ethics* II. 6–11.

SELECT INDEX OF TOPICS